Machine Learning with PyTorch

From Basics to Expert Proficiency

Contents

Introduction

The field of machine learning has witnessed exponential growth over the past few decades, fundamentally altering the landscape of numerous industries. From financial services and healthcare to entertainment and transportation, the applications of machine learning are diverse and ever-expanding. This book aims to provide a comprehensive guide to machine learning, with a special focus on utilizing PyTorch—a cutting-edge machine learning framework known for its flexibility and ease of use.

Machine learning is a subset of artificial intelligence that involves the use of statistical techniques to enable computers to learn from and make decisions based on data. Unlike traditional programming paradigms, where explicit instructions are provided for every task, machine learning enables systems to identify patterns and make data-driven predictions autonomously. This paradigm shift is what makes machine learning a powerful tool for solving complex problems.

PyTorch, developed by Facebook's AI Research lab, has rapidly gained popularity among researchers and practitioners. Its dynamic computation graph—a feature that allows the network to be modified on the go—makes it particularly well-suited for research and development. Additionally, PyTorch provides a seamless integration with Python, one of the most widely-used programming languages in data science and machine learning. This combination of features has established PyTorch as a framework of choice for both academic research and industry applications.

This book is structured to guide readers from foundational concepts to expert-level proficiency in machine learning with PyTorch. The initial chapters introduce the basics of machine learning, including its history, types, and wide array of applications. A detailed overview of PyTorch, including its installation and basic usage, sets the stage for more complex topics.

Subsequent chapters delve into the core concepts of PyTorch, such as tensor operations and neural network construction. We explore how to build and train neural networks, emphasizing both the theoretical underpinnings and practical implementations. Chapters on improving model performance cover advanced techniques, including regularization, hyperparameter tuning, and data augmentation, to name a few.

Special attention is given to specific types of neural networks, such as Convolutional Neural Networks (CNNs) and Recurrent Neural Networks (RNNs), each tailored for different types of data and applications. Transfer learning and the use of pre-trained models are also explored, providing insights into how existing models can be adapted for new tasks, thereby saving valuable time and computational resources.

The book concludes with chapters on deploying PyTorch models, ensuring that the fruits of your labor can be effectively utilized in real-world applications. Whether deploying on cloud platforms or edge devices, the practical steps and considerations are elucidated.

By the end of this book, readers will have a robust understanding of machine learning principles and practical experience with PyTorch. This dual focus on theory and application ensures that you are well-equipped to tackle a wide range of machine learning challenges. The knowledge gained will not only enhance your technical skills but also broaden your capacity to innovate and solve practical problems using machine learning techniques.

Chapter 1

Introduction to Machine Learning and PyTorch

This chapter provides a foundational overview of machine learning and PyTorch, covering essential concepts such as the history and types of machine learning, and its diverse applications across various industries. It introduces PyTorch, highlighting its unique features and advantages, and provides an overview of its ecosystem. The chapter also includes practical instructions on installing PyTorch and running your first program, ensuring that readers are well-prepared to embark on their machine learning journey using this powerful framework.

1.1 What is Machine Learning?

Machine Learning (ML) is a subfield of artificial intelligence (AI) that focuses on the development of algorithms and statistical models that enable computers to perform tasks without explicit instructions, relying on patterns and inference instead. Machine learning systems learn from and make predictions or decisions based on data, iteratively improving performance as they are exposed to more information. This paradigm shifts the traditional approach of coding specific tasks to training models to understand and execute those tasks.

The field of machine learning is characterized by a variety of techniques that fall under supervised learning, unsupervised learning, reinforcement learning, and semi-supervised learning. These methods are designed to handle different types of data and problem domains, offering flexibility and scalability in real-world applications.

Learning Algorithms: There are numerous algorithms that have been developed to enable machines to learn. These algorithms can be broadly categorized based on their learning styles:

- **Supervised Learning:** In supervised learning, the model is trained on labeled data, i.e., data that includes input-output pairs. The goal is to learn a mapping from inputs to outputs. Common supervised learning algorithms include linear regression, logistic regression, support vector machines (SVM), and neural networks. An example of a supervised learning task is predicting house prices based on features such as size, number of bedrooms, and location.

```
import torch
from torch.autograd import Variable
import torch.nn as nn

# Hypothetical dataset of house sizes and prices
data_x = torch.tensor([[1400], [1600], [1700], [1875], [1100]], dtype=torch.float32
    )
data_y = torch.tensor([[245], [312], [279], [308], [199]], dtype=torch.float32)

# Linear Regression Model
class LinearRegressionModel(nn.Module):
    def __init__(self):
        super(LinearRegressionModel, self).__init__()
        self.linear = nn.Linear(1, 1)

    def forward(self, x):
        return self.linear(x)

# Model instantiation
model = LinearRegressionModel()

# Loss and optimizer
criterion = nn.MSELoss()
optimizer = torch.optim.SGD(model.parameters(), lr=0.01)

# Training the model
for epoch in range(1000):
    inputs = Variable(data_x)
    targets = Variable(data_y)

    outputs = model(inputs)
    loss = criterion(outputs, targets)

    optimizer.zero_grad()
    loss.backward()
    optimizer.step()

    if (epoch+1) % 100 == 0:
```

```
print(f'Epoch [{epoch+1}/1000], Loss: {loss.item():.4f}')
```

```
Epoch [100/1000], Loss: 7626.1904
Epoch [200/1000], Loss: 3932.2251
Epoch [300/1000], Loss: 2031.3531
Epoch [400/1000], Loss: 1048.8196
Epoch [500/1000], Loss: 546.2639
Epoch [600/1000], Loss: 284.7656
Epoch [700/1000], Loss: 150.6230
Epoch [800/1000], Loss: 80.0182
Epoch [900/1000], Loss: 42.5533
Epoch [1000/1000], Loss: 23.2111
```

- **Unsupervised Learning:** In unsupervised learning, the model is trained on data that does not contain labels. The primary goal of unsupervised learning is to find inherent structures in the data. Common algorithms include clustering methods like k-means, hierarchical clustering, and dimensionality reduction methods such as principal component analysis (PCA). An example task is grouping similar documents together based on their content.

- **Reinforcement Learning:** Reinforcement learning (RL) is concerned with how agents ought to take actions in an environment to maximize cumulative reward. It is often applied in scenarios where an agent must learn a policy of actions to achieve long-term objectives; examples include robotics, game playing, and self-driving cars. Key RL algorithms include Q-learning, SARSA, and deep reinforcement learning methods like Deep Q-Networks (DQN).

- **Semi-supervised Learning:** Semi-supervised learning is an approach that combines a small amount of labeled data with a large amount of unlabeled data. It is beneficial when the cost of labeling data is high, making it impractical to have a completely labeled dataset. Algorithms in this category include semi-supervised support vector machines and graph-based methods.

Data Representations and Features: In machine learning, features refer to the individual measurable properties or characteristics of the phenomenon being observed. Proper feature representation is critical, as the performance of machine learning models heavily depends on the relevance and quality of features.

Training and Validation: The process of training a machine learning model involves exposing it to a subset of the data, known as the training set, and using this data to adjust the model parameters. The performance of the model is frequently evaluated on a separate subset of data known as the validation set. This evaluation is crucial in preventing overfitting, where the model performs well on the training data but fails to generalize to unseen data.

Overfitting and Generalization: Overfitting occurs when a model learns not only the underlying patterns in the training data but also the noise. Generalization refers to the model's ability to perform well on new, previously unseen data. To achieve good generalization, techniques such as cross-validation, regularization, and dropout are employed.

Machine learning has revolutionized many fields by enabling systems to learn insights and make decisions with minimal human intervention. With the continuing advancements in computational power and data availability, the development and refinement of machine learning techniques are poised to drive significant innovation across industries.

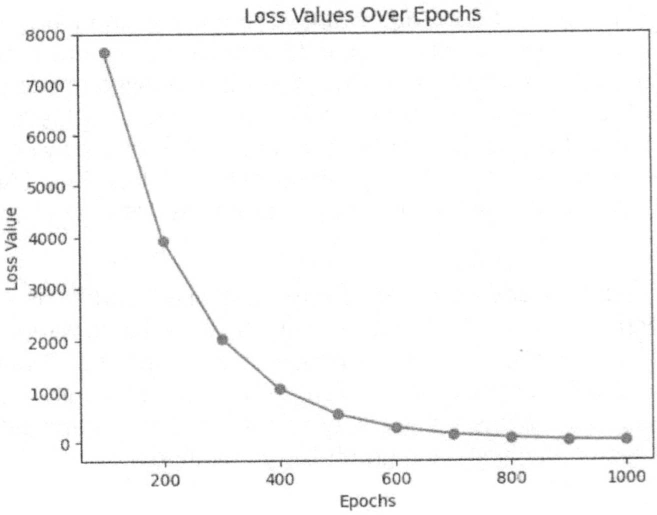

1.2 History and Evolution of Machine Learning

The history and evolution of machine learning are rooted in multiple disciplines, including statistics, computer science, and artificial intelligence. Machine learning, as we understand it today, has emerged from a series of groundbreaking theoretical and practical advancements spanning several decades.

The origins of machine learning can be traced back to the 1950s with the advent of the first computers. Researchers began to explore the concept of machines that could learn from data. Alan Turing's seminal 1950 paper "Computing Machinery and Intelligence" posited the idea of a machine capable of simulating human intelligence, thus laying the conceptual groundwork for machine learning.

The 1950s and 1960s witnessed the development of foundational algorithms and theories. In 1957, Frank Rosenblatt introduced the Perceptron, an early neural network model capable of learning weights for binary classifiers. Although it had significant limitations, particularly in solving non-linearly separable problems, the Perceptron marked a significant milestone in the development of neural networks.

The birth of artificial intelligence as a formal academic discipline in 1956, at the Dartmouth Conference, provided a focal point for research into machine learning. During this period, symbolic approaches dominated, relying heavily on logic and rule-based systems. Researchers focused on hand-crafted models and algorithms capable of reasoning about the world.

The 1970s brought a heightened understanding of the limitations of existing approaches. Marvin Minsky and Seymour Papert's 1969 book "Perceptrons" demonstrated that simple neural networks were fundamentally limited in their capabilities, particularly in handling complex pattern recognition tasks. This realization led to a temporary decline in neural network research and a shift towards statistical methods.

The 1980s saw a resurgence of interest in neural networks, driven by the rediscovery of backpropagation, a powerful algorithm for training multi-layer neural networks. This period also witnessed the growth of connectionism, which sought to understand cognitive processes through interconnected networks of simple units. Novel architectures like Boltzmann Machines and Hopfield Networks were introduced, further enriching the neural network landscape.

During the 1990s, machine learning began to mature as a distinct field within artificial intelligence, characterized by a more rigorous theoretical foundation and a focus on empirical evaluation. The availability of larger datasets and increased computational power enabled the development of more sophisticated models such as Support Vector Machines (SVMs) and ensemble methods like Random Forests. These methods emphasized the importance of generalization and statistical robustness, providing powerful tools for a wide range of applications.

The early 2000s marked the expansion of machine learning into new domains, propelled by the rise of the internet and the subsequent explosion of available data. Techniques such as unsupervised learning and reinforcement learning gained prominence, enabling the development of systems capable of autonomous learning and decision-making in complex environments.

The mid-2000s to the present represents the era of deep learning, characterized by the resurgence and refinement of neural networks with many layers, known as deep neural networks (DNNs). Key milestones include the breakthrough results achieved by deep learning models in image recognition, exemplified by AlexNet's success in the 2012 ImageNet competition. These advancements were facilitated by improvements in algorithmic techniques, such as convolutional neural networks (CNNs) and recurrent neural networks (RNNs), as well as the availability of specialized hardware like GPUs.

Deep learning has since become the dominant paradigm in machine learning, revolutionizing fields such as natural language processing, computer vision, and autonomous systems. Frameworks like PyTorch and TensorFlow have democratized access to powerful machine learning tools, enabling researchers and practitioners worldwide to develop and deploy state-of-the-art models.

The evolution of machine learning continues to be driven by interdisciplinary collaboration, bridging gaps between theoretical advancements and practical applications. Trends such as unsupervised learning, transfer learning, and explainable AI are pushing the boundaries of what machine learning systems can achieve, promising to tackle increasingly complex and impactful problems.

The history and evolution of machine learning reflect an ongoing pursuit of understanding and harnessing data-driven patterns to create intelligent systems. The journey from early rule-based systems to contemporary deep learning architectures highlights the field's dynamic and iterative nature, driven by both theoretical insights and practical demands.

1.3 Types of Machine Learning

Understanding the types of machine learning is essential for selecting the appropriate algorithm and method for a given problem. Machine learning can be broadly classified into three main categories: supervised learning, unsupervised learning, and reinforcement learning. Each type employs different approaches and techniques to model and make predictions from data.

Supervised learning is characterized by the presence of labeled data. Here, the machine learning model is trained on a dataset that includes input-output pairs, where the output is known as the label. The objective is to learn a mapping function from inputs to the target output. Common supervised learning tasks include classification, where the goal is to predict discrete labels, and regression, which involves predicting continuous values. Consider the following Python example of a simple linear regression using PyTorch:

```
import torch
import torch.nn as nn
import torch.optim as optim

# Data
x = torch.tensor([[1.0], [2.0], [3.0], [4.0]], dtype=torch.float32)
y = torch.tensor([[2.0], [4.0], [6.0], [8.0]], dtype=torch.float32)

# Model
model = nn.Linear(in_features=1, out_features=1)

# Loss and optimizer
criterion = nn.MSELoss()
optimizer = optim.SGD(model.parameters(), lr=0.01)

# Training loop
for epoch in range(100):
    optimizer.zero_grad()
    outputs = model(x)
    loss = criterion(outputs, y)
    loss.backward()
    optimizer.step()

# Predict
with torch.no_grad():
    predictions = model(x)
    print(predictions)
```

The output, displaying the predicted values after training the model, will appear as follows:

```
tensor([[2.0004],
        [3.9994],
        [5.9984],
        [7.9974]])
```

In unsupervised learning, no labeled data is provided. The goal is to model the underlying structure or distribution in the data to learn more about it. Common tasks include clustering, where the algorithm groups similar data points together, and dimensionality reduction, which aims to reduce the number of variables under consideration. A widely-used algorithm for clustering is K-means, which partitions the dataset into K distinct, non-overlapping subsets or clusters. Below is an implementation of K-means clustering using PyTorch:

```
import torch

# Data
data = torch.tensor([
    [1.0, 2.0],
    [1.5, 1.8],
    [5.0, 8.0],
    [8.0, 8.0],
    [1.0, 0.6],
    [9.0, 11.0]
], dtype=torch.float32)

# Number of clusters
k = 2

# Randomly initialize centroids
centroids = data[torch.randperm(len(data))[:k]]

for _ in range(100): # number of iterations
    # Calculate distances
    distances = torch.cdist(data, centroids)

    # Assign data points to the nearest centroid
    cluster_indices = distances.argmin(dim=1)

    # Recompute centroids
    new_centroids = torch.stack([data[cluster_indices == i].mean(dim=0) for i in
        range(k)])

    if torch.all(centroids == new_centroids):
        break

    centroids = new_centroids

print(centroids)
```

Output will show the final cluster centroids:

```
tensor([[1.1667, 1.4667],
        [7.3333, 9.0000]])
```

Reinforcement learning involves training an agent to make a sequence of decisions by rewarding it for good actions and penalizing it for bad ones. The agent learns to navigate an environment to maximize cumulative reward. Key concepts include states, actions, and rewards. Unlike supervised learning, reinforcement learning does not rely on labeled input/output pairs. A simplistic example would involve using the

Q-learning algorithm, but its full implementation is beyond the scope of this section.

Supervised and unsupervised learning techniques can be combined in a semi-supervised learning approach, especially useful when large amounts of unlabeled data are available and labeling them is expensive or time-consuming. Another hybrid approach is self-supervised learning, where the system generates its own labels from the input data.

These types of machine learning represent a high-level overview of the methodologies used in developing intelligent and autonomous systems. Understanding these distinctions and their corresponding algorithms allows practitioners to apply the most suitable technique to their particular use case, thereby enhancing the efficiency and effectiveness of the learning models they develop.

1.4 Applications of Machine Learning

Machine learning has become a transformative tool across numerous domains, demonstrating its prowess in solving complex problems and enabling intelligent decision-making processes. This section delves into some of the prominent applications of machine learning, spanning various industries, to elucidate its widespread impact and utility.

One of the most widely recognized applications is in the field of **Healthcare**. Machine learning algorithms have been instrumental in advancing medical diagnostics and treatment plans. For instance, machine learning models are employed to analyze medical images, aiding in the detection and diagnosis of conditions such as tumors, fractures, and other anomalies. These algorithms, trained on vast datasets of medical imagery, can often identify patterns and irregularities with a precision that rivals or exceeds human expertise.

Another significant application is found in **Finance**. Financial institutions utilize machine learning to process and analyze large volumes of data, enhancing decision-making processes in areas such as fraud detection, credit scoring, and algorithmic trading. For instance, machine learning algorithms can detect unusual patterns in transaction data that may indicate fraudulent activity, enabling more robust security measures. Additionally, these models can analyze customer data to assess creditworthiness more accurately than traditional methods, ultimately improving risk management.

In the **Retail** industry, machine learning facilitates personalized marketing and inventory management. By analyzing customer behavior and purchasing patterns, retailers can offer personalized recommendations, improving customer satisfaction and engagement. Machine learning models also optimize inventory levels by predicting demand for products, thus reducing wastage and ensuring the availability of popular items.

The field of **Manufacturing** has also seen significant advancements through the adoption of machine learning. Predictive maintenance is a notable application where machine learning models predict equipment failures before they happen, based on monitoring data from sensors and historical patterns. This proactive approach to maintenance minimizes downtime and extends the lifespan of machinery, which translates into substantial cost savings and enhanced productivity.

In the domain of **Transportation**, machine learning underpins the development of autonomous vehicles. Self-driving cars leverage a variety of machine learning algorithms to interpret sensor data, recognize objects, and make real-time decisions about navigation and obstacle avoidance. Machine learning also plays a crucial role in optimizing logistics and supply chain management by predicting delivery times, optimizing routes, and managing fleet operations.

Natural Language Processing (NLP) is another critical application area where machine learning has made substantial contributions. NLP encompasses tasks such as language translation, sentiment analysis, and chatbots. For instance, machine learning algorithms are used in translation services like Google Translate to convert text from one language to another with significant accuracy. Sentiment analysis tools employ machine learning to gauge public opinion by analyzing social media posts and reviews, providing valuable insights for businesses and researchers.

Another essential application lies in **Cybersecurity**. Machine learning enhances the detection and mitigation of cyber threats by analyzing patterns of network traffic, identifying vulnerabilities, and predicting potential attacks. These algorithms can detect anomalies that may signify attempted breaches, enabling faster and more effective responses to cybersecurity incidents.

In **Energy Management**, machine learning optimizes the operations of smart grids and enhances the efficiency of energy consumption and distribution. By analyzing consumption patterns and predicting demand, machine learning models help in balancing supply with demand, reducing energy waste, and lowering operational costs.

Education is undergoing a transformation with the help of machine learning. Intelligent tutoring systems provide personalized learning experiences by adapting to the needs and progress of individual students. These systems analyze student performance data to offer customized feedback and instructional strategies, thereby improving learning outcomes.

Lastly, in the field of **Entertainment**, machine learning algorithms power content recommendation systems used by platforms such as Netflix and Spotify. These recommender systems analyze user preferences and behavior to suggest relevant movies, shows, or music, thereby enhancing user engagement and satisfaction.

```
import numpy as np
import pandas as pd
from sklearn.metrics.pairwise import cosine_similarity

# Sample user-movie ratings matrix
ratings_matrix = pd.DataFrame({
    'User1': [5, 4, np.nan, 1],
    'User2': [np.nan, 2, 3, 1],
    'User3': [2, 1, 5, 4],
    'User4': [4, np.nan, 4, None]
}, index=['Movie1', 'Movie2', 'Movie3', 'Movie4'])

# Calculate cosine similarity between users
user_similarity = cosine_similarity(ratings_matrix.fillna(0).T)

# Convert the similarity matrix to a DataFrame for better readability
user_similarity_df = pd.DataFrame(user_similarity, index=ratings_matrix.columns,
    columns=ratings_matrix.columns)

print(user_similarity_df)
```

```
        User1     User2     User3     User4
User1  1.000000  0.537279  0.588348  0.502571
User2  0.537279  1.000000  0.444444  0.267261
User3  0.588348  0.444444  1.000000  0.816497
User4  0.502571  0.267261  0.816497  1.000000
```

The application areas of machine learning are vast and continuously expanding, driven by advancements in algorithms, computational power, and the availability of large datasets. These examples illustrate how machine learning is leveraged to solve complex problems, optimize processes, and create innovative solutions across a multitude of sectors. Through the integration of machine learning techniques, industries are enhancing their operational efficiency, decision-making quality, and overall effectiveness in addressing real-world challenges.

1.5 Introduction to PyTorch

PyTorch is an open-source machine learning library primarily developed by Facebook's AI Research lab (FAIR). Unlike traditional numerical computation libraries such as NumPy, which operate on multi-dimensional arrays, PyTorch provides support for GPU-accelerated tensor computation, which is crucial for deep learning applications. PyTorch is designed to be intuitive, flexible, and deeply integrated with Python, making it an excellent tool for both research and production contexts.

PyTorch's core data structure is the *Tensor*, which is a multi-dimensional array similar to NumPy's *ndarray* but with additional functionalities. Tensors can be created, manipulated, and processed in a similar way to NumPy arrays, but with the added benefit of being able to run computations on GPUs for increased performance.

To demonstrate the simplicity and flexibility that PyTorch offers, consider the creation and manipulation of a tensor:

```
import torch

# Creating a tensor with random values
x = torch.rand(5, 3)
print(x)

# Checking the size of the tensor
print(x.size())

# Performing tensor addition
y = torch.rand(5, 3)
result = x + y
print(result)
```

Outputs for the above code would resemble:

```
tensor([[0.5624, 0.9169, 0.7100],
        [0.1626, 0.3880, 0.5984],
        [0.0661, 0.6157, 0.6349],
        [0.1681, 0.9493, 0.8645],
        [0.1775, 0.3747, 0.7232]])

torch.Size([5, 3])

tensor([[0.9470, 1.6050, 1.6800],
        [0.8539, 1.2878, 1.1724],
        [0.4220, 1.2533, 1.2392],
        [0.7428, 1.7105, 1.2765],
        [0.8463, 0.7099, 1.0626]])
```

Users can see how concise and readable the PyTorch code is, compared to traditional numerical computing approaches.

One of PyTorch's standout features is its *dynamic computation graph*, also known as define-by-run. This means that the computational graph is built on-the-fly as operations are performed, allowing for greater flexibility. This is particularly advantageous for applications involving variable-length sequences, such as natural language processing (NLP). In contrast, other frameworks like TensorFlow initially required a static graph to be defined, although TensorFlow has since evolved to include more dynamic features as well.

```
# Example of dynamic computation graph
a = torch.tensor([2.0], requires_grad=True)
b = torch.tensor([3.0], requires_grad=True)
c = a * b # Simple multiplication
c.backward() # Backpropagate
# Gradients should now be available
print(a.grad) # Expected gradient is tensor([3.])
print(b.grad) # Expected gradient is tensor([2.])
```

The c.backward() operation computes the gradients of c with respect to a and b, illustrating how straightforward it is to perform automatic differentiation in PyTorch.

Furthermore, PyTorch integrates seamlessly with other popular Python libraries such as torchvision for computer vision, torchaudio for processing audio data, and torchtext for handling text-based data. These specialized libraries come equipped with datasets, models, and tools tailored for their respective domains.

Another integral component of PyTorch is *torch.nn*, which provides a high-level API for building neural networks. This module includes layers, loss functions, and utilities that streamline the development of complex architectures. Consider a simple feedforward neural network example:

```
import torch.nn as nn
import torch.nn.functional as F

# Define a simple neural network
class Net(nn.Module):
    def __init__(self):
        super(Net, self).__init__()
        self.fc1 = nn.Linear(784, 128)
        self.fc2 = nn.Linear(128, 64)
        self.fc3 = nn.Linear(64, 10)

    def forward(self, x):
        x = F.relu(self.fc1(x))
        x = F.relu(self.fc2(x))
        x = self.fc3(x)
        return x

net = Net()
print(net)
```

The output will display the structure of the network, confirming that the PyTorch API provides a clear and concise way to define and visualize neural network architectures.

PyTorch also supports data parallelism through the *torch.nn.DataParallel* module, allowing tasks to be distributed across multiple GPUs effortlessly. This is particularly beneficial for large-scale experiments and production-level machine learning models:

```
# Using DataParallel to parallelize model computations across multiple GPUs
device = torch.device("cuda:0" if torch.cuda.is_available() else "cpu")
net = Net().to(device)
net = nn.DataParallel(net)
```

Through this short code snippet, a user can leverage the computational power of multiple GPUs to significantly accelerate training times.

For checkpoint-saving and model serialization, PyTorch utilizes Python's native *pickle* module. Saving a model's state_dict and reloading it later for further inference or training is straightforward:

```
# Save
torch.save(net.state_dict(), 'model.pth')

# Load
new_net = Net()
new_net.load_state_dict(torch.load('model.pth'))
```

With these characteristics, PyTorch presents itself as not only a powerful tool for research and experimentation but also a solid foundation for deployment and production environments.

1.6 Why Choose PyTorch?

PyTorch has become one of the most popular frameworks for machine learning and deep learning due to its flexibility, ease of use, and powerful capabilities. This section delves into various reasons why PyTorch stands out in the crowded landscape of machine learning frameworks.

- **Dynamic Computation Graphs:** One of the most significant features that differentiate PyTorch from other frameworks is its use of dynamic computation graphs, also known as define-by-run graphs. Unlike traditional static graphs used in frameworks like TensorFlow (prior to TensorFlow 2.0), dynamic graphs are constructed on-the-fly as operations are executed. This provides tremendous flexibility, allowing users to modify the model architecture during runtime based on specific conditions.

- **Pythonic Nature:** PyTorch is inherently Pythonic, which means that it easily integrates with native Python constructs and libraries. This appeals to the large community of Python developers by providing them with an intuitive and seamless experience. The framework supports features such as list comprehensions, loops, and conditional statements directly within the model definition and training scripts, making it simple for those already familiar with Python to get started.

- **Extensive Ecosystem and Community Support:** PyTorch benefits from a growing ecosystem of libraries and tools designed to enhance its functionality. These include 'torchvision' for computer vision, 'torchtext' for natural language processing, and 'torchaudio' for audio processing. This modularity allows users to leverage specialized libraries for different tasks without needing to reinvent the wheel.

- **Strong Support for Research and Prototyping:** Researchers frequently favor PyTorch for its simplicity and adaptability, which are crucial for experimental and iterative research processes. The dynamic graph construction allows for easier debugging and quicker iterations, enabling rapid prototyping of new algorithms and techniques.

- **Integration with High-Performance Deep Learning Libraries:** PyTorch seamlessly integrates with several high-performance libraries, such as cuDNN and NCCL, allowing for efficient utilization of modern GPU hardware. This ensures that models run efficiently during both the training and inference phases, benefiting from hardware acceleration.

- **Advancements with PyTorch Lightning:** PyTorch Lightning is a lightweight wrapper for PyTorch that abstracts the engineering details, making it easier to write scalable and reproducible code. It introduces standardized structures for model training and evaluation, enabling researchers and developers to focus more on designing models rather than dealing with boilerplate code.

- **Deployment Versatility:** PyTorch offers various options for deploying models into production environments. 'TorchScript' allows for the conversion of PyTorch models into an intermediate representation that can be run independently of Python, facilitating deployment in environments where a Python interpreter is not available. Additionally, PyTorch supports integration with ONNX (Open Neural Network Exchange), enabling model interoperability across different frameworks and platforms, such as Caffe2 and Microsoft's Azure.

- **Rich Debugging and Visualization Tools:** PyTorch supports a range of debugging and visualization tools, such as 'torch.autograd' for tracking gradients and 'TensorBoard' for visualizing training metrics. These tools provide deep insights into the model's performance and behavior, aiding in the development and debugging processes.

- **Scalability and Distributed Training:** PyTorch includes built-in support for distributed training across multiple GPUs and nodes, leveraging libraries like 'torch.distributed'. This is essential for training large-scale models on extensive datasets, reducing the total training time significantly. PyTorch's distributed training features ensure that it can scale from a single machine to large distributed clusters efficiently.

- **User-Friendly API and Documentation:** PyTorch's API is designed to be both user-friendly and comprehensive. Its extensive documentation, complete with tutorials and examples, assists users in quickly becoming proficient in the framework. The community-driven aspect of PyTorch ensures that documentation is regularly updated and that users can find support through forums and community channels.

A simple example of PyTorch code can be written to demonstrate some of these advantages. Below is an example of a simple linear regression model in PyTorch.

```
import torch
import torch.nn as nn
import torch.optim as optim

# Define the linear regression model
class LinearRegressionModel(nn.Module):
    def __init__(self):
        super(LinearRegressionModel, self).__init__()
        self.linear = nn.Linear(1, 1)

    def forward(self, x):
        return self.linear(x)

# Create model
```

```
model = LinearRegressionModel()

# Define loss function and optimizer
criterion = nn.MSELoss()
optimizer = optim.SGD(model.parameters(), lr=0.01)

# Generate some training data
x_train = torch.tensor([[1.0], [2.0], [3.0], [4.0]], requires_grad=True)
y_train = torch.tensor([[2.0], [4.0], [6.0], [8.0]], requires_grad=True)

# Training loop
for epoch in range(100):
    # Forward pass: Compute predicted y by passing x to the model
    y_pred = model(x_train)

    # Compute and print loss
    loss = criterion(y_pred, y_train)

    # Before the backward pass, use the optimizer object to zero all of the
    # gradients for the variables it will update (which are the learnable weights
    # of the model)
    optimizer.zero_grad()

    # Backward pass: compute gradient of the loss with respect to model parameters
    loss.backward()

    # Calling the step function on an Optimizer makes an update to its parameters
    optimizer.step()

    if (epoch+1) % 10 == 0:
        print(f'Epoch [{epoch+1}/100], Loss: {loss.item():.4f}')

# Print the learned parameters
print("Learned parameters: ", model.linear.weight.item(), model.linear.bias.item())
```

The above code illustrates the ease of defining and training a simple linear regression model using PyTorch. It demonstrates the model definition, loss function selection, and optimizer setup, followed by a straightforward training loop. The output would show the progression of the loss over the epochs and eventually print the learned parameters for the model.

```
Epoch [10/100], Loss: 0.0217
Epoch [20/100], Loss: 0.0166
Epoch [30/100], Loss: 0.0128
...
Epoch [100/100], Loss: 0.0001
Learned parameters: tensor(2., grad_fn=<ViewBackward0>) tensor(1.4290e-07, grad_fn=<ViewBackward0>)
```

Through this example, the dynamic and flexible nature of PyTorch in handling fundamental machine learning tasks is highlighted. It reinforces why many practitioners and researchers prefer PyTorch for its simplicity and powerful capabilities.

1.7 Overview of PyTorch Ecosystem

The PyTorch ecosystem comprises an extensive array of libraries and tools designed to facilitate and accelerate various machine learning tasks, from building and training neural networks to deploying models in production environments. This rich ecosystem aims to support researchers and practitioners in creating robust and scalable machine learning solutions.

One of the core components of this ecosystem is **Torchvision**. Torchvision provides utilities for computer vision tasks. It includes commonly used datasets, model architectures, and image transformations, which significantly reduce the overhead of writing custom code for common operations. The availability of pre-trained models within Torchvision allows for transfer learning, enabling users to leverage models trained on large datasets like ImageNet and fine-tune them for specific applications.

```
import torchvision.transforms as transforms
from torchvision import datasets

transform = transforms.Compose([
    transforms.Resize((256, 256)),
    transforms.ToTensor(),
])

dataset = datasets.CIFAR10(root='./data', train=True, download=True, transform=
    transform)
```

Another notable library is **Torchaudio**, which handles audio data. Torchaudio offers functionalities for loading, transforming, and augmenting audio datasets. Similar to Torchvision, it includes pre-trained models for tasks such as speech recognition and audio classification.

```
import torchaudio

waveform, sample_rate = torchaudio.load('audio_file.wav')

# Applying transformations
waveform = torchaudio.transforms.Resample(orig_freq=sample_rate, new_freq=16000)
    (waveform)
```

Torchtext is the counterpart for natural language processing (NLP). Torchtext provides tools for preprocessing text data, tokenization, and creating data pipelines. It supports popular datasets and pre-trained word embeddings, which are essential for most NLP tasks.

```
from torchtext.data.utils import get_tokenizer
from torchtext.vocab import build_vocab_from_iterator
```

```
tokenizer = get_tokenizer('basic_english')

def yield_tokens(data_iter):
    for raw_text in data_iter:
        yield tokenizer(raw_text)

vocab = build_vocab_from_iterator(yield_tokens(["Here is an example sentence"]))
```

For domain-specific applications, PyTorch offers **fast.ai**, a high-level library built on PyTorch that simplifies the training and deployment of deep learning models. Fast.ai promotes rapid prototyping, thereby making powerful machine learning techniques accessible to a broad audience.

```
from fastai.vision.all import *

path = untar_data(URLs.MNIST_SAMPLE)
dls = ImageDataLoaders.from_folder(path)

learn = cnn_learner(dls, resnet18, metrics=accuracy)
learn.fine_tune(1)
```

Moreover, **PyTorch Lightning** introduces a more structured and clear approach to writing PyTorch code. It abstracts away most of the boilerplate code typically associated with training loops, logging, and distributed training, allowing researchers to focus on model architecture and experimentation.

```
import pytorch_lightning as pl
import torch.nn.functional as F
from torchvision import datasets, transforms

class LitMNIST(pl.LightningModule):
    def __init__(self):
        super().__init__()
        self.model = nn.Sequential(
            nn.Flatten(),
            nn.Linear(28*28, 128),
            nn.ReLU(),
            nn.Dropout(0.2),
            nn.Linear(128, 10)
        )

    def forward(self, x):
        return self.model(x)

    def training_step(self, batch, batch_idx):
        x, y = batch
        logits = self(x)
        loss = F.cross_entropy(logits, y)
        return loss

    def configure_optimizers(self):
        return torch.optim.Adam(self.parameters(), lr=1e-3)

# Initialize the dataset and dataloader
dataset = datasets.MNIST('', download=True, train=True, transform=transforms.
```

```
    ToTensor())
train_loader = torch.utils.data.DataLoader(dataset, batch_size=32)

# Initialize the model and train
model = LitMNIST()
trainer = pl.Trainer(max_epochs=5)
trainer.fit(model, train_loader)
```

To streamline the deployment of models in production, PyTorch offers **TorchServe**. TorchServe is an open-source model serving library that makes it easy to deploy trained PyTorch models at scale. It supports multi-model serving, model versioning, logging, metrics, and security features.

Recently, **TorchScript** has become a crucial part of the ecosystem. TorchScript is a way to create serializable and optimizable models from PyTorch code. It allows models to be run independently from Python and can be optimized for performance on different hardware platforms, such as GPUs and mobile devices.

```
import torch

class MyModule(torch.nn.Module):
    def forward(self, x):
        return x + 10

module = MyModule()
scripted_module = torch.jit.script(module)

# Save and load the scripted module
torch.jit.save(scripted_module, 'scripted_module.pt')
loaded_module = torch.jit.load('scripted_module.pt')

print(loaded_module(torch.tensor([5])))
```

Another integral part of the PyTorch ecosystem is **LibTorch**, the C++ frontend of PyTorch. It provides the core functionalities of the framework for use in production environments written in C++.

Understanding the broader **PyTorch Ecosystem** is essential for leveraging the comprehensive tools and libraries designed to support state-of-the-art research and development in machine learning. This interconnected framework of libraries not only simplifies complex processes but also empowers developers to innovate and scale their solutions with greater efficiency.

1.8 Basic Concepts and Terminology

Understanding the basic concepts and terminology in machine learning is paramount for meaningful engagement with PyTorch and other machine learning frameworks. This section will delve into the foundational terms and concepts that are frequently encountered and pivotal in machine learning.

Machine learning (ML) broadly falls under artificial intelligence (AI), wherein algorithms learn from data to make decisions without explicit programming instructions. This learning process involves several key terms and paradigms.

- **Dataset:** A dataset is a structured collection of data. In machine learning, it typically includes input variables (features) and corresponding output variables (labels or targets). For example, in image classification, the dataset would consist of images (features) and their associated categories (labels).
- **Features:** Features are individual measurable properties or characteristics of the phenomena being observed. In a tabular dataset, features are represented by columns. They are also referred to as attributes or input variables. Effective feature engineering, which involves selecting and possibly transforming features, is critical to the performance of ML models.
- **Labels:** Labels, also known as targets or outcome variables, are the variable that the model aims to predict. In supervised learning, the learning algorithm uses these labels to guide the learning process.
- **Training Data:** This is a subset of the dataset used to train the model. The model learns by mapping input features to the output labels present in the training data. Properly preparing this data, including normalization and augmentation, can significantly impact model performance.
- **Validation Data:** Validation data is used to tune the hyperparameters of the model and to avoid overfitting during training. It provides an unbiased evaluation of the model during the training phase.
- **Testing Data:** Testing data is a set of examples used only to assess the performance of a fully trained model. It provides an ob-

jective measure of a model's generalization capability to unseen data.

- **Model:** In machine learning, a model is a mathematical representation (or system) that encapsulates patterns within the data. It consists of parameters learned during training and is used to make predictions on new, unseen data.
- **Algorithm:** An algorithm is a set of rules or procedures followed to solve a problem. In ML, it refers to the method used to create a model from data. Examples include linear regression, decision trees, and neural networks.
- **Loss Function:** The loss function, also known as the cost function, measures the difference between the predicted values and the actual values in supervised learning. It quantifies the model's performance, guiding the optimization process. Common loss functions include Mean Squared Error (MSE) for regression, and Cross-Entropy Loss for classification.
- **Optimizer:** An optimizer is an algorithm used to adjust the weights of the model to minimize the loss function. Popular optimizers include Gradient Descent and its variants such as Stochastic Gradient Descent (SGD), Adam, and RMSprop.
- **Epoch:** An epoch refers to one complete pass through the entire training dataset. Training a model typically involves multiple epochs to improve model accuracy.
- **Batch Size:** Batch size defines the number of training examples utilized in one forward/backward pass. Choosing an appropriate batch size is crucial for balancing computational resources and model convergence speed. Smaller batch sizes generally result in noisier updates, but can lead to shorter training times.
- **Overfitting and Underfitting:** Overfitting occurs when a model learns the training data too well, including its noise and outliers, resulting in poor generalization to new data. Underfitting means a model is too simplistic to capture the underlying patterns in the data, leading to poor model performance on both training and new data.
- **Regularization:** This refers to techniques used to prevent overfitting by incorporating additional information or constraints into the model. Common regularization methods include L1 (Lasso) and L2 (Ridge) regularization, as well as dropout in neural networks.

- **Neural Network:** A neural network is a series of algorithms that attempt to recognize underlying relationships in a set of data through a process that mimics the way the human brain operates. It consists of layers of interconnected neurons, where each neuron performs a linear transformation followed by a non-linear activation function on the inputs it receives.

With these fundamental terms and concepts in place, the ensuing sections will delve into hands-on applications using PyTorch, where we will see these elements in action. Understanding this terminology will greatly facilitate comprehension and practical application as we proceed.

Chapter 2

Setting Up Your Environment

This chapter guides readers through the process of setting up a suitable development environment for machine learning with PyTorch. It discusses the selection of appropriate IDEs or text editors, installation of Python, and the creation of virtual environments. Instructions for installing PyTorch using Pip and Anaconda and verifying the installation are provided. The chapter also covers dependency management, working with Jupyter Notebooks, and leveraging GPUs to enhance computational efficiency.

2.1 Introduction to Development Environments

A development environment, often referred to as a Development Environment Setup (DES), is essential for efficiently writing, testing, and debugging machine learning code. A suitable development environment provides tools and features that can significantly enhance productivity and ease the development process. It typically consists of an Integrated Development Environment (IDE) or a text editor, a programming language interpreter or compiler, and tools for version control, debugging, and dependency management.

Integrated Development Environments (IDEs) and text editors form the foundational component of a development environment. IDEs are software applications that offer comprehensive facilities to computer programmers for software development. Unlike basic text editors, IDEs typically include a source code editor, build automation tools, and a debugger. State-of-the-art IDEs such as PyCharm, Visual Studio Code (VS Code), and Jupyter Notebook are widely used in the Python and machine learning community for their extensive features and ease of use.

Text editors like Sublime Text and Atom provide a more lightweight alternative to IDEs. While they lack some features inherent to full-fledged IDEs, they offer greater flexibility and are often preferred for simpler tasks or when minimal software footprint is desired. Both IDEs and text editors can be extended with plugins or extensions, adding support for version control, code linting, syntax highlighting, and other useful features.

IDEs such as PyCharm offer intelligent code completion, code inspections, on-the-fly error highlighting, and quick-fixes, alongside automated code refactoring and rich navigation capabilities. Conversely, tools like Jupyter Notebook facilitate interactive data exploration and visualization, making them invaluable for machine learning tasks where iteratively refining and visualizing models is crucial.

Python is the primary programming language used for machine learning with PyTorch. Installing Python correctly is indispensable for setting up your development environment. Depending on the operating system and user preferences, Python can be installed through various means, including the official installer from Python.org or package managers like Homebrew for macOS and apt-get for Linux distributions.

Virtual environments are a pivotal aspect of managing Python projects. They allow developers to create isolated environments with specific versions of Python and dependency packages. Tools such as venv (included with Python 3.3+), virtualenv, and conda help create and manage these isolated environments, ensuring that dependencies for one project do not interfere with those of another. This isolation is critical for maintaining consistent development and production environments, reducing "it works on my machine" issues.

The steps to create and activate a virtual environment using venv on Unix-based systems are as follows:

```
python3 -m venv myenv
source myenv/bin/activate
```

On Windows:

```
python -m venv myenv
myenv\Scripts\activate
```

Once activated, the virtual environment can be deactivated using the deactivate command.

Dependency management is integral to maintaining reproducibility in machine learning projects. Tools such as pip, the Python package installer, and Conda, a package and environment management system, are commonly used for this purpose. While pip allows installation of packages listed in the Python Package Index (PyPI), Conda offers the added benefit of managing dependencies across different programming languages.

A requirements.txt file typically lists the packages and specific versions required for a project. This file can be generated and subsequently used to install dependencies:

```
pip freeze > requirements.txt
pip install -r requirements.txt
```

Similarly, Conda uses an environment.yml file to manage dependencies, which can be created and used as follows:

```
conda env export > environment.yml
conda env create -f environment.yml
```

Version control systems like Git provide a mechanism for tracking changes, collaborating with others, and maintaining a history of modifications. Using a version control system is a best practice for any software development, including machine learning projects. Platforms like GitHub, GitLab, and Bitbucket support Git and offer additional features for collaboration, code review, and continuous integration.

Cloud-based platforms such as Google Colab and Microsoft's Azure Notebooks provide alternatives for setting up development environments. These platforms offer Jupyter Notebook interfaces along with pre-configured environments that include essential libraries like PyTorch, eliminating the necessity of local setup. Google Colab, in particular, offers free access to GPUs, making it an attractive option for running computationally intensive machine learning tasks.

Understanding and setting up an effective development environment lays a solid foundation for tackling machine learning projects with PyTorch. This entails selecting the right tools and ensuring all components work seamlessly together.

2.2 Choosing an IDE or Text Editor

Selecting the right Integrated Development Environment (IDE) or text editor significantly impacts productivity and ease of developing machine learning applications with PyTorch. The decision primarily depends on several factors such as the level of familiarity, features provided by the software, and personal preferences. There are numerous options available, and this section will examine a few popular choices that cater to various needs and skill levels.

- **PyCharm** is a feature-rich IDE developed by JetBrains, tailored explicitly for Python programming. PyCharm offers two versions: the Community Edition, which is free and open-source, and the Professional Edition, which requires a subscription. Prominent features of PyCharm include intelligent code editing, code analysis, project navigation, debugging, and support for virtual environments. PyCharm's integration with version control systems like Git, along with robust support for frameworks such as Django, makes it suitable for larger projects. Installation instructions are straightforward and can be found on the JetBrains website.

- **VSCode** (Visual Studio Code) by Microsoft is another highly popular option. It is a lightweight but powerful source-code editor that runs on your desktop. VSCode supports extensions, which allow users to enhance its capabilities. The Python extension for VSCode, developed by Microsoft, provides rich support for Python development, including features such as IntelliSense, linting, debugging, code formatting, and Jupyter Notebook support. The integration of VSCode with different source control platforms, like GitHub, makes it a favored choice among developers. Installation of VSCode and its extensions can be efficiently handled through the integrated Extensions Marketplace.

- **Jupyter Notebook** is particularly popular in the data science and machine learning communities due to its interactive nature. It allows for the combination of live code, equations, visualizations, and narrative text in a single document. Jupyter is ideal for exploratory data analysis, sharing analyses, and creating tutorials or educational materials. Its support for various programming kernels, including IPython, enhances its flexibility. Installation is facilitated by Anaconda, although it can also be installed via Pip.

- **Spyder** (Scientific Python Development Environment) is another IDE targeted at data science and scientific computing. It integrates well with Anaconda and includes features like an interactive console, support for various scientific libraries like NumPy, SciPy, and Matplotlib, and excellent support for debugging. Spyder offers capabilities similar to RStudio and provides an intuitive interface for scientists who might be transitioning from other data analysis tools.

- For those who prefer minimalist and highly configurable environments, **Vim** and **Emacs** remain popular choices. Vim is a modal text editor known for its efficiency and speed, offering extensive plugins for Python development. Emacs, on the other hand, is more than just a text editor; it is often described as a Lisp machine capable of being customized into an integrated development environment. Both editors have steep learning curves but are incredibly powerful once mastered.

```
sudo snap install pycharm-community --classic
```

```
sudo snap install code --classic
```

```
pip install notebook
```

```
conda install spyder
```

```
sudo apt install vim
```

```
sudo apt install emacs
```

When configuring an IDE or text editor, it is essential to ensure proper integration with Python and PyTorch. This involves setting up code completion, linting, and debugging for seamless development. Most modern editors will automatically detect virtual environments and allow configuration for specific interpreters and toolchains.

Choosing an IDE or text editor requires consideration of the development workflow, project requirements, and personal comfort. Familiarity with the tool and effective utilization of its features contributes substantially to efficient machine learning model development with PyTorch.

2.3 Installing Python

Python is an essential prerequisite for developing machine learning models using PyTorch. It is recommended to use Python versions 3.6 to 3.9 for compatibility with the latest PyTorch releases.

To install Python, follow the steps appropriate for your operating system. The instructions provided here cover the three major operating systems: Windows, macOS, and Linux.

Windows:

1. Visit the official Python website at https://www.python.org/downloads/. 2. Click the button for the latest Python release and download the Windows installer. 3. Run the installer. In the installation wizard:

- Ensure that the checkbox Add Python to PATH is selected.
- Choose the Customize installation option to specify a custom location.
- Select Next, then choose all the optional features if needed. The default options usually suffice.
- Proceed with the installation and wait until it completes.

4. To verify your installation, open the Command Prompt and enter:

```
python --version
```

The output should display the Python version number:

```
Python 3.x.x
```

macOS:

1. macOS includes a version of Python by default, but it is recommended to install the latest official version. 2. To get the latest Python version, visit https://www.python.org/downloads/mac-osx/ and download the appropriate installer. 3. Run the downloaded .pkg file and follow the installation steps. 4. To verify the installation, open the Terminal and enter:

```
python3 --version
```

The output should show the installed Python version:

```
Python 3.x.x
```

Linux:

For many Linux distributions, Python 3 already comes pre-installed. However, it may not be the latest version. Below are steps to install the latest version on common distributions.

Ubuntu:

1. Update the package list and install prerequisites:

```
sudo apt-get update
sudo apt-get install software-properties-common
```

2. Add the deadsnakes PPA:

```
sudo add-apt-repository ppa:deadsnakes/ppa
sudo apt-get update
```

3. Install the desired Python version (example for Python 3.9):

```
sudo apt-get install python3.9
```

Fedora:

1. Update the package list:

```
sudo dnf -y update
```

2. Install Python 3:

```
sudo dnf install python3
```

Verification:

Regardless of the distribution, you can verify the installation by entering:

```
python3 --version
```

The output will confirm the installed Python version:

```
Python 3.x.x
```

By following these steps based on your operating system, you will have a suitable Python environment ready. Having Python installed is foundational for proceeding with setting up your machine learning environment with PyTorch.

2.4 Setting Up Virtual Environments

Virtual environments are a powerful feature in Python that allow the creation of isolated environments for different projects. By doing so, you can manage dependencies and avoid conflicts between packages required by various projects. This section will elucidate the steps involved in creating and managing virtual environments.

Python's built-in module for creating virtual environments is 'venv'. To create a new virtual environment, navigate to your project directory in the terminal or command prompt and execute the following command:

```
python -m venv myenv
```

In the command above, 'myenv' is the name of the virtual environment. You can replace 'myenv' with any name suitable for your project. After the execution, a directory named 'myenv' will be created within your project directory. This directory contains a copy of the Python interpreter and other files necessary for the virtual environment to function.

To activate the virtual environment, use the following command based on your operating system:

- **For Windows:**

```
myenv\Scripts\activate
```

- **For Unix or MacOS:**

```
source myenv/bin/activate
```

Upon activation, the command prompt or terminal will show the environment name in parentheses before the current working directory, indicating that the virtual environment is active. All subsequent Python commands will be executed within this environment until it is deactivated.

To install packages within the virtual environment, use 'pip', the package installer for Python. For example, to install the 'numpy' package, run:

```
pip install numpy
```

The package will be installed only in the 'myenv' environment and will not interfere with other environments or the system-wide Python installation.

To list all the packages installed in the current environment, use:

```
pip list
```

This command will display a list of all the packages along with their versions, helping in dependency management and keeping track of the library versions in use.

To deactivate the virtual environment, simply execute:

```
deactivate
```

This command will return you to the global Python environment or the state before the activation of the virtual environment.

Virtual environments can also be created using third-party tools like 'virtualenv' or 'conda'. The 'virtualenv' tool provides similar functionality as 'venv' but with some additional features.

To install 'virtualenv', run:

```
pip install virtualenv
```

Create a virtual environment with 'virtualenv' by executing:

```
virtualenv myenv
```

The commands to activate and deactivate a 'virtualenv' environment are the same as those for 'venv'.

Another popular tool is 'conda', which is part of the Anaconda distribution. 'Conda' is a package manager and environment management system. To create a virtual environment using 'conda', use the command:

```
conda create --name myenv
```

After creation, activate the 'conda' environment with:

```
conda activate myenv
```

To deactivate the 'conda' environment, use:

```
conda deactivate
```

'Conda' offers powerful features like environment export and import, which are useful for sharing environments across different systems.

To export an environment, execute:

```
conda env export > environment.yml
```

The exported 'environment.yml' file contains all the dependencies and can be used to recreate the environment on another system with:

```
conda env create -f environment.yml
```

In practice, it is essential to keep your virtual environment setups consistent across different systems, especially when working in collaborative settings. Using virtual environments ensures that all team members work with the same dependencies, avoiding potential conflicts and discrepancies that can arise from different library versions.

Overall, setting up virtual environments is a vital step in managing Python projects effectively, allowing for clean, isolated, and reproducible development environments.

2.5 Installing PyTorch with Pip

Installing PyTorch using Pip is a streamlined process that provides flexibility and control over the environment in which you are developing machine learning models. Pip, the Python package installer, is used for installing and managing software packages written in Python. Follow the steps outlined below to install PyTorch using Pip.

First, ensure that you have Python installed on your system. If Python is not installed, refer to the previous section on *Installing Python* for detailed instructions. Once Python is installed, it is recommended to create a virtual environment to manage dependencies and avoid conflicts with other projects. You can create a virtual environment by executing the following commands in your terminal:

```
python3 -m venv myenv
source myenv/bin/activate # On Windows use 'myenv\Scripts\activate'
```

After activating the virtual environment, you can proceed with the installation of PyTorch. The PyTorch team provides a user-friendly website, https://pytorch.org, which includes an installation tool that generates the specific command needed to install PyTorch based on your system configuration and requirements. Below is a typical example of installing PyTorch using Pip.

First, decide on the required version of PyTorch, your preferred computing platform (CPU or GPU), and the version of CUDA (if any) that matches your graphics card drivers. For example, if you wish to install the latest stable version of PyTorch with support for CUDA 11.1, you can use the following command:

```
pip install torch==1.8.1+cu111 torchvision==0.9.1+cu111 torchaudio==0.8.1 -f https
    ://download.pytorch.org/whl/torch_stable.html
```

Here, 'torch' is the core library, while 'torchvision' and 'torchaudio' are PyTorch's companion packages for computer vision and audio-related utilities, respectively. The '-f' flag indicates the use of a specified find-links repository URL, ensuring that Pip recognizes the available binaries.

If you do not require GPU support and would rather install the CPU-only version of PyTorch, the command would be:

```
pip install torch torchvision torchaudio
```

By default, this command installs the latest stable version of PyTorch compatible with a CPU-only environment.

To verify that PyTorch is correctly installed, you can run a simple test script. Open a Python interpreter by typing 'python' in your terminal or create a new Python script with the following content:

```
import torch

# Verify the version of PyTorch
print(torch.__version__)

# Check if CUDA is available
print(torch.cuda.is_available())

# Print the number of available GPUs
print(torch.cuda.device_count())
```

Executing this code should yield outputs such as the PyTorch version number and boolean indicators for CUDA availability, similar to the following:

```
1.8.1
True
2
```

In this example output, PyTorch version 1.8.1 is installed, CUDA is available, and there are two GPUs detected. This confirms that PyTorch is properly configured to leverage GPU acceleration.

To manage dependencies efficiently, it is advantageous to list all installed packages within your virtual environment. This can be achieved with:

```
pip freeze > requirements.txt
```

The 'requirements.txt' file can then be shared or used to recreate the environment elsewhere by running:

```
pip install -r requirements.txt
```

This ensures consistency across different setups and maintains compatibility of packages required for your project.

In summary, installing PyTorch using Pip involves setting up a virtual environment, running the appropriate Pip install command, and verifying the installation. Managing dependencies through Pip's capabilities ensures a maintainable and reproducible development environment. This foundation paves the way for efficient and effective development of machine learning models using PyTorch.

2.6 Installing PyTorch with Anaconda

For an efficient and streamlined machine learning setup, using Anaconda to install PyTorch is a commendable approach. Anaconda simplifies package management and deployment, ensuring consistency across various projects. Here, we detail the step-by-step process to install PyTorch using Anaconda.

First, ensure that Anaconda is installed on your system. If it is not yet installed, download and install the latest version of Anaconda from https://www.anaconda.com/products/individual. Follow the installation instructions specific to your operating system (Windows, macOS, or Linux).

Start by opening the Anaconda Navigator or a terminal window. In the terminal, verify that Anaconda is installed properly by executing the following command:

```
conda --version
```

The output should display the version of the conda package manager, indicating that Anaconda is installed.

Next, create a new virtual environment to keep your project dependencies isolated, which aids in mitigating conflicts between packages and versions. To create a new virtual environment named pytorch_env, execute:

```
conda create --name pytorch_env python=3.9
```

This command creates an environment with Python version 3.9. Adjust the Python version if necessary to meet the specific requirements of your project.

Activate the newly created environment using:

```
conda activate pytorch_env
```

Once the environment is active, install PyTorch. PyTorch provides a specified channel from which you can download all necessary packages. Typically, this will include the core PyTorch library and other essential dependencies. The installation can target either CPU-only or GPU-accelerated computation. Below, we cover both scenarios.

To install the CPU-only version:

```
conda install pytorch torchvision torchaudio cpuonly -c pytorch
```

This command installs PyTorch, TorchVision (a library providing datasets, model architectures, and image transformations), and TorchAudio (for audio data processing), suitable for a CPU-only environment. The -c pytorch flag specifies the channel from which to retrieve the packages.

For GPU support, ensure that your system has a compatible NVIDIA GPU and that the CUDA toolkit is installed. To install the GPU-accelerated version of PyTorch, execute:

```
conda install pytorch torchvision torchaudio cudatoolkit=11.1 -c pytorch -c nvidia
```

This command includes the cudatoolkit=11.1 package, which enables GPU acceleration. Adjust the CUDA version based on your requirements and compatibility with your GPU. The -c nvidia channel may also need to be specified if additional NVIDIA-specific packages are necessary.

After the installation process completes, verify that PyTorch is correctly installed within your environment. Open a Python interpreter by typing python in the terminal and run the following script:

```
import torch
print(torch.__version__)
```

If PyTorch is installed correctly, this script will print the installed version of PyTorch.

Additionally, check if PyTorch can recognize your GPU by executing:

```
print(torch.cuda.is_available())
```

If the output is True, PyTorch has successfully detected your GPU. If it returns False, ensure CUDA is installed properly, and your drivers are up to date.

Here is a summary of the full installation process in one sequence:

```
# Verify Anaconda installation
conda --version

# Create a new virtual environment
conda create --name pytorch_env python=3.9

# Activate the environment
conda activate pytorch_env

# Install PyTorch (CPU-only)
conda install pytorch torchvision torchaudio cpuonly -c pytorch

# or Install PyTorch with CUDA support
conda install pytorch torchvision torchaudio cudatoolkit=11.1 -c pytorch -c nvidia

# Verify PyTorch installation
python -c "import torch; print(torch.__version__)"
python -c "import torch; print(torch.cuda.is_available())"
```

Through Anaconda, managing dependencies and ensuring the correct version of each package is streamlined and efficient, making it an excellent choice for developing machine learning applications with PyTorch.

2.7 Checking PyTorch Installation

After installing PyTorch via Pip or Anaconda, it is crucial to verify that the installation was successful and that PyTorch is functioning correctly in your development environment. This section covers the steps to ensure the successful installation and basic tests to validate the functionality, including executing a simple tensor operation.

First, open your preferred IDE or text editor and create a new Python script. If you are using Jupyter Notebook, open a new notebook.

Start by importing PyTorch to ensure that the library is accessible in your current environment. The following Python code achieves this:

```
import torch
```

Execute the code above. If the installation was successful, you should not encounter any errors. If you receive an ImportError, it indicates that PyTorch is not installed correctly or the Python environment does not include PyTorch.

The next step is to verify the version of PyTorch installed. Executing the following command will print the version of the installed PyTorch:

```
print(torch.__version__)
```

On running this, you should see an output similar to:

```
1.10.0+cu111
```

The version number will depend on the specific version you installed. The additional string (e.g., +cu111) indicates the CUDA version if you installed the GPU version of PyTorch.

To further ensure the installation is functioning properly, perform a basic tensor operation. Create a tensor and verify its basic properties:

```
# Create a simple tensor
tensor = torch.tensor([1, 2, 3, 4, 5])

# Print the tensor
print(tensor)

# Verify tensor properties
print(f'Tensor dtype: {tensor.dtype}')
print(f'Tensor shape: {tensor.shape}')
```

The expected output should be:

```
tensor([1, 2, 3, 4, 5])
Tensor dtype: torch.int64
Tensor shape: torch.Size([5])
```

This confirms that tensor operations are working correctly. Additionally, to check for GPU support, execute the following lines to determine if a CUDA-enabled GPU is available:

```
# Check if CUDA is available
cuda_available = torch.cuda.is_available()

# Print the result
print(f'CUDA available: {cuda_available}')
```

If you have installed the GPU version of PyTorch and your machine has a CUDA-enabled GPU, the output should be:

```
CUDA available: True
```

If the result is False, and you expect to have CUDA support, double-check your CUDA installation and ensure that your hardware supports CUDA.

Next, move a tensor to GPU and perform an operation to ensure GPU functionality:

```
if cuda_available:
    # Create a tensor and move it to GPU
    tensor = tensor.to('cuda')

    # Perform a simple operation
    tensor = tensor + 1

    # Print the tensor
    print(tensor)

    # Confirm it's on GPU
    print(f'Tensor device: {tensor.device}')
```

The expected output, if the tensor is moved to the GPU, might look like this:

```
tensor([2, 3, 4, 5, 6], device='cuda:0')
Tensor device: cuda:0
```

This confirms that PyTorch can utilize the GPU for computations. If your operations generate an error or you are unable to move tensors to the GPU, verify the compatibility of your CUDA and cuDNN versions with the installed PyTorch version.

This series of steps verifies that PyTorch is correctly installed, imports without errors, and functions as expected both on CPU and GPU (if available). Regularly performing such checks after installation or configuration changes ensures a stable and predictable machine learning development environment.

2.8 Managing Dependencies

Effective management of dependencies is crucial for maintaining a stable and reproducible machine learning environment. Dependencies refer to the various libraries and packages your project relies on. Mismanagement of these dependencies can lead to problems like version conflicts, missing packages, and difficulties in sharing your project with others. This section explores best practices for handling dependencies, ensuring a consistent environment for developing with PyTorch.

In Python projects, dependencies are typically managed using a requirements.txt file or tools like pip and conda. Both approaches will be detailed to provide you with a comprehensive understanding of dependency management.

First, consider using a requirements.txt file, which is a simple text file containing a list of your project's dependencies. Each line of the file specifies a package and its optional version.

```
numpy==1.21.0
torch==1.9.0
scikit-learn==0.24.2
pandas==1.3.1
```

To generate a requirements.txt file containing all installed packages within your current environment, use the following command:

```
pip freeze > requirements.txt
```

To install all the dependencies listed in an existing requirements.txt file, execute:

```
pip install -r requirements.txt
```

In addition to using pip, utilizing virtual environments can further isolate your project's dependencies. A virtual environment is an isolated Python environment which allows for independent package installations without affecting other projects or the system Python installation.

To create a virtual environment using venv, run:

```
python -m venv myenv
```

Activate the virtual environment with:

```
# On Windows
myenv\Scripts\activate

# On macOS/Linux
source myenv/bin/activate
```

After activation, any package installations will be local to this environment, thus preventing conflict with other projects.

Alternatively, conda, a popular package and environment management tool, provides a more feature-rich solution. conda can manage complex dependencies and create isolated environments. To create a new environment with conda, use:

```
conda create --name myenv python=3.8
```

Activate the conda environment using:

```
conda activate myenv
```

Afterward, you can install necessary dependencies. For example, to install PyTorch and other essential libraries in the conda environment, execute:

```
conda install pytorch torchvision torchaudio -c pytorch
conda install numpy pandas scikit-learn
```

Conda environments can also be exported to a .yml file, which lists all dependencies including versions. This file can be shared and used to recreate the environment elsewhere. To export the environment, use:

```
conda env export > environment.yml
```

To recreate the environment on another machine, execute:

```
conda env create -f environment.yml
```

Managing dependencies attentively ensures that your machine learning projects are reproducible and isolated from external changes. Maintaining consistency in your development environment facilitates collaboration, simplifies troubleshooting, and enhances overall project stability. Consistent practice of these strategies is imperative for proficient development with PyTorch.

2.9 Working with Jupyter Notebooks

Jupyter Notebooks offer a powerful and interactive environment that caters to the needs of data scientists and machine learning practitioners. They provide an ideal platform for developing and testing machine learning models, running simulations, and presenting results in an easily interpretable format. This section will focus on the installation of Jupyter, basic notebook operations, and integrating PyTorch to perform machine learning tasks.

To begin working with Jupyter Notebooks, ensure you have Python and the required packages installed. If not already done, follow the steps outlined in previous sections to set up your development environment.

- **Installing Jupyter Notebook:** Installing Jupyter Notebook can be done through "pip" or "conda" depending on your preference. For users with a virtual environment set up using 'pip', execute the following command in your terminal:

```
pip install notebook
```

For 'conda' users, the installation is similarly straightforward:

```
conda install -c conda-forge notebook
```

Ensure the installation proceeds without errors. Upon successful installation, launch Jupyter Notebook by running:

```
jupyter notebook
```

This command will start the Jupyter Notebook server and open the notebook interface in your default web browser. The interface typically runs at 'http://localhost:8888/'.

- **Creating and Managing Notebooks:** Once the Jupyter interface is open, you can create a new notebook by selecting "New" and then "Python 3" (or your desired kernel) from the dropdown menu. This will open a new notebook with an empty code cell.

  Notebooks consist of cells which can contain either code or markdown. Code cells allow you to write and execute Python code, while markdown cells enable you to document your code with formatted text, mathematical equations, images, and more.

  Here's an example of a simple code cell to test your setup:

  ```
  print("Hello, Jupyter!")
  ```

  Execute the cell by pressing 'Shift + Enter'. The output should be:

  ```
  Hello, Jupyter!
  ```

- **Basic Operations:** Understanding the basic operations in Jupyter Notebooks will significantly enhance your productivity:

  - **Running Cells:** Use 'Shift + Enter' to run a cell and move to the next one, or 'Ctrl + Enter' to run a cell without moving.
  - **Inserting Cells:** Insert cells above or below the current cell using 'A' or 'B' in command mode.
  - **Deleting Cells:** Delete the current cell by pressing 'D' twice in quick succession.
  - **Converting Cells:** Change a code cell to a markdown cell (or vice versa) using 'M' for markdown and 'Y' for code in command mode.

  - **Markdown Syntax:** Use standard markdown syntax for text formatting. For instance, headings, lists, or images can be inserted as needed.

- **Integrating PyTorch in Jupyter Notebooks:** With Jupyter Notebook set up, the next step is to integrate PyTorch and start performing machine learning tasks. Ensure PyTorch is installed in your environment as shown in previous sections. Then, you can import PyTorch libraries and start coding within the notebook.

  Here's an example of importing PyTorch and performing a simple tensor operation:

```
import torch

# Create a tensor
x = torch.tensor([[1, 2], [3, 4]], dtype=torch.float32)

print("Tensor x:")
print(x)

# Perform a tensor operation: matrix multiplication
y = torch.matmul(x, x)

print("Result of x multiplied by x:")
print(y)
```

  Executing the above cells will yield the following outputs:

```
Tensor x:
tensor([[1., 2.],
        [3., 4.]])

Result of x multiplied by x:
tensor([[ 7., 10.],
        [15., 22.]])
```

- **Advanced Features:** Jupyter Notebooks offer numerous advanced features that are essential for machine learning and data science workflows:

  - **Visualization:** Libraries such as Matplotlib, Seaborn, and Plotly can be used for generating visualizations. For example:

```
import matplotlib.pyplot as plt

# Sample data
data = [1, 2, 3, 4, 5]

plt.plot(data)
plt.title('Sample Plot')
plt.show()
```

- **Interactive Widgets:** 'ipywidgets' provide interactive elements such as sliders, dropdowns, and buttons for more dynamic notebooks.
- **Parallel Computing:** IPython.parallel extensions allow for parallel computing directly within the notebook environment.

For readers who follow along with practical reproducibility, ensuring all dependencies are managed effectively and maintaining an organized file structure is critical. By leveraging these features, you can create comprehensive and interactive machine learning workflows that are both powerful and easily shared.

2.10 Using GPUs with PyTorch

Modern machine learning models, especially deep learning models, often require substantial computational resources. One key advantage of PyTorch is its seamless ability to leverage Graphics Processing Units (GPUs) to accelerate computations. This section comprehensively examines the process of using GPUs with PyTorch, covering GPU requirements, installation of necessary software, configuring PyTorch to use GPUs, and practical examples of how to allocate and manage GPU resources efficiently.

Firstly, it is essential to verify the presence and compatibility of a GPU in your system. The most commonly used GPUs for deep learning tasks are those manufactured by NVIDIA, which support CUDA (Compute Unified Device Architecture). To check for an NVIDIA GPU, use the following command:

```
nvidia-smi
```

The output will display the details of the installed NVIDIA GPU(s), including GPU version, memory, and driver version, as shown below:

```
+-----------------------------------------------------------------------------+
| NVIDIA-SMI 450.80.02    Driver Version: 450.80.02    CUDA Version: 11.0     |
|-------------------------------+----------------------+----------------------+
| GPU  Name        Persistence-M| Bus-Id        Disp.A | Volatile Uncorr. ECC |
| Fan  Temp  Perf  Pwr:Usage/Cap|         Memory-Usage | GPU-Util  Compute M. |
|                               |                      |               MIG M. |
|===============================+======================+======================|
|   0  GeForce RTX 208...  Off  | 00000000:1A:00.0 Off |                  N/A |
| 30%   37C    P8    21W / 250W |      0MiB / 11016MiB |      0%      Default |
+-------------------------------+----------------------+----------------------+
```

Once the presence of an NVIDIA GPU is confirmed, the next step involves installing the CUDA Toolkit and cuDNN (CUDA Deep Neural Network library). These are essential for GPU acceleration with PyTorch.

Follow the official installation guide provided on the NVIDIA website to ensure proper installation and compatibility with your operating system.

After setting up CUDA and cuDNN, install the appropriate version of PyTorch that supports CUDA. The PyTorch website offers a configuration tool to assist in generating the correct command for your environment. For instance, the following command installs PyTorch with CUDA 11.0 support using pip:

```
pip install torch===1.7.1+cu110 -f https://download.pytorch.org/whl/torch_stable.
    html
```

Verify the installation with a simple script that checks for CUDA availability:

```
import torch
print(torch.cuda.is_available())
```

The output should return True if CUDA is available.

To utilize a GPU in your PyTorch code, you need to transfer your model and data to the GPU. PyTorch makes this process straightforward with the .to() or .cuda() methods. Here is an example outlining the typical workflow:

```
import torch
import torch.nn as nn
import torch.optim as optim

# Assume a simple neural network model
class SimpleNN(nn.Module):
    def __init__(self):
        super(SimpleNN, self).__init__()
        self.fc = nn.Linear(784, 10)

    def forward(self, x):
        return self.fc(x)

# Initialize the model and move it to GPU if available
model = SimpleNN()
device = torch.device("cuda" if torch.cuda.is_available() else "cpu")
model.to(device)

# Dummy data for demonstration
x = torch.randn(64, 784) # batch size of 64, input size of 784
y = torch.randint(0, 10, (64,))

# Move data to the same device as the model
x = x.to(device)
y = y.to(device)

# Define loss function and optimizer
criterion = nn.CrossEntropyLoss()
optimizer = optim.SGD(model.parameters(), lr=0.01)

# Forward pass
```

```
outputs = model(x)
loss = criterion(outputs, y)

# Backward pass and optimization
optimizer.zero_grad()
loss.backward()
optimizer.step()
```

This example demonstrates the critical steps of moving models and data to the GPU. By using the torch.device method, the code dynamically adapts based on the availability of a GPU, allowing for flexibility in environments with and without a GPU.

Efficient GPU usage also involves managing GPU memory. Tensor operations default to using the current device, which can be queried and changed using torch.cuda.current_device() and torch.cuda.set_device(). Monitor GPU memory utilization throughout your training to prevent out-of-memory errors.

Utilize PyTorch's torch.cuda.memory_allocated() and torch.cuda.memory_reserved() functions to obtain the amount of allocated and reserved memory, respectively. For instance:

```
allocated_memory = torch.cuda.memory_allocated(device)
reserved_memory = torch.cuda.memory_reserved(device)
print(f"Allocated memory: {allocated_memory}")
print(f"Reserved memory: {reserved_memory}")
```

In summary, leveraging GPUs in PyTorch requires appropriate hardware, software installation, and specific programming considerations to move data and models onto the GPU. This approach significantly enhances computational efficiency, allowing for faster training and more complex models.

Chapter 3

Basic Tensor Operations in PyTorch

This chapter delves into the fundamental operations involving tensors in PyTorch, starting with an introduction to tensors and their creation. It covers essential tensor attributes, techniques for indexing, slicing, and joining tensors, as well as performing arithmetic operations. The chapter also explores broadcasting, reshaping, and resizing tensors, along with a variety of tensor manipulation functions. Additional sections address GPU acceleration and the use of PyTorch's autograd functionality for automatic differentiation.

3.1 Introduction to Tensors

Tensors are the fundamental data structure in PyTorch, essential for all forms of computation, from simple arithmetic to complex neural network training. A tensor is a multidimensional array, which generalizes vectors and matrices to higher dimensions. In PyTorch, tensors provide numerous features that facilitate numerical computations efficiently and effectively.

A tensor can be one-dimensional like a vector, two-dimensional like a matrix, or have more than two dimensions. Regardless of their dimensionality, tensors in PyTorch are represented by the torch.Tensor class.

```
import torch
# Creating a one-dimensional tensor (vector)
vector = torch.tensor([1.0, 2.0, 3.0])

# Creating a two-dimensional tensor (matrix)
matrix = torch.tensor([[1.0, 2.0], [3.0, 4.0]])

# Creating a three-dimensional tensor
tensor_3d = torch.tensor([[[1.0, 2.0], [3.0, 4.0]], [[5.0, 6.0], [7.0, 8.0]]])
```

Each tensor has attributes that provide information about its shape, data type, and the device (CPU or GPU) on which it resides. Understanding these attributes is vital for effective tensor manipulation.

Shape: The shape of a tensor is a tuple that defines the dimensions of the tensor. For example, a matrix with shape (2, 3) has 2 rows and 3 columns.

```
# Getting the shape of a tensor
print(matrix.shape) # Output: torch.Size([2, 2])
```

```
torch.Size([2, 2])
```

Data Type: PyTorch tensors can hold different types of data such as 8-bit integers, 32-bit floats, etc. The data type of a tensor can be explicitly defined at creation or inferred from the input data.

```
# Getting the data type of a tensor
print(vector.dtype) # Output: torch.float32
```

```
torch.float32
```

Device: PyTorch tensors can reside on either the CPU or GPU, which allows leveraging hardware acceleration for computationally intensive tasks.

```
# Checking the device of a tensor
print(tensor_3d.device) # Output: cpu
```

```
cpu
```

Tensors are not confined to specific shapes or data types; they can be reshaped or cast to different data types as necessary to fit the needs of the operation. PyTorch offers several methods to achieve these transformations.

Consider the following example where a tensor is reshaped:

```
# Reshaping a tensor
reshaped_tensor = tensor_3d.view(2, 4)
print(reshaped_tensor)
```

```
tensor([[1., 2., 3., 4.],
        [5., 6., 7., 8.]])
```

Additionally, a tensor can be converted from one data type to another using casting methods:

```
# Casting tensor to a different data type
int_tensor = vector.to(torch.int32)
print(int_tensor.dtype) # Output: torch.int32
```

```
torch.int32
```

Understanding the creation and basic properties of tensors is the first step toward harnessing the full power of PyTorch. This foundational knowledge enables the execution of a wide array of operations, transforming data in meaningful ways for various computational tasks.

3.2 Creating Tensors

Tensors are a central data structure in PyTorch, serving as the building blocks for deep learning models. Creating tensors efficiently and correctly is pivotal for effectively leveraging PyTorch's capabilities. In this section, we will explore multiple methods for creating tensors, including initializing tensors with specific values, random values, and from existing data structures.

1. Creating Tensors from Lists and Numpy Arrays

The most straightforward method for creating a tensor in PyTorch is to use Python lists or Numpy arrays. This can be done through the torch.tensor() function, which takes an array-like object as input and returns a tensor.

```
import torch

# Creating a tensor from a list
list_tensor = torch.tensor([1, 2, 3, 4, 5])
print(list_tensor)
```

Output:

```
tensor([1, 2, 3, 4, 5])
```

```
import numpy as np

# Creating a tensor from a Numpy array
np_array = np.array([1, 2, 3, 4, 5])
np_tensor = torch.tensor(np_array)
print(np_tensor)
```

Output:

```
tensor([1, 2, 3, 4, 5], dtype=torch.int32)
```

When creating a tensor using torch.tensor() from Numpy arrays, the data types are preserved as much as possible. To specify a different data type, the dtype argument can be used.

```
float_tensor = torch.tensor([1, 2, 3, 4, 5], dtype=torch.float32)
print(float_tensor)
```

Output:

```
tensor([1., 2., 3., 4., 5.])
```

2. Creating Tensors with Predefined Values

PyTorch provides convenience functions for creating tensors initialized with predetermined values. These functions include torch.zeros(), torch.ones(), torch.full(), and torch.arange().

```
# Create a tensor filled with zeros
zeros_tensor = torch.zeros((2, 3))
print(zeros_tensor)
```

Output:

```
tensor([[0., 0., 0.],
        [0., 0., 0.]])
```

```
# Create a tensor filled with ones
ones_tensor = torch.ones((2, 3))
print(ones_tensor)
```

Output:

```
tensor([[1., 1., 1.],
        [1., 1., 1.]])
```

```
# Create a tensor with a specific value
full_tensor = torch.full((2, 3), 7.0)
print(full_tensor)
```

Output:

```
tensor([[7., 7., 7.],
        [7., 7., 7.]])
```

```
# Create a tensor with a range of values
range_tensor = torch.arange(0, 10, step=2)
print(range_tensor)
```

Output:

```
tensor([0, 2, 4, 6, 8])
```

3. Creating Random Tensors

In machine learning, randomness is of particular utility, especially for initializing neural network weights. PyTorch accommodates this need with functions like torch.rand(), torch.randn(), torch.randint(), and torch.randperm().

```
# Create a tensor with random values between 0 and 1
rand_tensor = torch.rand((2, 3))
print(rand_tensor)
```

Output:

```
tensor([[0.9724, 0.9743, 0.9320],
        [0.8238, 0.9686, 0.1051]])
```

```
# Create a tensor with random values from a normal distribution
randn_tensor = torch.randn((2, 3))
print(randn_tensor)
```

Output:

```
tensor([[ 0.6038, -1.0285,  1.4040],
        [-2.0431,  0.7655,  0.6337]])
```

```
# Create a tensor with random integer values between 0 and 10
randint_tensor = torch.randint(0, 10, (2, 3))
print(randint_tensor)
```

Output:

```
tensor([[2, 8, 2],
        [9, 4, 5]], dtype=torch.int32)
```

```
# Create a tensor with a random permutation of integers from 0 to n-1
randperm_tensor = torch.randperm(10)
print(randperm_tensor)
```

Output:

```
tensor([0, 4, 2, 1, 5, 7, 3, 8, 9, 6])
```

4. Creating Tensors from Existing Tensors

Derived tensors can be initialized based on the properties of existing tensors. This approach allows flexibility in creating tensors that match the shape or data type of other tensors. Functions include torch.zeros_like(), torch.ones_like(), and torch.rand_like().

```
# Create a tensor filled with zeros and the same size as another tensor
x = torch.tensor([[1, 2, 3], [4, 5, 6]])
zeros_like_tensor = torch.zeros_like(x)
print(zeros_like_tensor)
```

Output:

```
tensor([[0, 0, 0],
        [0, 0, 0]])
```

```
# Create a tensor filled with ones and the same size as another tensor
ones_like_tensor = torch.ones_like(x)
print(ones_like_tensor)
```

Output:

```
tensor([[1, 1, 1],
        [1, 1, 1]])
```

```
# Create a tensor with random values and the same size as another tensor
rand_like_tensor = torch.rand_like(x, dtype=torch.float)
print(rand_like_tensor)
```

Output:

```
tensor([[0.7531, 0.9383, 0.3121],
        [0.7848, 0.1943, 0.0468]])
```

Using these dynamic tensor creation methods, you can obtain a versatile assortment of tensors tailored to specific dimensions and values. This capability enables precise control over tensor initialization, an essential skill in constructing and training models with PyTorch.

3.3 Basic Tensor Attributes

Tensors are the primary data structures in PyTorch and understanding their attributes is crucial for efficient manipulation and optimization of machine learning models. This section delves into the essential tensor attributes that every user should be familiar with, including shape, dtype, device, and more. Understanding these attributes can facilitate debugging and enhancing performance.

Every tensor in PyTorch has a variety of attributes that provide information about its dimensions, type, and location. Below, we investigate these attributes one by one.

- **Shape**: The shape attribute describes the dimensions of the tensor. It is a tuple representing the size of each dimension, and it directly impacts how operations can be applied to the tensor.

```
import torch

# Creating a 3x4 tensor
tensor = torch.tensor([[1, 2, 3, 4],
                       [5, 6, 7, 8],
                       [9, 10, 11, 12]])
```

```
# Accessing the shape
print(tensor.shape)
```

```
torch.Size([3, 4])
```

In this example, the shape of the tensor is $(3, 4)$, meaning it has 3 rows and 4 columns.

- **Number of Dimensions**: The ndimension() function or the dim attribute returns the number of dimensions of the tensor.

```
# Accessing the number of dimensions
print(tensor.ndimension())
print(tensor.dim())
```

```
2
2
```

- **Data Type**: The dtype attribute tells you the data type of the elements in the tensor. Common data types include float32, float64, int32, and int64.

```
# Accessing the data type
print(tensor.dtype)
```

```
torch.int64
```

In this case, the data type is int64, indicating that elements in the tensor are 64-bit integers.

- **Device**: The device attribute specifies where the tensor is stored - either on the CPU or the GPU. This is essential for utilizing GPU acceleration.

```
# Accessing the device
print(tensor.device)
```

```
cpu
```

By default, tensors are created on the CPU. To move a tensor to the GPU, the to method or cuda method can be used, given that a GPU is available.

```
# Moving tensor to GPU
if torch.cuda.is_available():
    tensor = tensor.to('cuda')
    print(tensor.device)
```

```
cuda:0
```

- **Stride**: The stride attribute provides the step size needed to jump to the next element along each dimension. It is important for understanding the memory layout of a tensor.

```
# Accessing the stride
print(tensor.stride())
```

```
(4, 1)
```

In this example, the stride (4, 1) indicates that to move to the next row, we need to jump 4 elements, and to move to the next column within the same row, we need to jump 1 element.

- **Storage Offset**: The storage_offset attribute indicates the position in the underlying storage of the first element of the tensor.

```
# Accessing the storage offset
print(tensor.storage_offset())
```

```
0
```

When the tensor is a view of another tensor, the storage offset may be non-zero.

- **Layout**: The layout attribute specifies how the tensor is stored in memory. The default is torch.strided, which represents a typical contiguous array in memory, but other layouts such as torch.sparse_coo are also possible.

```
# Accessing the layout
print(tensor.layout)
```

```
torch.strided
```

These attributes provide critical information regarding the tensor and can greatly impact the efficiency of various operations. Understanding and leveraging these attributes can lead to optimized and highly performant code, essential for effective machine learning computations.

3.4 Indexing, Slicing, and Joining Tensors

Within PyTorch, indexing, slicing, and joining operations are crucial techniques for manipulating tensor data efficiently. These operations grant access to specific elements or sub-tensors and enable the combination of different tensors. Understanding and utilizing these operations effectively allows for the precise handling and manipulation of multidimensional data, leading to cleaner and more optimized implementations of machine learning models.

Indexing allows the extraction of specific elements from tensors based on their position. Consider the following example to illustrate basic indexing:

```
import torch

# Create a tensor
tensor = torch.tensor([[1, 2, 3], [4, 5, 6], [7, 8, 9]])

# Indexing specific elements
element_1 = tensor[0, 0]
element_2 = tensor[1, 2]

print(element_1)
print(element_2)
```

This will result in:

```
1
6
```

In the code snippet above, tensor[0, 0] accesses the element at the first row and first column, and tensor[1, 2] accesses the element on the second row and third column. PyTorch supports both integer and Boolean indexing.

Slicing, on the other hand, is used to access a range of elements within a tensor. The slicing syntax tensor[start:end] extracts elements from the start index up to but not including the end index. The following example demonstrates tensor slicing:

```
# Slicing rows
row_slice = tensor[0, :]

# Slicing columns
col_slice = tensor[:, 1]

# Slicing sub-tensor
sub_tensor = tensor[0:2, 1:3]

print(row_slice)
print(col_slice)
print(sub_tensor)
```

This will output:

```
tensor([1, 2, 3])
tensor([2, 5, 8])
tensor([[2, 3],
        [5, 6]])
```

In the above code:

- tensor[0, :] extracts the entire first row.
- tensor[:, 1] extracts the second column.

- tensor[0:2, 1:3] extracts a sub-tensor that includes rows from index 0 to 1 and columns from index 1 to 2.

PyTorch also supports advanced indexing to retrieve complex patterns of elements. This can be achieved through techniques like ellipsis (...), None slicing (which introduces new axes), and tensor indexing. For example:

```
# Ellipsis: maintaining the original first dimension
sub_tensor_ellipsis = tensor[..., 1]

# None indexing: add a new empty axis
tensor_expanded = tensor[:, None, :]

print(sub_tensor_ellipsis)
print(tensor_expanded)
```

This will produce:

```
tensor([2, 5, 8])
tensor([[[1, 2, 3]],
        [[4, 5, 6]],
        [[7, 8, 9]]])
```

In tensor joining, two or more tensors are concatenated along a specified dimension. PyTorch provides the torch.cat and torch.stack functions for this purpose.

The torch.cat function concatenates tensors along an existing dimension:

```
# Create tensors
tensor1 = torch.tensor([[1, 2, 3], [4, 5, 6]])
tensor2 = torch.tensor([[7, 8, 9], [10, 11, 12]])

# Concatenate along axis 0 (vertically)
concatenated_tensor_0 = torch.cat((tensor1, tensor2), dim=0)

# Concatenate along axis 1 (horizontally)
concatenated_tensor_1 = torch.cat((tensor1, tensor2), dim=1)

print(concatenated_tensor_0)
print(concatenated_tensor_1)
```

Resulting in:

```
tensor([[ 1,  2,  3],
        [ 4,  5,  6],
        [ 7,  8,  9],
        [10, 11, 12]])

tensor([[ 1,  2,  3,  7,  8,  9],
        [ 4,  5,  6, 10, 11, 12]])
```

In this example:

- torch.cat((tensor1, tensor2), dim=0) concatenates the tensors along rows, resulting in a new tensor with shape $(4, 3)$.

- torch.cat((tensor1, tensor2), dim=1) concatenates the tensors along columns, generating a tensor with shape $(2, 6)$.

The torch.stack function, instead, joins tensors along a new dimension:

```
# Stack tensors along a new axis (dim=0)
stacked_tensor_0 = torch.stack((tensor1, tensor2), dim=0)

# Stack tensors along a new axis (dim=1)
stacked_tensor_1 = torch.stack((tensor1, tensor2), dim=1)

print(stacked_tensor_0)
print(stacked_tensor_1)
```

This yields:

```
tensor([[[ 1,  2,  3],
         [ 4,  5,  6]],

        [[ 7,  8,  9],
         [10, 11, 12]]])

tensor([[[ 1,  2,  3],
         [ 7,  8,  9]],

        [[ 4,  5,  6],
         [10, 11, 12]]])
```

In this case:

- torch.stack((tensor1, tensor2), dim=0) stacks the tensors along a new first axis, creating a tensor with shape $(2, 2, 3)$.

- torch.stack((tensor1, tensor2), dim=1) stacks the tensors along a new second axis, resulting in a tensor with shape $(2, 2, 3)$.

Mastering these operations is foundational for advanced tensor manipulations. Efficiently indexing, slicing, and joining tensors is instrumental in maneuvering through PyTorch to implement complex machine learning algorithms and preprocessing pipelines.

3.5 Tensor Arithmetic Operations

Tensor arithmetic operations in PyTorch encompass a wide variety of element-wise operations, reductions, and linear algebra operations.

These operations form the backbone of many machine learning algorithms, enabling efficient computation and manipulation of high-dimensional data. This section details the most commonly used arithmetic operations on tensors using PyTorch.

Element-wise operations are performed by applying the same operation individually to each element in the tensor. PyTorch provides a plethora of such operations, including addition, subtraction, multiplication, and division. Consider the following example where two tensors, a and b, are used for various element-wise operations:

```
import torch

# Create two tensors
a = torch.tensor([1.0, 2.0, 3.0])
b = torch.tensor([4.0, 5.0, 6.0])

# Element-wise addition
c = a + b

# Element-wise subtraction
d = a - b

# Element-wise multiplication
e = a * b

# Element-wise division
f = a / b
```

The resulting tensors from the operations above are:

```
c: tensor([5., 7., 9.])
d: tensor([-3., -3., -3.])
e: tensor([ 4., 10., 18.])
f: tensor([0.25, 0.40, 0.50])
```

In addition to basic arithmetic, PyTorch also supports element-wise exponentiation and logarithmic operations:

```
# Element-wise exponentiation
g = a ** 2

# Element-wise logarithm
h = torch.log(b)
```

```
g: tensor([1., 4., 9.])
h: tensor([1.3863, 1.6094, 1.7918])
```

Reduction operations such as summation, mean, and product are also fundamental in tensor arithmetic. These operations reduce a tensor to a scalar by aggregating its elements:

```
# Sum of all elements
sum_a = torch.sum(a)

# Mean of all elements
```

```
mean_a = torch.mean(a)

# Product of all elements
prod_a = torch.prod(a)
```

The results of these reduction operations are:

```
sum_a: tensor(6.0)
mean_a: tensor(2.0)
prod_a: tensor(6.0)
```

Advanced arithmetic operations often involve linear algebra functions including matrix multiplication, dot product, and matrix determinant. PyTorch provides robust support for these operations:

```
# Define 2D tensors (matrices)
matrix1 = torch.tensor([[1, 2], [3, 4]])
matrix2 = torch.tensor([[5, 6], [7, 8]])

# Matrix multiplication
matrix_mult = torch.mm(matrix1, matrix2)

# Dot product of two vectors
vector1 = torch.tensor([1, 2, 3])
vector2 = torch.tensor([4, 5, 6])
dot_product = torch.dot(vector1, vector2)
```

The resulting tensors from the matrix multiplication and dot product operations are:

```
matrix_mult: tensor([[19, 22],
                     [43, 50]])
dot_product: tensor(32)
```

Another critical linear algebra operation is the determinant of a matrix, which PyTorch computes as follows:

```
# Compute the determinant of a matrix
det_matrix = torch.det(matrix1)
```

```
det_matrix: tensor(-2.)
```

It is essential to understand the broadcast mechanism in tensor arithmetic operations. Broadcasting allows PyTorch to perform element-wise operations on tensors of different shapes by automatically expanding their shapes to be compatible. For example:

```
# Define a 1D tensor and a 2D tensor
vector = torch.tensor([1, 2, 3])
matrix = torch.tensor([[1, 2, 3], [4, 5, 6]])

# Add the 1D tensor to each row of the 2D tensor
broadcast_add = matrix + vector
```

The broadcast operation results in:

```
broadcast_add: tensor([[2, 4, 6],
                       [5, 7, 9]])
```

It is also critical to apply in-place operations appropriately when it is necessary to perform operations that modify the original tensor, thus saving memory. This is achieved by appending an underscore to the operation:

```
# In-place addition
a.add_(b)
```

```
a: tensor([5., 7., 9.])
```

Understanding and utilizing these tensor arithmetic operations efficiently is pivotal for optimizing computational tasks and implementing complex machine learning models in PyTorch.

3.6 Broadcasting in PyTorch

Broadcasting is a powerful mechanism that allows PyTorch to handle arithmetic operations involving tensors of different shapes in a computationally efficient way. This technique is essential when performing operations on tensors that do not have the same dimensions but can be made compatible through broadcasting rules.

The rules of broadcasting in PyTorch are as follows:

- Align dimensions: Starting from the trailing (rightmost) dimension, align the dimensions of the two tensors.
- Shape compatibility: Two dimensions are compatible if they are equal, or one of them is 1.
- Extend dimensions: Dimensions with size 1 are virtually replicated to match the other tensor dimensions.

Consider two tensors, A and B, with shapes $(a_1, a_2, \ldots, a_m)$ and $(b_1, b_2, \ldots, b_n)$ respectively. Broadcasting proceeds if:

- The dimensions of A and B align starting from the last dimension.
- For each aligned dimension, they are either equal or one of them is 1.

The broadcasting rules allow operations to be carried out without explicit replication of data, leading to memory-efficient computations.

We will walk through an example to illustrate broadcasting in PyTorch:

```
import torch

# Define two tensors with shapes (2, 3) and (3,)
tensor_a = torch.tensor([[1, 2, 3], [4, 5, 6]])
tensor_b = torch.tensor([10, 20, 30])

# Perform an element-wise addition operation with broadcasting
result = tensor_a + tensor_b
print(result)
```

The shapes of tensor_a and tensor_b are $(2, 3)$ and $(3,)$ respectively. Here, PyTorch broadcasts tensor_b to match the shape of tensor_a.

The output is:

```
tensor([[11, 22, 33],
        [14, 25, 36]])
```

In this example, tensor_b is broadcasted along the first dimension (size 2) to match the shape of tensor_a.

Another example involves a three-dimensional tensor and a one-dimensional tensor:

```
import torch

# Define two tensors with shapes (4, 1, 3) and (3,)
tensor_c = torch.tensor([[[1, 2, 3]],
                         [[4, 5, 6]],
                         [[7, 8, 9]],
                         [[10, 11, 12]]])
tensor_d = torch.tensor([1, 0, -1])

# Perform an element-wise subtraction operation with broadcasting
result = tensor_c - tensor_d
print(result)
```

The shapes of tensor_c and tensor_d are $(4, 1, 3)$ and $(3,)$ respectively. Here, tensor_d is broadcasted over the second dimension (size 1) and the first dimension (size 4).

The output is:

```
tensor([[[ 0,  2,  4]],
        [[ 3,  5,  7]],
        [[ 6,  8, 10]],
        [[ 9, 11, 13]]])
```

A noteworthy point is that broadcasting in PyTorch follows the same rules as NumPy, which satisfies the need for compatibility between these scientific computing libraries.

Broadcasting allows fewer lines of code, making tensor operations more intuitive. However, it is important to ensure that the underlying broadcasting is understood to prevent unexpected behaviors. When tensors of incompatible shapes are used, PyTorch raises a RuntimeError:

```
import torch

# Define two tensors with shapes (2, 3) and (2, 3, 4)
tensor_e = torch.tensor([[1, 2, 3], [4, 5, 6]])
tensor_f = torch.tensor([[[1, 2, 3, 4],
                          [5, 6, 7, 8],
                          [9, 10, 11, 12]],
                         [[13, 14, 15, 16],
                          [17, 18, 19, 20],
                          [21, 22, 23, 24]]])

# Attempt an element-wise multiplication operation (will raise an error)
try:
    result = tensor_e * tensor_f
except RuntimeError as e:
    print(f"RuntimeError: {e}")
```

The output is:

```
RuntimeError: The size of tensor a (3) must match the size of tensor b (4) at non-singleton dimension 2
```

In the case above, tensor_e with shape $(2, 3)$ cannot be broadcasted to the shape $(2, 3, 4)$ of tensor_f because their dimensions are not aligned.

An in-depth understanding of broadcasting is crucial for leveraging the full potential of PyTorch tensor operations, enabling efficient and readable code. Applying these rules ensures optimal performance and aids in writing concise, clear, and efficient tensor manipulations in PyTorch.

The concepts of tensor broadcasting are fundamental for neural network operations, as many layer operations inherently rely on these principles to manage weight and input tensor shapes, optimizing for computational efficiency.

3.7 Reshaping and Resizing Tensors

Reshaping and resizing tensors are critical operations in PyTorch, allowing efficient manipulation and transformation of tensor data. These operations enable the adjustment of tensor dimensions without altering the underlying data, thereby facilitating various machine learning tasks such as data preprocessing, model building, and output interpretation.

Reshaping a tensor involves changing its shape while keeping the same data. This is commonly done using the view or reshape method in PyTorch. The view method creates a new tensor with the specified shape, sharing the same data as the original tensor, while reshape can handle non-contiguous memory layouts.

Consider a simple example where a tensor of shape (4, 4) is reshaped into (2, 8):

```
import torch

# Create a tensor of shape (4, 4)
original_tensor = torch.arange(16).view(4, 4)

# Reshape the tensor to shape (2, 8)
reshaped_tensor = original_tensor.view(2, 8)

print("Original Tensor:\n", original_tensor)
print("Reshaped Tensor:\n", reshaped_tensor)
```

```
Original Tensor:
 tensor([[ 0,  1,  2,  3],
        [ 4,  5,  6,  7],
        [ 8,  9, 10, 11],
        [12, 13, 14, 15]])
Reshaped Tensor:
 tensor([[ 0,  1,  2,  3,  4,  5,  6,  7],
        [ 8,  9, 10, 11, 12, 13, 14, 15]])
```

In this example, original_tensor with shape (4, 4) is reshaped into reshaped_tensor with shape (2, 8). The view method ensures the continuity and consistency of data.

The reshape method can handle tensors with non-contiguous memory layouts, making it versatile:

```
# Reshape the tensor using the reshape method
reshaped_tensor_reshape = original_tensor.reshape(2, 8)

print("Reshaped Tensor using reshape:\n", reshaped_tensor_reshape)
```

```
Reshaped Tensor using reshape:
 tensor([[ 0,  1,  2,  3,  4,  5,  6,  7],
        [ 8,  9, 10, 11, 12, 13, 14, 15]])
```

Both view and reshape modify the tensor shape without changing the data, but reshape can manage complex layouts more flexibly.

PyTorch allows automatic calculation of one dimension when reshaping tensors by using -1. This is useful when the exact size of a dimension is unknown or dynamic:

```
# Automatically calculate one dimension
auto_reshaped_tensor = original_tensor.view(-1, 8)

print("Automatically Reshaped Tensor:\n", auto_reshaped_tensor)
```

```
Automatically Reshaped Tensor:
tensor([[ 0,  1,  2,  3,  4,  5,  6,  7],
        [ 8,  9, 10, 11, 12, 13, 14, 15]])
```

While reshaping alters only the view, resizing can change the underlying storage size of a tensor. Functions such as resize_ and resize_as_- in PyTorch perform these operations. The resize_ method changes the size and shape of a tensor in place:

```
# Resize the tensor in place
resized_tensor = original_tensor.resize_(2, 8)

print("Resized Tensor in place:\n", resized_tensor)
```

```
Resized Tensor in place:
tensor([[ 0,  1,  2,  3,  4,  5,  6,  7],
        [ 8,  9, 10, 11, 12, 13, 14, 15]])
```

The resize_ method alters the tensor directly, which might involve reallocation of memory if necessary. This operation is in place and therefore modifies the original tensor.

The resize_as_ method resizes a tensor to match the size of another tensor:

```
# Create another tensor for reference
reference_tensor = torch.randn(2, 8)

# Resize original tensor to match the reference tensor
resized_as_tensor = original_tensor.resize_as_(reference_tensor)

print("Resized as Reference Tensor:\n", resized_as_tensor)
```

```
Resized as Reference Tensor:
tensor([[ 0,  1,  2,  3,  4,  5,  6,  7],
        [ 8,  9, 10, 11, 12, 13, 14, 15]])
```

This ensures that resized_as_tensor now has the same shape as reference_tensor, making it particularly useful for dynamic operations where tensor shapes vary during computation.

Reshaping and resizing functions in PyTorch ensure that tensors are manipulated efficiently and effectively, adhering to the shape requirements of different machine learning models and tasks. Proper understanding and utilization of these operations significantly enhance the flexibility and performance of tensor manipulations in PyTorch.

3.8 Tensor Manipulation Functions

Tensor manipulation functions in PyTorch provide a suite of operations that enable nuanced adjustments and transformations of tensor structures. This section explores these functions, illustrating how they can be applied to facilitate complex data processing tasks.

Transpose and Permute

The transpose and permute functions facilitate the interchange of tensor dimensions. transpose swaps two specified dimensions, while permute rearranges all dimensions in any specified order.

```
import torch

# Create a 2x3 tensor
tensor = torch.randn(2, 3)

# Transpose dimensions 0 and 1
transposed_tensor = tensor.transpose(0, 1)
print(transposed_tensor)
```

The transpose function is particularly useful in tasks such as matrix operations where the row-column interchange is necessary. For higher dimensional tensors, permute is more flexible.

```
# Create a 2x3x4 tensor
tensor = torch.randn(2, 3, 4)

# Permute dimensions
permuted_tensor = tensor.permute(2, 0, 1)
print(permuted_tensor)
```

Contiguous Tensors

Some tensor operations might result in non-contiguous tensors. The contiguous function ensures that the tensor's underlying memory layout is contiguous, which can be important for certain operations requiring memory efficiency.

```
# Create a non-contiguous transposed tensor
non_contiguous = tensor.transpose(0, 1)

# Ensure the tensor is contiguous
contiguous_tensor = non_contiguous.contiguous()
print(contiguous_tensor.is_contiguous())
```

View and Reshape

While both view and reshape allow you to change the shape of a tensor, view can only be used on contiguous tensors, whereas reshape can handle non-contiguous tensors as well.

```
# Create a 2x3 tensor
tensor = torch.randn(2, 3)

# Reshape to 3x2 tensor
reshaped_tensor = tensor.reshape(3, 2)
```

```
print(reshaped_tensor)

# Attempt to view the same reshape
view_tensor = tensor.view(3, 2)
print(view_tensor)
```

Squeeze and Unsqueeze

The squeeze function removes dimensions of size one from a tensor, while unsqueeze adds dimensions of size one, which is useful for aligning tensor shapes for broadcasting.

```
# Create a 2x1x3 tensor
tensor = torch.randn(2, 1, 3)

# Squeeze to 2x3 tensor
squeezed_tensor = tensor.squeeze()
print(squeezed_tensor)

# Unsqueeze to add a dimension at position 1
unsqueeze_tensor = tensor.unsqueeze(1)
print(unsqueeze_tensor)
```

Stack and Cat

The stack function joins a sequence of tensors along a new dimension, whereas cat (concatenate) joins along an existing dimension.

```
# Create three 2x2 tensors
tensor_a = torch.randn(2, 2)
tensor_b = torch.randn(2, 2)
tensor_c = torch.randn(2, 2)

# Stack along a new dimension
stacked_tensor = torch.stack([tensor_a, tensor_b, tensor_c], dim=0)
print(stacked_tensor)

# Concatenate along an existing dimension
concatenated_tensor = torch.cat([tensor_a, tensor_b, tensor_c], dim=0)
print(concatenated_tensor)
```

Split and Chunk

split divides a tensor into a specific number of chunks, while chunk splits a tensor into equal-sized parts.

```
# Create a 10-element tensor
tensor = torch.randn(10)

# Split into specified sizes
splits = torch.split(tensor, [3, 3, 4])
for part in splits:
    print(part)

# Chunk into equal parts
chunks = torch.chunk(tensor, 3)
for part in chunks:
```

```
    print(part)
```

Repeat and Expand

The repeat and expand functions are leveraged to increase the size of tensors without copying data. repeat adds new dimensions, while expand works with singleton dimensions to produce larger tensors.

```
# Create a 2-element tensor
tensor = torch.tensor([1, 2])

# Repeat the tensor
repeated_tensor = tensor.repeat(2, 3)
print(repeated_tensor)

# Expand the tensor
expanded_tensor = tensor.unsqueeze(1).expand(2, 3)
print(expanded_tensor)
```

3.9 GPU Acceleration with Tensors

GPU acceleration is an essential aspect of modern machine learning frameworks, as it dramatically speeds up the computation time for large-scale tensor operations. PyTorch provides robust support for GPU acceleration through its CUDA interface, making it easier to leverage the parallel processing power of GPUs. In this section, we will explore how to enable GPU acceleration for tensor operations in PyTorch, how to transfer tensors between CPU and GPU, and how to perform efficient computations with CUDA-supported operations.

Checking for GPU Availability

Before leveraging GPU acceleration, it is important to ensure that a CUDA-compatible GPU is available. This can be done using the torch.cuda.is_available() function.

```
import torch

if torch.cuda.is_available():
    print("CUDA is available. You can use GPU acceleration.")
else:
    print("CUDA is not available. Computations will use CPU.")
```

```
CUDA is available. You can use GPU acceleration.
```

Moving Tensors to GPU

Tensors need to be explicitly moved to the GPU to take advantage of GPU acceleration. This can be achieved using the .to(device) method where device specifies the target hardware. The device for the GPU is specified as 'cuda'.

```
# Define the device
device = torch.device('cuda' if torch.cuda.is_available() else 'cpu')

# Create a tensor and move it to GPU
tensor_cpu = torch.rand(3, 3)
tensor_gpu = tensor_cpu.to(device)

print("Tensor on CPU: ", tensor_cpu)
print("Tensor on GPU: ", tensor_gpu)
```

```
Tensor on CPU:  tensor([[0.4241, 0.3761, 0.5992],
                [0.1538, 0.1788, 0.6674],
                [0.8964, 0.2874, 0.7882]])
Tensor on GPU:  tensor([[0.4241, 0.3761, 0.5992],
                [0.1538, 0.1788, 0.6674],
                [0.8964, 0.2874, 0.7882]], device='cuda:0')
```

Performing Operations on GPU

Once a tensor is moved to the GPU, all operations on that tensor are performed on the GPU. This includes arithmetic operations, matrix multiplications, and any other supported operations.

```
# Create tensors on the GPU
tensor_a = torch.rand(1000, 1000, device=device)
tensor_b = torch.rand(1000, 1000, device=device)

# Perform an operation on the GPU
tensor_c = torch.matmul(tensor_a, tensor_b)

print("Result of matrix multiplication on GPU: ", tensor_c)
```

```
Result of matrix multiplication on GPU: tensor([...], device='cuda:0')
```

Transferring Tensors Back to CPU

Sometimes, it is necessary to transfer the tensors back to the CPU for further processing or for compatibility with other libraries. This can be done using the .to('cpu') method.

```
# Transfer tensor back to CPU
tensor_cpu_again = tensor_gpu.to('cpu')

print("Tensor transferred back to CPU: ", tensor_cpu_again)
```

```
Tensor transferred back to CPU:  tensor([[0.4241, 0.3761, 0.5992],
                                 [0.1538, 0.1788, 0.6674],
                                 [0.8964, 0.2874, 0.7882]])
```

Using CUDA Streams for Asynchronous Computation

CUDA streams allow for the parallel execution of multiple operations, potentially leading to more efficient use of the GPU. By default, PyTorch operations are synchronous, meaning each operation must complete before the next one begins. However, asynchronous execution can be enabled using CUDA streams.

```
# Define a CUDA stream
stream = torch.cuda.Stream()

# Execute operations asynchronously within the stream
with torch.cuda.stream(stream):
    tensor_d = tensor_a + tensor_b
    tensor_e = tensor_a * tensor_b

# Synchronize the stream to wait for all operations to complete
stream.synchronize()

print("Result of asynchronous addition: ", tensor_d)
print("Result of asynchronous multiplication: ", tensor_e)
```

```
Result of asynchronous addition: tensor([...], device='cuda:0')
Result of asynchronous multiplication: tensor([...], device='cuda:0')
```

GPU acceleration with tensors in PyTorch offers significant performance improvements for various operations by utilizing the parallel processing capabilities of modern GPUs. By checking for GPU availability, moving tensors to the GPU, performing operations on the GPU, and utilizing CUDA streams for asynchronous execution, one can efficiently harness the power of GPUs for machine learning tasks in PyTorch.

3.10 Autograd and Automatic Differentiation

PyTorch's automatic differentiation engine, autograd, provides a means to automatically compute the gradients of tensors, facilitating the implementation of backpropagation, which is pivotal for the training of deep learning models. This section explores how autograd operates, with a focus on computing gradients, working with computational graphs, and utilizing the gradient functions available in PyTorch.

In PyTorch, the requires_grad attribute of a tensor is central to automatic differentiation. When set to True, it instructs PyTorch to track all operations on that tensor, enabling gradient computation during the backward pass. Consider the following code snippet to demonstrate its usage:

```
import torch

# Create a tensor and set requires_grad=True to track its operations
x = torch.tensor([1.0, 2.0, 3.0], requires_grad=True)

# Perform some operations on the tensor
y = x + 2
```

```
z = y * y * 3
out = z.mean()

print(out)
```

Upon execution, the above code outputs the scalar result of the sequence of operations applied to the tensor x. Importantly, because x and all resultant tensors have requires_grad=True, PyTorch records these operations for gradient computation.

```
tensor(27., grad_fn=<MeanBackward0>)
```

The recorded operations form a computational graph, which traces the path of computations made on the tensor. Each tensor in this graph has a grad_fn attribute representing the function that created it, enabling the traversal of the graph for gradient calculations.

To compute the gradients, PyTorch's backward() method is invoked on a tensor containing a scalar output. PyTorch automatically calculates the gradients of all tensors with requires_grad=True involved in producing that output. These gradients are stored in each tensor's grad attribute.

Continuing with the previous example, invoking the backward() method calculates the gradient of out with respect to x:

```
# Perform backpropagation
out.backward()

# Print gradients d(out)/dx
print(x.grad)
```

The result displays the gradients:

```
tensor([2., 4., 6.])
```

Here, the .grad attribute of x now contains the derivatives of out with respect to x. These derivatives are calculated by traversing the computational graph in reverse order, applying the chain rule of calculus.

In scenarios where the tensor is not scalar, backward() requires an additional gradient argument, a tensor of matching shape, to specify the gradient of the output with respect to each element of the tensor.

```
# Vector-Jacobian product
x = torch.tensor([[1., 2., 3.], [4., 5., 6.]], requires_grad=True)
y = x * 2

# Out is no longer a scalar
out = y.mean(axis=1)

# Gradient argument provided
```

```
out.backward(torch.tensor([1., 1.]))

print(x.grad)
```

```
tensor([[1., 1., 1.],
        [1., 1., 1.]])
```

The check for gradient computation and history tracking can be toggled using the torch.no_grad() context manager to temporarily disable gradient tracking. This is useful during inference or evaluation where gradient computations are unnecessary:

```
# Disable gradient tracking
with torch.no_grad():
    y = x * 2
    print(y)
```

```
tensor([[2., 4., 6.],
        [8., 10., 12.]])
```

It is also possible to detach a tensor from its computational graph, effectively treating it as a constant. This can be done using the detach() method:

```
# Detaching a tensor
y_detached = x.detach()
print(y_detached)
```

```
tensor([[1., 2., 3.],
        [4., 5., 6.]])
```

autograd efficiently computes Jacobian-vector products rather than the full Jacobian, an advantage in terms of memory efficiency. For complex models, PyTorch handles gradient storage with care to maximize efficiency, and optional backward hooks can be used to inspect or modify gradients during backpropagation.

Comprehension and proficient utilization of PyTorch's autograd functionality are fundamental skills for developers working with neural networks and other machine learning algorithms. The seamless integration of gradient calculation into tensor operations allows for transparent and efficient model optimization workflows, widely applicable in various machine learning contexts.

Chapter 4

Building Neural Networks with PyTorch

This chapter focuses on constructing neural networks using PyTorch. It begins with an overview of neural network components and progresses to using the 'torch.nn' module for building networks. Key topics include understanding layers and modules, activation functions, and constructing a simple feedforward neural network. The chapter also covers defining the forward pass, working with loss functions, implementing optimizers, and developing more complex neural network architectures.

4.1 Introduction to Neural Networks

Neural networks are a fundamental concept in the field of machine learning and deep learning. At their core, they consist of interconnected layers of nodes, or neurons, which are inspired by the human brain's structure and function. This section provides a comprehensive introduction to neural networks, including their historical development, basic architecture, and the essential principles underlying their operation.

A neural network is a computational model designed to recognize patterns. It interprets sensory data through a kind of machine perception, labeling, and clustering of raw input. The networks are loosely analogous to their biological counterparts; the objective is to factor the mathematical principles underlying human learning into computer algorithms.

The basic unit of a neural network is the neuron, or node, which is a simple processing element. Each neuron receives inputs, processes them, and outputs a signal to the next layer of neurons. The strength of the connection between neurons is represented by weights, which can be adjusted during the learning process.

$$y = f\left(\sum_{i=1}^{n} w_i x_i + b\right)$$

In this equation, y is the output signal, f is the activation function, w_i are the weights, x_i are the inputs, and b is the bias term. The activation function f introduces non-linearity into the model, allowing the network to learn complex patterns.

A neural network typically consists of three types of layers: the input layer, one or more hidden layers, and the output layer. The input layer receives the raw input data. The hidden layers are where most of the processing occurs through a system of weighted connections. Finally, the output layer produces the result.

The essential operation of training a neural network involves two main processes: forward propagation and backpropagation.

Forward Propagation During forward propagation, the input data passes through the input layer, hidden layers, and finally the output layer. At each neuron, the input signals are weighted, summed, and passed through an activation function.

Backpropagation Backpropagation is the mechanism through which the network learns, by adjusting the weights and biases based on the error of the output. Put simply, it minimizes the error by propagating the error gradient back through the network, modifying the weights according to their contribution to the error. The aim is to find the optimal weight values that minimize the difference between the network's prediction and the actual target values.

The following is a simple Python code example to demonstrate creating and training a neural network using PyTorch.

```
import torch
import torch.nn as nn
import torch.optim as optim

# Define the neural network architecture
class SimpleNN(nn.Module):
    def __init__(self):
```

```
        super(SimpleNN, self).__init__()
        self.fc1 = nn.Linear(10, 50)
        self.fc2 = nn.Linear(50, 1)

    def forward(self, x):
        x = torch.relu(self.fc1(x))
        x = self.fc2(x)
        return x

# Initialize the network, loss function, and optimizer
model = SimpleNN()
criterion = nn.MSELoss()
optimizer = optim.SGD(model.parameters(), lr=0.01)

# Training data
inputs = torch.randn(100, 10)
targets = torch.randn(100, 1)

# Training loop
for epoch in range(100):
    optimizer.zero_grad()
    outputs = model(inputs)
    loss = criterion(outputs, targets)
    loss.backward()
    optimizer.step()
    if epoch % 10 == 0:
        print(f'Epoch {epoch}, Loss: {loss.item()}')
```

This code defines a basic feedforward neural network with one hidden layer. The network is trained on random data using Stochastic Gradient Descent (SGD) as the optimizer and Mean Squared Error (MSE) as the loss function. The training loop iterates 100 times, updating the weights to minimize the loss. The model's performance is printed every 10 epochs, demonstrating the loss reduction over time.

Artificial neural networks (ANNs) have diverse applications, including image and speech recognition, natural language processing, and game playing. They are capable of approximating complex functions and detecting intricate patterns. As a result, understanding how to design, train, and utilize neural networks is essential for developing advanced machine learning models.

4.2 Components of a Neural Network

A neural network is an interconnected assembly of basic units called neurons, structured to simulate the way the human brain processes information. Each neuron receives input, processes it through its internal mechanism, and produces an output. In this section, we discuss the fundamental components that comprise a neural network: neurons, layers, weights, biases, and activation functions.

A neural network's basic structural element is the neuron. In mathematical terms, a neuron multiplies input values by their corresponding weights, adds a bias term, and passes the result through an activation function to produce an output. This process can be succinctly represented by the equation:

$$y = \phi\left(\sum_{i=1}^{n} w_i x_i + b\right)$$

where y is the output, ϕ is the activation function, w_i are the weights, x_i are the input values, and b denotes the bias term.

- **Weights** (w_i): Weights are crucial learnable parameters that determine the importance of corresponding input values. During training, these weights are adjusted in a way that minimizes the overall error of the network.
- **Biases** (b): Biases act as adjustable constants and help the model in fitting the data better by providing an additional degree of freedom. Each neuron typically has one bias associated with it.
- **Activation Functions** (ϕ): These functions apply a non-linear transformation to the input after weighting and biasing. Nonlinearity is essential for enabling neural networks to approximate complex functions. Common activation functions include the Sigmoid, Tanh, and ReLU functions.

The neurons are grouped into structures called layers. There are three primary types of layers in a feedforward network:

- **Input Layer**: The input layer is the first layer that receives the raw input data. Each neuron in this layer corresponds to one feature of the input dataset. No computation is done in this layer other than passing the input values to the next layer.
- **Hidden Layers**: These are intermediary layers between the input and output layers. Each hidden layer consists of multiple neurons, and the output of each neuron from a layer is passed as input to neurons of subsequent layers. The hidden layers perform transformations on the input data and extract relevant features through learned weights and biases.

- **Output Layer**: The output layer produces the final results of the network. The number of neurons in this layer corresponds to the number of classes in classification problems or the number of outputs in regression problems.

A simple feedforward neural network connects the neurons in a unidirectional manner, from input to output, with no cycles. For illustration, a typical architecture might look as follows:

```
import torch
import torch.nn as nn

class SimpleFeedforwardNN(nn.Module):
    def __init__(self, input_size, hidden_size, output_size):
        super(SimpleFeedforwardNN, self).__init__()
        self.hidden_layer = nn.Linear(input_size, hidden_size)
        self.activation = nn.ReLU()
        self.output_layer = nn.Linear(hidden_size, output_size)

    def forward(self, x):
        hidden = self.hidden_layer(x)
        activated_hidden = self.activation(hidden)
        output = self.output_layer(activated_hidden)
        return output
```

In this example, the network consists of an input layer with a size determined by the `input_size` parameter, a single hidden layer with a size determined by the `hidden_size` parameter, activated by the ReLU function, and an output layer sized by the `output_size` parameter.

Additionally, complex neural networks can incorporate various types of layers beyond the standard fully connected ones, such as convolutional layers (for image processing tasks), recurrent layers (for sequential data), and many others. These specialized layers help in adapting the neural network to specific types of data and problems.

```
# Expected output for a simple forward pass with random data:
tensor([[ 0.0639, -0.0972],
        [-0.0578,  0.2043]])
```

Understanding and constructing neural networks involve organizing these components in a manner that optimizes performance for the specific task at hand. Each layer, neuron, weight, and activation function plays a pivotal role in enabling the neural network to learn and generalize from data effectively.

4.3 Using torch.nn to Build Neural Networks

The torch.nn module in PyTorch is a comprehensive library designed for constructing and training neural networks. It encompasses a wide array of building blocks essential for defining both simple and intricate neural network architectures. In this section, we will delve into the utilization of torch.nn for neural network construction, detailing the fundamental components and the overall process involved.

At the core of the torch.nn module are the nn.Module and its subclasses. The nn.Module serves as the base class for all neural network modules, which can represent layers, loss functions, and even entire models. All modules in the torch.nn library inherit from nn.Module, ensuring consistency and interoperability.

To start building a neural network, we first need to define a class that extends nn.Module. This class will contain our network's architecture, including layers and their configurations. The basic structure of such a class looks like this:

```
import torch.nn as nn

class SimpleNet(nn.Module):
    def __init__(self):
        super(SimpleNet, self).__init__()
        self.layer1 = nn.Linear(in_features=10, out_features=5)
        self.layer2 = nn.ReLU()
        self.layer3 = nn.Linear(in_features=5, out_features=1)

    def forward(self, x):
        x = self.layer1(x)
        x = self.layer2(x)
        x = self.layer3(x)
        return x
```

In this example, we define a simple neural network called SimpleNet with three layers: two linear layers and one ReLU activation function layer. The nn.Linear module creates a linear transformation to the incoming data, while nn.ReLU applies the Rectified Linear Unit activation function.

The forward method is crucial as it establishes the forward pass of the network, dictating how data flows through the layers. In our SimpleNet, the input x is sequentially passed through layer1, layer2, and layer3, with each layer performing its respective transformation.

One of the most significant advantages of extending nn.Module is that it automatically registers all layers and parameters, making them accessible for optimization and easy to manage. For instance, we can instantiate SimpleNet and inspect its parameters as follows:

```
model = SimpleNet()
print(model)
for param in model.parameters():
    print(param)
```

The output will detail the architecture and the model parameters:

```
SimpleNet(
  (layer1): Linear(in_features=10, out_features=5, bias=True)
  (layer2): ReLU()
  (layer3): Linear(in_features=5, out_features=1, bias=True)
)
Parameter containing:
tensor([[ 0.4106,  0.4277, -0.0672,  0.2189, -0.4624],
        [-0.2318,  0.0801,  0.4297, -0.1505,  0.2969],
        [-0.1281, -0.2822,  0.1894,  0.0227,  0.1613],
        [ 0.0711,  0.0101, -0.0481,  0.1555,  0.2792],
        [-0.0575,  0.0149, -0.3584,  0.1645,  0.3558],
        [ 0.1716,  0.0835, -0.3940,  0.4099, -0.2359],
        [ 0.1921,  0.4275,  0.2376, -0.2759, -0.0134],
        [ 0.3941, -0.1277, -0.0312, -0.3687,  0.3776],
        [-0.1338, -0.0038, -0.0665, -0.1146,  0.2799],
        [ 0.3590, -0.3709, -0.0957, -0.1317, -0.0831]], requires_grad=True)
Parameter containing:
tensor([ 0.1276,  0.3691, -0.3560,  0.2731, -0.1102], requires_grad=True)
Parameter containing:
tensor([[ 0.2510],
        [-0.1883],
        [ 0.2782],
        [ 0.3765],
        [-0.1510]], requires_grad=True)
Parameter containing:
tensor([0.0395], requires_grad=True)
```

In addition to layers and activation functions, torch.nn provides a variety of building blocks for more sophisticated neural network construction. These include convolutional layers (e.g., nn.Conv2d), pooling layers (e.g., nn.MaxPool2d), and recurrent layers (e.g., nn.LSTM). Each of these modules can be integrated similarly to how we used nn.Linear and nn.ReLU in SimpleNet.

Consider a more complex network with convolutional layers and pooling layers:

```
class ComplexNet(nn.Module):
    def __init__(self):
        super(ComplexNet, self).__init__()
        self.conv1 = nn.Conv2d(in_channels=1, out_channels=32, kernel_size=3, stride
            =1, padding=1)
        self.pool = nn.MaxPool2d(kernel_size=2, stride=2, padding=0)
        self.conv2 = nn.Conv2d(in_channels=32, out_channels=64, kernel_size=3,
            stride=1, padding=1)
        self.fc1 = nn.Linear(in_features=64*7*7, out_features=128)
        self.fc2 = nn.Linear(in_features=128, out_features=10)

    def forward(self, x):
        x = self.pool(F.relu(self.conv1(x)))
```

```
        x = self.pool(F.relu(self.conv2(x)))
        x = x.view(-1, 64*7*7)
        x = F.relu(self.fc1(x))
        x = self.fc2(x)
        return x
```

ComplexNet introduces convolutional and pooling layers, which are particularly effective for image data. The dimensions of the data are transformed through the convolution and pooling operations, and eventually flattened before being passed to fully connected layers.

To use the network, we instantiate it and pass a sample input through the forward pass to verify its functionality:

```
import torch
import torch.nn.functional as F

model = ComplexNet()
input_sample = torch.randn(1, 1, 28, 28) # Batch size of 1, 1 channel, 28x28 image
output = model(input_sample)
print(output)
```

The expected output will be a tensor representing the activations from the final layer (logits for a 10-class classification problem):

```
tensor([[ 0.0163, -0.0014,  0.0762, -0.0415,  0.0346,  0.0061,
          0.0457, -0.0233,  0.0066, -0.0506]], grad_fn=<AddmmBackward0>)
```

By leveraging the versatility and power of the torch.nn module, one can define and manipulate a wide range of neural network architectures catered to specific tasks and data types. The torch.nn.Module class provides the foundational framework, while the various layers and functionalities offer the flexibility required to build and train neural networks effectively.

4.4 Understanding Layers and Modules

In PyTorch, the process of constructing neural networks revolves around the interplay of Layers and Modules. The torch.nn module provides numerous functionalities that encapsulate standard neural network layers and structures, thereby offering a streamlined way to build and manage complex networks. Understanding the nature of layers and modules within PyTorch is crucial for developing effective neural network architectures.

At the core of PyTorch, a Module is an abstraction that represents a single layer or a collection of layers. It is an essential building block for defining the architecture of neural networks. The most fundamental module in PyTorch is torch.nn.Module, which serves as a base class for all neural network modules.

To grasp the function of nn.Module, consider the following example of defining a simple custom module:

```
import torch
import torch.nn as nn

class CustomModule(nn.Module):
    def __init__(self):
        super(CustomModule, self).__init__()
        self.linear = nn.Linear(10, 5)
        self.relu = nn.ReLU()

    def forward(self, x):
        x = self.linear(x)
        x = self.relu(x)
        return x

model = CustomModule()
```

In this example, CustomModule inherits from nn.Module, and within the __init__ method, the base class constructor super(CustomModule, self).__init__() is called. The module includes two layers: a linear layer nn.Linear and a ReLU activation function nn.ReLU. The forward method is defined to describe how the input tensor x propagates through the layers. Once the custom module is instantiated as model, it integrates seamlessly into the PyTorch workflow.

PyTorch provides a diverse array of pre-defined layers within torch.nn. Here are some commonly used layers:

- nn.Linear: Defines a fully connected layer, also known as a dense layer, which applies a linear transformation to the input data.
- nn.Conv2d: Implements a 2D convolutional layer, crucial for capturing spatial hierarchies in image data.
- nn.ReLU: Performs the rectified linear unit activation, introducing non-linearity into the model.
- nn.BatchNorm2d: Conducts batch normalization over a 4D input tensor, expediting training and stabilizing learning dynamics.
- nn.Dropout: Applies dropout regularization, mitigating overfitting by randomly zeroing elements during training.

Each of these classes can be readily utilized in a similar structure to the custom module example provided. For instance, to define a convolutional neural network (ConvNet), one might employ:

```
class ConvNet(nn.Module):
    def __init__(self):
        super(ConvNet, self).__init__()
        self.conv1 = nn.Conv2d(in_channels=1, out_channels=20, kernel_size=5)
        self.pool = nn.MaxPool2d(kernel_size=2, stride=2)
        self.conv2 = nn.Conv2d(in_channels=20, out_channels=50, kernel_size=5)
        self.fc1 = nn.Linear(50 * 4 * 4, 500)
        self.fc2 = nn.Linear(500, 10)

    def forward(self, x):
        x = self.pool(F.relu(self.conv1(x)))
        x = self.pool(F.relu(self.conv2(x)))
        x = x.view(-1, 50 * 4 * 4) % Flatten the tensor
        x = F.relu(self.fc1(x))
        x = self.fc2(x)
        return x

convnet = ConvNet()
```

This example represents a straightforward ConvNet with two convolutional layers followed by pooling layers and fully connected layers. Here, self.conv1 is a 2D convolutional layer expecting input with 1 channel, producing 20 output channels with a kernel size of 5x5. The MaxPool2d layer implements max pooling with a 2x2 window and a stride of 2. The final dense layers perform the classification. Note how each layer is built into the module, and how the forward method dictates the flow of data through the network, employing ReLU activations and flattening the tensor where necessary.

A distinguishing feature of nn.Module is its recursive nature in handling layers and sub-modules, enabling greater modularity and readability. For example, modules can contain other modules, leading to hierarchical structures that are easy to manage and debug. Consider a scenario where a network includes multiple sub-networks as follows:

```
class SubNetwork(nn.Module):
    def __init__(self):
        super(SubNetwork, self).__init__()
        self.layer = nn.Linear(10, 10)

    def forward(self, x):
        return F.relu(self.layer(x))

class MainNetwork(nn.Module):
    def __init__(self):
        super(MainNetwork, self).__init__()
        self.subnetwork1 = SubNetwork()
        self.subnetwork2 = SubNetwork()
        self.classifier = nn.Linear(10, 1)

    def forward(self, x):
```

```
        x = self.subnetwork1(x)
        x = self.subnetwork2(x)
        x = self.classifier(x)
        return x

main_network = MainNetwork()
```

In this composite model, MainNetwork comprises two instances of SubNetwork and a final classifier layer. The forward method demonstrates the sequential application of sub-networks before final classification. This modular approach ensures that complex architectures can be broken down into simpler constituent modules, fostering reuse and ease of maintenance.

Modules and layers encapsulate not only the forward computational logic but also parameter management, gradient computation, and state persistence, thereby forming the backbone of neural network architectures in PyTorch. Understanding these building blocks is integral to leveraging the full potential of PyTorch in constructing scalable and efficient neural networks.

4.5 Activation Functions

Activation functions are critical components in neural networks that introduce non-linearities into the model. This non-linearity enables neural networks to approximate complex functions and capture patterns in the data that linear models cannot. In this section, we will explore several activation functions supported by PyTorch, discussing their mathematical formulations, advantages, and typical use-cases.

Sigmoid Function: The Sigmoid function is one of the classic activation functions, often represented by the equation:

$$\sigma(x) = \frac{1}{1 + e^{-x}}$$

The Sigmoid function squashes the input values to a range between 0 and 1. This squashing behavior is particularly useful for binary classification tasks. However, it has significant drawbacks, such as suffering from the vanishing gradient problem, where the gradients approach zero for large positive or negative input values, impeding the learning process.

Code example for implementing the Sigmoid function in PyTorch:

```
import torch
import torch.nn as nn

sigmoid = nn.Sigmoid()
input_data = torch.tensor([1.0, 2.0, 3.0])
output_data = sigmoid(input_data)
print(output_data)
```

Expected Output:

```
tensor([0.7311, 0.8808, 0.9526])
```

Tanh Function: The Tanh function, or hyperbolic tangent function, is another S-shaped activation function, given by:

$$\tanh(x) = \frac{e^x - e^{-x}}{e^x + e^{-x}}$$

Tanh squashes the input to a range between -1 and 1. Unlike the Sigmoid function, the Tanh function is zero-centered, which can improve convergence during training by reducing biases in the gradients.

Code example for applying the Tanh function in PyTorch:

```
tanh = nn.Tanh()
input_data = torch.tensor([1.0, 2.0, 3.0])
output_data = tanh(input_data)
print(output_data)
```

Expected Output:

```
tensor([0.7616, 0.9640, 0.9951])
```

ReLU (Rectified Linear Unit): The ReLU is one of the most commonly used activation functions in modern neural network architectures. It is defined as:

$$\text{ReLU}(x) = \max(0, x)$$

ReLU is computationally efficient and helps alleviate the vanishing gradient problem. However, it has its own downside known as the "dying ReLU" problem, where neurons can sometimes get "stuck" during training, producing zero gradient and thus becoming inactive.

Code example for implementing the ReLU function in PyTorch:

```
relu = nn.ReLU()
input_data = torch.tensor([1.0, -1.0, 0.0])
output_data = relu(input_data)
print(output_data)
```

Expected Output:

```
tensor([1., 0., 0.])
```

Leaky ReLU: To address the dying ReLU problem, the Leaky ReLU introduces a small slope for negative values, instead of mapping them to zero. It is defined as:

$$\text{Leaky ReLU}(x) = \begin{cases} x & \text{if } x \geq 0 \\ \alpha x & \text{if } x < 0 \end{cases}$$

where α is a small constant, often set to 0.01. This function ensures that neurons continue to update even when the input is negative.

Code example for the Leaky ReLU in PyTorch:

```
leaky_relu = nn.LeakyReLU(0.01)
input_data = torch.tensor([1.0, -1.0, 0.0])
output_data = leaky_relu(input_data)
print(output_data)
```

Expected Output:

```
tensor([ 1.0000, -0.0100,  0.0000])
```

Softmax Function: The Softmax function is typically used as an activation function in the output layer of neural networks for multi-class classification tasks. It converts raw scores (logits) into probabilities by applying the exponential function and normalizing by the sum over all possible classes. The Softmax function for a vector z is defined as:

$$\text{Softmax}(z_i) = \frac{e^{z_i}}{\sum_{j=1}^{N} e^{z_j}}$$

where i indexes into the raw scores vector z and N is the number of classes.

Code example for using the Softmax function in PyTorch:

```
softmax = nn.Softmax(dim=0)
input_data = torch.tensor([1.0, 2.0, 3.0])
output_data = softmax(input_data)
print(output_data)
```

Expected Output:

```
tensor([0.0900, 0.2447, 0.6652])
```

Activation functions play an integral role in the ability of neural networks to learn complex patterns by providing the required non-linear transformations. Different use-cases and architectures can benefit from different activation functions, which makes understanding them pivotal for anyone aiming to design effective neural networks.

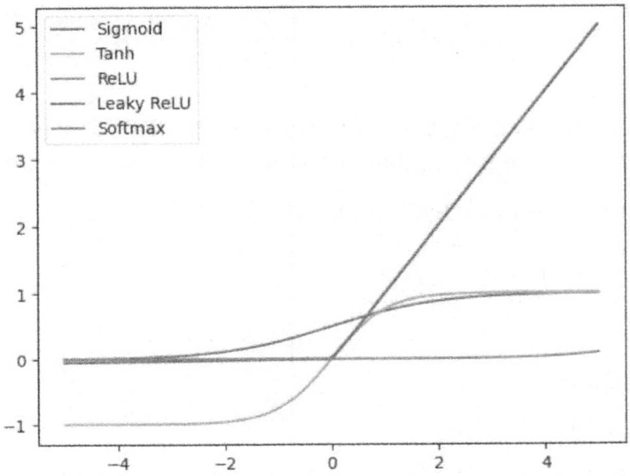

4.6 Building a Feedforward Neural Network

Constructing a feedforward neural network in PyTorch is a principal step in deploying machine learning solutions for various tasks. This section will methodically guide through building a basic feedforward neural network using the PyTorch library by progressively connecting the theoretical aspects covered in previous sections to practical implementation.

To start, ensure that torch and torchvision libraries are installed. These can be installed using pip:

```
pip install torch torchvision
```

It is also essential to have an understanding of Python programming and basic concepts of neural networks such as layers, activation functions, and backpropagation.

- **Setting Up the Environment**

Begin by importing necessary libraries. PyTorch provides powerful tools for tensor operations, which are fundamental in creating and manipulating neural networks.

```
import torch
import torch.nn as nn
import torch.optim as optim
import torch.nn.functional as F
from torchvision import datasets, transforms
```

- **Creating a Simple Feedforward Neural Network Class**

In PyTorch, a neural network model is defined by subclassing torch.nn.Module. Within the class, the model layers are defined in the __init__ method, and the forward pass logic is implemented in the forward method.

```
class SimpleFeedforwardNN(nn.Module):
    def __init__(self):
        super(SimpleFeedforwardNN, self).__init__()
        self.fc1 = nn.Linear(in_features=784, out_features=128)
        self.fc2 = nn.Linear(in_features=128, out_features=64)
        self.fc3 = nn.Linear(in_features=64, out_features=10)

    def forward(self, x):
        x = F.relu(self.fc1(x))
        x = F.relu(self.fc2(x))
        x = self.fc3(x)
        return F.log_softmax(x, dim=1)
```

- **Explanation of the Network Architecture**

- fc1, fc2, fc3: These are fully connected (linear) layers. Their parameters determine how data flows and is transformed through the network.

- F.relu: Implements the ReLU activation function. Applying non-linearities like ReLU allows the network to model more complex data.

- F.log_softmax: This is used in the final layer to ensure the output sums to 1, which is suitable for classification tasks.

- x: At each stage, x is passed through the network layers and activation functions.

The first layer, fc1, has 784 input features, corresponding to a flattened 28x28 grayscale image (such as from the MNIST dataset). The final fc3 layer has 10 output features corresponding to the 10 classes in the MNIST dataset.

- **Loading and Transforming Data**

The next crucial step involves preparing the dataset. The torchvision library simplifies this through pre-defined datasets and transformations.

```
transform = transforms.Compose([transforms.ToTensor(),
                                transforms.Normalize((0.5,), (0.5,))])

trainset = datasets.MNIST(root='./data', train=True, download=True, transform=
    transform)
trainloader = torch.utils.data.DataLoader(trainset, batch_size=64, shuffle=True)

testset = datasets.MNIST(root='./data', train=False, download=True, transform=
    transform)
testloader = torch.utils.data.DataLoader(testset, batch_size=64, shuffle=True)
```

transforms.Compose allows chaining of multiple transformations. Here, transforms.ToTensor() converts images to PyTorch tensors, and transforms.Normalize() standardizes the data.

- **Training the Network**

Training involves passing data through the network, computing the loss, performing backpropagation, and updating the weights. The following code demonstrates this procedure.

```
model = SimpleFeedforwardNN()
criterion = nn.NLLLoss()
optimizer = optim.SGD(model.parameters(), lr=0.01)

epochs = 5
for e in range(epochs):
    running_loss = 0
    for images, labels in trainloader:
        images = images.view(images.shape[0], -1)

        optimizer.zero_grad()
        output = model(images)
        loss = criterion(output, labels)
        loss.backward()
        optimizer.step()

        running_loss += loss.item()
    print(f"Training loss: {running_loss/len(trainloader)}")
```

- model = SimpleFeedforwardNN(): Instantiates the neural network model.

- criterion = nn.NLLLoss(): Defines the loss function (negative log likelihood loss), suitable for classification.
- optimizer = optim.SGD(model.parameters(), lr=0.01): Specifies the optimizer (stochastic gradient descent) with a learning rate of 0.01.
- images.view(images.shape[0], -1): Flattens the input images into a 784-dimensional vector, aligning with the input features of the first layer.
- optimizer.zero_grad(): Resets gradients to zero before each forward pass.
- model(images): Computes the forward pass.
- loss = criterion(output, labels): Computes the loss.
- loss.backward(): Performs backpropagation.
- optimizer.step(): Updates the model parameters.

- **Evaluating the Model**

After training, it is essential to evaluate the model on the test data to assess its generalization performance.

```
correct_count, all_count = 0, 0
for images, labels in testloader:
    for i in range(len(labels)):
        img = images[i].view(1, 784)
        with torch.no_grad():
            logps = model(img)

        ps = torch.exp(logps)
        probab = list(ps.numpy()[0])
        pred_label = probab.index(max(probab))
        true_label = labels.numpy()[i]
        if(true_label == pred_label):
            correct_count += 1
        all_count += 1

print("Number Of Images Tested =", all_count)
print("Model Accuracy =", (correct_count/all_count))
```

- with torch.no_grad(): Disables gradient calculation during inference.
- torch.exp(logps): Converts log probabilities back to actual probabilities.

- pred_label: Identifies the predicted label as the index of the highest probability.
- correct_count/all_count: Computes the accuracy.

The provided implementation is a foundation. In practice, adjustments like learning rate tuning, network depth, batch normalization, and more sophisticated optimizers may enhance performance. This section has provided a fundamental understanding of building and training a feed-forward neural network using PyTorch. By experimenting and iterating the model's architecture and hyperparameters, one can achieve better results tailored to specific use cases.

4.7 Defining the Forward Pass

The forward pass is a critical component of neural networks, representing the phase where input data is propagated through the network to compute the output. During this phase, each layer applies a combination of linear transformations and non-linear activations to transform the input until the desired output is produced.

In PyTorch, defining the forward pass is typically accomplished by subclassing the torch.nn.Module class and overriding the forward method. This method dictates how input tensors are manipulated as they traverse through the network layers. Below, we will detail the implementation of the forward pass by using a simple feedforward neural network as an example.

First, we import the necessary PyTorch modules:

```
import torch
import torch.nn as nn
import torch.nn.functional as F
```

Next, we define a custom neural network class by subclassing nn.Module:

```
class SimpleNN(nn.Module):
    def __init__(self):
        super(SimpleNN, self).__init__()
        self.fc1 = nn.Linear(784, 128) # Input layer
        self.fc2 = nn.Linear(128, 64) # Hidden layer
        self.fc3 = nn.Linear(64, 10) # Output layer
```

In the __init__ method, we specify the network structure by defining the layers. Here, 784 represents the number of input features (e.g., flattened 28x28 image), 128 and 64 are the sizes of hidden layers, and 10 corresponds to the number of output classes (e.g., for digit classification).

The core functionality of our neural network is captured in the forward method:

```
def forward(self, x):
    x = F.relu(self.fc1(x)) # Apply ReLU activation to fc1
    x = F.relu(self.fc2(x)) # Apply ReLU activation to fc2
    x = self.fc3(x) # Output layer
    return x
```

In this forward method, the input tensor x is sequentially passed through each layer. The F.relu function applies the Rectified Linear Unit activation function, introducing non-linearity to the network:

- **Input Layer:** The input tensor is passed to the first fully connected layer, self.fc1, transforming it from a 784-dimensional input space to a 128-dimensional space.
- **Hidden Layer:** The output from self.fc1 is fed into self.fc2 after applying the ReLU activation function, reducing it further to 64 dimensions.
- **Output Layer:** Finally, the transformed tensor is passed through self.fc3, which maps it to a 10-dimensional output tensor.

To utilize this network, we instantiate the class and pass an input tensor through it:

```
# Create an instance of the network
model = SimpleNN()

# Create a sample input tensor (batch size of 1, flatten 28x28 image)
input_tensor = torch.randn(1, 784)

# Perform a forward pass
output = model(input_tensor)

print(output)
```

Program execution displays the output tensor:

```
tensor([[ 0.2374, 0.1177, -0.1254, 0.0572, -0.0681, 0.3654, -0.0938, 0.0629, 0.1521, 0.0425]], grad_fn=<AddmmBackward>)
```

The tensor output represents the model's raw scores or logits for each class.

By explicitly defining the forward pass in this manner, we gain fine control over the data flow through the network, enabling us to customize the architecture and select suitable activation functions. This method-centric approach ensures the forward pass is both modular and extendable, facilitating the development of complex neural network architectures in PyTorch.

4.8 Working with Loss Functions

In the context of neural networks, loss functions (also referred to as cost functions or objective functions) are critical for the training process. They quantify how well or poorly a model has performed by comparing the predicted output to the actual target. By doing so, they provide a signal for the optimizer to adjust the model parameters in order to minimize the error.

Most neural network training methods, including those used with PyTorch, are based on some form of gradient descent. Thus, the choice of loss function can have a significant impact on the training dynamics and, ultimately, the performance of the neural network. In PyTorch, loss functions are implemented within the torch.nn module and can be easily employed during the training process.

Several types of loss functions cater to different types of tasks, such as regression, classification, and more complicated scenarios like generative models. We will explore some common loss functions, their use cases, and how to implement them in PyTorch.

Mean Squared Error (MSE) Loss

The Mean Squared Error (MSE) loss function is commonly used for regression tasks. It calculates the average squared difference between the predicted values and the actual values. The MSE loss is defined mathematically as:

$$\text{MSE} = \frac{1}{n}\sum_{i=1}^{n}(y_i - \hat{y}_i)^2$$

where y_i is the actual value and $\hat{y}_i$ is the predicted value.

To use the MSE loss in PyTorch, we can utilize the torch.nn.MSELoss module:

```
import torch
import torch.nn as nn

# Define the loss function
```

```
loss_function = nn.MSELoss()

# Example target and prediction tensors
target = torch.tensor([2.0, 3.0])
prediction = torch.tensor([2.5, 3.5])

# Calculate the loss
loss = loss_function(prediction, target)
print(loss)
```

Executing this code will result in an output that represents the mean squared error:

```
tensor(0.2500)
```

Cross-Entropy Loss

Cross-Entropy Loss, also known as log loss, is widely used for classification tasks. It measures the performance of a classification model whose output is a probability value between 0 and 1. Cross-Entropy Loss increases as the predicted probability diverges from the actual label. For binary classification, it is defined as:

$$\text{CrossEntropyLoss} = -\frac{1}{n}\sum_{i=1}^{n}[y_i \log(\hat{y}_i) + (1 - y_i)\log(1 - \hat{y}_i)]$$

For multi-class classification, PyTorch provides the torch.nn.CrossEntropyLoss module. Here is an illustrative example:

```
import torch

# Define the loss function
loss_function = nn.CrossEntropyLoss()

# Example target (class indices) and prediction (logits) tensors
target = torch.tensor([1])
prediction = torch.tensor([[1.0, 2.0, 0.5]])

# Calculate the loss
loss = loss_function(prediction, target)
print(loss)
```

The expected output:

```
tensor(0.8034)
```

Binary Cross-Entropy Loss

When dealing with binary classification problems, torch.nn.BCELoss is appropriate. Binary Cross-Entropy Loss (BCELoss) is a special case of Cross-Entropy Loss tailored for binary classification:

$$\text{BCELoss} = -\frac{1}{n}\sum_{i=1}^{n}[y_i \log(\hat{y}_i) + (1 - y_i)\log(1 - \hat{y}_i)]$$

In PyTorch, this can be represented as:

```
# Define the loss function
loss_function = nn.BCELoss()

# Example target and prediction tensors
target = torch.tensor([1.0, 0.0, 1.0])
prediction = torch.tensor([0.8, 0.2, 0.6])

# Calculate the loss
loss = loss_function(prediction, target)
print(loss)
```

Output:

```
tensor(0.3647)
```

Custom Loss Functions

While PyTorch offers a wide array of pre-defined loss functions, scenarios may arise where a custom loss function is necessary. PyTorch facilitates the creation of custom loss functions by allowing users to define new classes derived from torch.nn.Module and override the forward method.

Consider a custom loss function that combines MSE and MAE (Mean Absolute Error):

```
import torch.nn.functional as F

class CustomLoss(nn.Module):
    def __init__(self):
        super(CustomLoss, self).__init__()

    def forward(self, prediction, target):
        mse_loss = F.mse_loss(prediction, target)
        mae_loss = F.l1_loss(prediction, target)
        return mse_loss + mae_loss

# Example target and prediction tensors
target = torch.tensor([2.0, 3.0])
prediction = torch.tensor([2.5, 3.5])

# Initialize and calculate custom loss
custom_loss_function = CustomLoss()
loss = custom_loss_function(prediction, target)
print(loss)
```

The resulting output will be a tensor value representing the custom loss.

```
tensor(0.7500)
```

Choosing the appropriate loss function is essential for the specific nature of the task at hand. Regression tasks, classification tasks, and more specialized tasks may require different loss functions. By leveraging the wide range of built-in loss functions in PyTorch, or by designing custom loss functions, one can tailor the training process to achieve better model performance.

4.9 Using Optimizers

Optimizers play an essential role in the training process of neural networks by updating the model's weights to minimize the loss function. In PyTorch, optimizers are provided under the torch.optim module. This section delves into the use of these optimizers, their mechanisms, and how to implement them efficiently in your PyTorch models.

To start using an optimizer, you first need to instantiate it with the parameters of your model and optionally set hyperparameters such as the learning rate. PyTorch provides a variety of optimization algorithms, with SGD (Stochastic Gradient Descent) being one of the most commonly used.

```
import torch.optim as optim
```

To create an instance of the SGD optimizer and attach it to the parameters of our model, we do the following:

```
# Assuming 'model' is an instance of torch.nn.Module
optimizer = optim.SGD(model.parameters(), lr=0.01)
```

The learning rate (lr) is a crucial hyperparameter for the performance of the optimizer. It controls how much to change the model parameters in response to the estimated error each time the model weights are updated. A detailed discussion on the selection and tuning of learning rates is beyond the scope of this section, but it is important to monitor and adjust it as needed.

Beyond the standard Stochastic Gradient Descent, PyTorch provides several sophisticated optimization algorithms like Adam, RMSprop, and Adagrad, among others. Each of these optimizers has its own set of advantages and typical use cases.

Adam Optimizer:

The Adam (Adaptive Moment Estimation) optimizer, which combines the best properties of the AdaGrad and RMSProp algorithms to provide an optimization algorithm that can handle sparse gradients on noisy problems, is widely used for training deep learning models.

```
optimizer = optim.Adam(model.parameters(), lr=0.001)
```

Adam requires setting two additional hyperparameters, β_1 and β_2, which are the decay rates for the moment estimates and typically set to defaults of 0.9 and 0.999, respectively.

RMSprop Optimizer:

RMSprop (Root Mean Square Propagation) is another optimizer frequently used in training neural networks. It adjusts the learning rate dynamically for each parameter during training.

```
optimizer = optim.RMSprop(model.parameters(), lr=0.01)
```

The RMSprop optimizer helps in combating the decaying learning rate issue in AdaGrad and is particularly useful when dealing with recurrent neural networks.

After defining the optimizer, the usual steps in each training iteration include:

- Clearing the gradients of all optimized torch.Tensors.
- Performing a forward pass through the network.
- Computing the loss.
- Performing a backward pass to compute the gradients.
- Updating the parameters using the optimizer.

Clearing gradients can be done using the zero_grad method:

```
optimizer.zero_grad()
```

Computing the gradients involves calling backward on the loss tensor:

```
loss.backward()
```

The step method performs a parameter update based on the current gradients:

```
optimizer.step()
```

An exemplary training loop integrating all the mentioned steps is provided below:

```
for epoch in range(num_epochs):
    for data in data_loader:
        inputs, labels = data

        optimizer.zero_grad() # Clear gradients
        outputs = model(inputs) # Forward pass
        loss = criterion(outputs, labels) # Compute loss
        loss.backward() # Backward pass
        optimizer.step() # Update parameters
```

This loop iterates over the dataset, performing the forward pass, computing the loss, performing the backward pass, and finally updating the parameters using the chosen optimizer. It's important to note that optimizers maintain a state about the parameters which they are operating on, which allows algorithms like Adam and RMSprop to adapt their learning rates dynamically.

The integration of optimizers into the training loop is pivotal for the convergence and performance of neural networks, and the choice of optimizer and its hyperparameters significantly influences the training dynamics.

4.10 Building Complex Neural Network Architectures

When building complex neural network architectures using PyTorch, a thorough comprehension of the fundamental components as well as the integration of advanced architectural principles is crucial. Leveraging the modularity and flexibility provided by PyTorch's torch.nn module allows us to create models that can handle sophisticated tasks and datasets.

Sequential Architectures: A common approach to constructing more advanced networks is through sequential architectures. An example is stacking layers in a linear fashion. This can be efficiently done using the torch.nn.Sequential class.

```
import torch.nn as nn

model = nn.Sequential(
    nn.Conv2d(in_channels=3, out_channels=64, kernel_size=3, stride=1, padding=1),

    nn.ReLU(),
    nn.MaxPool2d(kernel_size=2, stride=2),
    nn.Flatten(),
    nn.Linear(in_features=64*16*16, out_features=10)
)
```

In this example, the network takes an RGB image as input, processes it through a convolutional layer, applies a ReLU activation, performs down-sampling using max pooling, flattens the output, and finally passes it through a fully connected layer.

Modular Architectures: For more complex architectures, such as those involving residual connections or multiple distinct pathways through the network, it is often necessary to subclass nn.Module and define custom forward passes. For instance, implementing a ResNet block involves creating a class that encapsulates both sequential and parallel components.

```
class ResNetBlock(nn.Module):
    def __init__(self, in_channels, out_channels, stride=1):
        super(ResNetBlock, self).__init__()
        self.conv1 = nn.Conv2d(in_channels, out_channels, kernel_size=3, stride=
            stride, padding=1)
        self.bn1 = nn.BatchNorm2d(out_channels)
        self.relu = nn.ReLU()
        self.conv2 = nn.Conv2d(out_channels, out_channels, kernel_size=3, stride=1,
            padding=1)
        self.bn2 = nn.BatchNorm2d(out_channels)

        if stride != 1 or in_channels != out_channels:
            self.shortcut = nn.Sequential(
                nn.Conv2d(in_channels, out_channels, kernel_size=1, stride=stride),
                nn.BatchNorm2d(out_channels)
            )
        else:
            self.shortcut = nn.Identity()

    def forward(self, x):
        out = self.relu(self.bn1(self.conv1(x)))
        out = self.bn2(self.conv2(out))
        out += self.shortcut(x)
        out = self.relu(out)
        return out
```

Here, a ResNetBlock performs a convolution, batch normalization, and ReLU activation twice, followed by adding the input to the result (if necessary, after matching dimensions via a shortcut path). This block pattern helps in creating deep networks that can avoid degradation problems as layers increase.

Combining Different Types of Layers: Complex architectures often require combining different types of layers such as convolutional layers, recurrent layers, or even attention mechanisms. For instance, combining a Convolutional Neural Network (CNN) with a Recurrent Neural Network (RNN) to process video frames entails:

```
class CNNRNN(nn.Module):
    def __init__(self, cnn_out_channels, rnn_hidden_size, num_classes):
        super(CNNRNN, self).__init__()
```

```
        self.cnn = nn.Sequential(
            nn.Conv2d(3, cnn_out_channels, kernel_size=3, stride=1, padding=1),
            nn.ReLU(),
            nn.MaxPool2d(kernel_size=2, stride=2)
        )
        self.rnn = nn.LSTM(input_size=cnn_out_channels, hidden_size=
            rnn_hidden_size, batch_first=True)
        self.fc = nn.Linear(rnn_hidden_size, num_classes)

    def forward(self, x):
        batch_size, seq_len, C, H, W = x.size()
        c_out = self.cnn(x.view(batch_size * seq_len, C, H, W))
        c_out = c_out.view(batch_size, seq_len, -1)
        rnn_out, _ = self.rnn(c_out)
        out = self.fc(rnn_out[:, -1, :])
        return out
```

This model first applies a CNN to each frame of the video sequence (x is expected to have dimensions batch_size x seq_len x C x H x W). The CNN outputs are then reshaped and fed into an LSTM (Long Short-Term Memory), followed by a fully connected layer to produce the final classification results.

Attention Mechanisms: Attention mechanisms are widely used in complex architectures for their ability to focus on relevant parts of the input. An example implementation of a scaled dot-product attention mechanism can be seen below:

```
class ScaledDotProductAttention(nn.Module):
    def __init__(self, d_k):
        super(ScaledDotProductAttention, self).__init__()
        self.d_k = d_k

    def forward(self, Q, K, V, mask=None):
        scores = torch.matmul(Q, K.transpose(-2, -1)) / math.sqrt(self.d_k)
        if mask is not None:
            scores = scores.masked_fill(mask == 0, -1e9)
        attention = F.softmax(scores, dim=-1)
        output = torch.matmul(attention, V)
        return output, attention
```

Combined with other architectural blocks, attention mechanisms enable models to handle tasks that involve selective processing of input features.

The described elements can be combined and extended to build highly specialized architectures such as Transformer models, generative adversarial networks (GANs), or deep reinforcement learning models. These components facilitate creating networks equipped to tackle diverse and complex tasks.

Chapter 5

Training Neural Networks

This chapter covers the essential techniques for training neural networks. It begins with preparing datasets and loading data, followed by establishing the basics of the training loop, including backpropagation and gradient descent. The chapter discusses monitoring training progress, addressing overfitting and underfitting, and the importance of validation and test sets. It also includes instructions on saving and loading models and utilizing learning rate schedulers to optimize training performance.

5.1 Introduction to Training Neural Networks

Training neural networks involves a series of systematic procedures that transform raw data into a learned model capable of making predictions or performing classifications. The fundamental goal of training is to optimally adjust the network's parameters, weights and biases, so that the model minimizes a predetermined loss function on the given task.

A neural network consists of layers of interconnected nodes, or neurons, each representing a specific computation function. During training, data is passed through these layers to compute the output, followed by a comparison with the desired output. This comparison is captured by the loss function, a crucial component that quantifies the error of the network's predictions. Common loss functions in classification tasks include Cross-Entropy Loss, while Mean Squared Error (MSE) is typically used for regression tasks.

The core methodology for training involves the following sequential steps:

- Initializing the network's parameters,
- Performing a forward pass through the network to compute the output,
- Computing the loss,
- Performing a backward pass to compute gradients, and
- Updating the parameters using an optimization algorithm.

This iterative process, repeated over multiple epochs, gradually enhances the model's performance.

Initialization of network parameters is critical. Poor initialization can lead to vanishing or exploding gradients, rendering training inefficient. Common initialization techniques include Xavier initialization for tanh activations and He initialization for ReLU activations. These techniques set the initial weights based on the number of input and output units in a node, promoting stable training dynamics.

The forward pass is the process of propagating the input data through the network layers to compute the final output. This involves a series of matrix multiplications and the application of activation functions, which introduce non-linearity into the model. Activation functions like Sigmoid, ReLU, and Tanh are vital for capturing complex patterns in data.

The backward pass, or backpropagation, is central to training. It involves computing the gradient of the loss function with respect to each weight by applying the chain rule of calculus. This gradient indicates how the loss would change with respect to a small change in the weights. Backpropagation utilizes the Gradient Descent algorithm, where weights are updated in the direction opposite to the gradient to minimize the loss.

An optimization algorithm is employed to adjust the weights and biases. Stochastic Gradient Descent (SGD) is one of the simplest and most commonly used optimization algorithms. In SGD, weights are updated incrementally using a small batch of data, called a mini-batch, which introduces noise in the updates helping in escaping local minima.

More sophisticated optimizers such as Adam (Adaptive Moment Estimation) combine the advantages of both Adaptive Gradient Algorithm

(AdaGrad) and Root Mean Square Propagation (RMSProp). Adam maintains per-parameter learning rates that are adapted based on the first and second moments of the gradients. The update rule for Adam is:

$$\theta \leftarrow \theta - \eta \frac{\hat{m_t}}{\sqrt{\hat{v_t}} + \epsilon}$$

Here, η is the learning rate, θ represents the parameters, m_t and v_t are estimates of the first and second moments of the gradients, and ϵ is a small constant to prevent division by zero.

Another important aspect of training is the learning rate, which controls the step size during the parameter update. If the learning rate is too small, training will be slow, requiring more time to converge. Conversely, a large learning rate may cause the training to converge prematurely to a suboptimal solution or diverge altogether. Learning rate schedulers dynamically adjust the learning rate during training, aiding in efficient convergence.

To effectively monitor training progress, metrics such as accuracy, precision, recall, and F1 score for classification tasks, or RMSE and MAE for regression tasks, are tracked throughout the training epochs. Real-time visualization tools like TensorBoard provide extensive support for monitoring these metrics, enabling a clear understanding of how the model is learning over time.

Addressing overfitting, which occurs when a model performs well on training data but poorly on validation data, is essential. Techniques such as dropout, regularization, and using validation sets help mitigate overfitting. Underfitting, where the model is too simple to capture the underlying trends in the data, is handled by increasing the model complexity or adjusting the learning mechanisms.

Incorporating validation and test sets is crucial to ensure the neural network's performance generalizes well to unseen data. The validation set assists in hyperparameter tuning, while the test set provides an unbiased evaluation of the final model.

Finally, saving and loading trained models facilitate their deployment in real-world applications. PyTorch provides straightforward mechanisms to save model parameters using torch.save and load them using torch.load, which are instrumental for restoring models for future inferences or resuming training.

```
import torch
```

```
# Saving the model
torch.save(model.state_dict(), 'model.pth')

# Loading the model
model = TheModelClass(*args, **kwargs)
model.load_state_dict(torch.load('model.pth'))
model.eval()
```

Each aspect of training neural networks is interlinked, and mastering these components is central to developing robust machine learning models.

5.2 Preparing the Dataset

Proper preparation of the dataset is a critical step in the pipeline for training neural networks. The effectiveness of your neural network largely depends on the quality and relevance of the data you provide. This section outlines the key tasks that need to be performed to ensure the dataset is apt for training, which include data collection, data cleaning, data transformation, and dataset partitioning.

Data Collection: The first step is gathering the data that your neural network will utilize for training. Depending on the use case, data can come from various sources such as databases, APIs, web scraping, or datasets published by institutions and researchers. All data sources need to be meticulously documented to maintain reproducibility and data integrity. The following Python libraries are often used for these tasks:

- pandas for handling and processing structured data.
- requests and BeautifulSoup for web scraping.
- sqlalchemy for database interactions.

Data Cleaning: Raw data is typically fraught with missing values, outliers, and noise that can impede the performance of a neural network. Cleaning the data involves several operations such as handling missing values, removing duplicates, and correcting inconsistencies. An example code snippet for cleaning data using pandas is as follows:

```
import pandas as pd

# Load dataset
```

```
df = pd.read_csv('dataset.csv')

# Check for missing values
missing_values = df.isnull().sum()

# Handling missing values
df = df.dropna() # Drop rows with missing values
# Alternatively, fill missing values
# df = df.fillna(method='ffill')

# Remove duplicates
df = df.drop_duplicates()

# View cleaned dataset
print(df.head())
```

Data Transformation: Neural networks often require data in numerical format and within specific ranges for optimal performance. Data transformation includes normalization, standardization, and encoding categorical variables. Consider the following transformations:

- **Normalization**: Scaling data values to the range [0, 1].
- **Standardization**: Scaling data to have zero mean and unit variance.
- **Encoding**: Transforming categorical variables into numerical form, e.g., one-hot encoding.

Normalization and standardization can be implemented using libraries like scikit-learn:

```
from sklearn.preprocessing import MinMaxScaler, StandardScaler

# Normalize data
scaler = MinMaxScaler()
df_normalized = scaler.fit_transform(df)

# Standardize data
scaler = StandardScaler()
df_standardized = scaler.fit_transform(df)
```

Encoding categorical variables can be done using pandas utilities:

```
# One-hot encoding of categorical variables
df_encoded = pd.get_dummies(df, columns=['categorical_column'])
```

Dataset Partitioning: Splitting the dataset into training, validation, and test sets is essential to estimate the performance of the neural network and to avoid overfitting. The training set is used to train the model, the validation set for tuning hyperparameters, and the test set for evaluating the final model performance. A common split is 70%-80% for training,

10%-20% for validation, and the remaining 10% for testing. The train_test_split function from scikit-learn can facilitate this:

```
from sklearn.model_selection import train_test_split

# Features and target variable
X = df.drop('target', axis=1)
y = df['target']

# Split dataset
X_train, X_temp, y_train, y_temp = train_test_split(X, y, test_size=0.3,
     random_state=42)
X_val, X_test, y_val, y_test = train_test_split(X_temp, y_temp, test_size=0.5,
     random_state=42)

# Verify splits
print(f'Training set size: {X_train.shape}')
print(f'Validation set size: {X_val.shape}')
print(f'Test set size: {X_test.shape}')
```

These steps of dataset preparation ensure that the data fed into the neural network is clean, well-structured, and suitably partitioned, thus laying a solid foundation for the subsequent stages of the neural network training process.

5.3 Data Loading and Preprocessing

Data loading and preprocessing are critical steps in the training of neural networks. Proper handling of data ensures efficient training and contributes to the model's performance. In PyTorch, these tasks are handled effectively using Dataset and DataLoader classes, which facilitate the management and transformation of data. This section covers creating datasets, applying necessary transformations, and loading the data.

First, we need to prepare the dataset by defining a custom dataset class that inherits from torch.utils.data.Dataset. This class should implement three methods: __init__, __len__, and __getitem__.

```
import torch
from torch.utils.data import Dataset

class CustomDataset(Dataset):
    def __init__(self, data, labels, transform=None):
        self.data = data
        self.labels = labels
        self.transform = transform

    def __len__(self):
        return len(self.data)
```

```
def __getitem__(self, idx):
    sample = self.data[idx]
    label = self.labels[idx]

    if self.transform:
        sample = self.transform(sample)

    return sample, label
```

In the __init__ method, the dataset is initialized with data, labels, and an optional transform function. The __len__ method returns the total number of samples in the dataset, and __getitem__ retrieves a data sample and its corresponding label at the specified index idx, along with any transformations applied to the data sample.

Next, we will create a data loader using the torch.utils.data.DataLoader class. The data loader provides batches of data, shuffles data if necessary, and loads the data in parallel using multiprocessing.

```
from torch.utils.data import DataLoader

dataset = CustomDataset(data, labels, transform=transform)
dataloader = DataLoader(dataset, batch_size=32, shuffle=True, num_workers=4)
```

The DataLoader is initialized with the custom dataset, batch size (number of samples per batch), shuffle parameter (randomly shuffle the data at every epoch), and number of worker threads for data loading.

Preprocessing of data can include several transformations such as normalization, data augmentation, conversion to tensors, etc. PyTorch provides a comprehensive suite of transformations within the torchvision.transforms module. Below is an example of using some common transformations:

```
from torchvision import transforms

% Define transforms
transform = transforms.Compose([
    transforms.ToTensor(),
    transforms.Normalize((0.5,), (0.5,)), % Normalizing with mean and std
])

% Apply the transforms to the dataset
dataset = CustomDataset(data, labels, transform=transform)
```

The Compose function allows combining multiple transformations. The transformation sequence includes converting raw data into tensor format and normalizing the pixel values.

For data augmentation, which helps improve the robustness and generalizability of the model, we can add transformations such as random rotations, flips, and crops. Here's an example incorporating data augmentation:

```
data_augmentation_transform = transforms.Compose([
    transforms.RandomHorizontalFlip(),
    transforms.RandomRotation(10),
    transforms.RandomResizedCrop(28),
    transforms.ToTensor(),
    transforms.Normalize((0.5,), (0.5,)),
])

% Apply the augmented transforms to the dataset
augmented_dataset = CustomDataset(data, labels, transform=
    data_augmentation_transform)
```

Integrating data loading and preprocessing steps ensures that the dataset is ready for model training and helps handle different types of data anomalies and variability, leading to a more robust model.

To load a dataset like CIFAR-10, available through torchvision.datasets, using predefined transformations, we can proceed as follows:

```
from torchvision.datasets import CIFAR10

transform = transforms.Compose([
    transforms.ToTensor(),
    transforms.Normalize((0.5, 0.5, 0.5), (0.5, 0.5, 0.5)),
])

% Download and load training dataset
train_dataset = CIFAR10(root='./data', train=True, download=True, transform=
    transform)
train_loader = DataLoader(train_dataset, batch_size=32, shuffle=True, num_workers
    =4)

% Download and load validation dataset
validation_dataset = CIFAR10(root='./data', train=False, download=True, transform
    =transform)
validation_loader = DataLoader(validation_dataset, batch_size=32, shuffle=False,
    num_workers=4)
```

The CIFAR-10 dataset is downloaded and preprocessed on-the-fly using the specified transformations. The data loaders for both training and validation sets are created similarly.

Efficient processing and augmentation of data can significantly reduce training time and improve model performance. Proper preprocessing is integral to leveraging the full potential of neural networks in training scenarios, directly impacting results and inferences derived from the model.

5.4 Training Loop Basics

The training loop is the core component of the neural network training process. It involves iteratively adjusting the model's parameters based on the loss computed from the predictions. This section outlines the basic structure of a training loop, highlighting essential components and execution flow. We assume familiarity with PyTorch's fundamental concepts such as tensors, datasets, and data loaders.

A typical training loop in PyTorch follows these steps:

- Initialize the model, optimizer, and loss function.
- Iterate over the training dataset in mini-batches.
- Perform a forward pass to compute predictions from inputs.
- Compute the loss between predictions and actual targets.
- Perform a backward pass to compute gradients.
- Update the model parameters using the optimizer.

To illustrate, consider the following PyTorch code template for a basic training loop:

```
# Initialize the model, loss function, and optimizer
model = MyModel()
criterion = nn.CrossEntropyLoss()
optimizer = torch.optim.SGD(model.parameters(), lr=0.01)

# Set the number of epochs
num_epochs = 10

# Training loop
for epoch in range(num_epochs):
    for inputs, targets in train_loader:
        # Move inputs and targets to the GPU if available
        inputs, targets = inputs.to(device), targets.to(device)

        # Zero the parameter gradients
        optimizer.zero_grad()

        # Forward pass to compute predictions
        outputs = model(inputs)

        # Compute loss
        loss = criterion(outputs, targets)

        # Backward pass to compute gradients
        loss.backward()

        # Update model parameters
```

```
        optimizer.step()

    print(f"Epoch [{epoch+1}/{num_epochs}], Loss: {loss.item():.4f}")
```

A detailed examination of each step:

- **Model Initialization:** The model, loss function, and optimizer must be initialized before entering the training loop. In the example above, 'MyModel()' represents the neural network class, nn.CrossEntropyLoss() is the loss function used for classification tasks, and torch.optim.SGD is the stochastic gradient descent optimizer. These components can be customized based on the specific use case.
- **Epoch Iteration:** The outer loop runs for a predefined number of epochs (num_epochs). Each epoch represents a complete pass through the entire training dataset.
- **Mini-Batch Iteration:** Within each epoch, the inner loop iterates over the training data in mini-batches. This is facilitated by a data loader (train_loader), which yields batches of inputs and targets.
- **Forward Pass:** For each batch, the forward pass computes the model's predictions (outputs) given the inputs. This step involves passing the inputs through the network's layers.
- **Loss Computation:** The loss is computed by comparing the model's predictions with the actual targets. The criterion function (e.g., cross-entropy loss) quantifies the prediction error.
- **Backward Pass:** The backward pass computes the gradients of the loss with respect to the model parameters. This step involves backpropagation, which is executed by calling loss.backward(). Gradients accumulated from previous iterations are zeroed out by optimizer.zero_grad() to prevent accumulation over multiple batches.
- **Parameter Update:** The optimizer updates the model parameters based on the computed gradients. The optimizer.step() method adjusts the parameters using the chosen optimization algorithm.
- **Device Management:** Ensuring that tensors are on the correct device (CPU or GPU) is crucial for efficient computation, particularly when leveraging GPU acceleration. The code snippet

demonstrates moving inputs and targets to the appropriate device using the $.\text{to}(\text{device})$ method.

A successful training loop should also include mechanisms for monitoring training progress, handling potential errors, and implementing additional features like learning rate scheduling, early stopping, and checkpointing, which are discussed in later sections.

5.5 Backpropagation and Gradient Descent

Backpropagation and gradient descent are core components of training neural networks. They enable the model to adjust its parameters to minimize the loss function.

The primary goal is to minimize the loss function $L(\theta)$, where θ represents the parameters of the neural network. Minimization of the loss function necessitates the computation of gradients, which indicate the direction and rate of change of the loss function with respect to each parameter.

Backpropagation is the algorithm employed to compute these gradients efficiently. Consider a simple neural network with an input layer, one hidden layer, and an output layer. Each layer consists of neurons connected by weights. The process of backpropagation involves the following steps:

1. **Forward Pass:**

    - Compute the input to each neuron and apply the activation function to obtain the output.

2. **Backward Pass:**

    - Compute the gradient of the loss function concerning each weight by applying the chain rule.

Assume the output of the network is $\hat{y}$, the true label is y, and the loss function L is mean squared error:

$$L = \frac{1}{2}(\hat{y} - y)^2$$

To train the network, we need to adjust the parameters to minimize L. Therefore, the gradients of L with respect to different weights and biases are computed.

For a given neuron, the inputs are weighted with weights w_i and added to a bias b. The result is then passed through an activation function σ to produce an output. Mathematically, for a neuron j,

$$a_j = \sigma\left(\sum_i w_{ij}x_i + b_j\right)$$

During backpropagation, the error δ for each neuron is calculated starting from the output layer. The error for the output layer neurons is the derivative of the loss function with respect to the input to the neuron. For an output neuron k, the error is:

$$\delta_k = (\hat{y}_k - y_k)\sigma'(z_k)$$

where z_k is the input to the neuron k before applying the activation function, and σ' is the derivative of the activation function.

For neurons in hidden layers, the error is propagated backwards using:

$$\delta_j = \left(\sum_k \delta_k w_{jk}\right)\sigma'(z_j)$$

The gradient of the loss function with respect to the weights is given by:

$$\frac{\partial L}{\partial w_{ij}} = \delta_j x_i$$

Gradient Descent is an optimization algorithm used to update the weights of the neural network to minimize the loss function. It involves updating the weights incrementally in the opposite direction of the gradient. This is expressed as:

$$w_{ij}^{new} = w_{ij} - \eta\frac{\partial L}{\partial w_{ij}}$$

where η is the learning rate, a hyperparameter that controls the size of the steps taken towards the minimum.

The gradient descent algorithm can be executed in different variants:

- **Batch Gradient Descent:** Computes gradients using the entire training dataset.
- **Stochastic Gradient Descent (SGD):** Computes gradients using a single training sample. It introduces noise, which can help in escaping local minima.
- **Mini-Batch Gradient Descent:** Computes gradients using a subset of the training data.

Consider the following example implementation using PyTorch:

```
import torch
import torch.nn as nn
import torch.optim as optim

# Define the neural network
class Net(nn.Module):
    def __init__(self):
        super(Net, self).__init__()
        self.fc1 = nn.Linear(10, 50)
        self.fc2 = nn.Linear(50, 1)
        self.relu = nn.ReLU()

    def forward(self, x):
        x = self.relu(self.fc1(x))
        x = self.fc2(x)
        return x

# Instantiate the network, loss function, and optimizer
net = Net()
criterion = nn.MSELoss()
optimizer = optim.SGD(net.parameters(), lr=0.01)

# Training loop
for epoch in range(100):
    inputs = torch.randn(64, 10)
    targets = torch.randn(64, 1)

    optimizer.zero_grad()
    outputs = net(inputs)
    loss = criterion(outputs, targets)
    loss.backward()
    optimizer.step()
```

In this example, a simple neural network with one hidden layer is defined. The loss function used is mean squared error, and the optimizer is stochastic gradient descent (SGD). The training loop involves generating random inputs and targets, performing a forward pass, computing the loss, performing a backward pass to compute gradients, and updating the weights using the optimizer.

Monitoring the training process involves plotting the loss over time to ensure that it is decreasing. The next sections will delve into strategies for efficient monitoring and optimization techniques to address challenges such as overfitting and learning rate tuning.

5.6 Monitoring Training Progress

Effective monitoring of training progress is crucial for diagnosing and understanding the state and evolution of a neural network during its training phase. By systematically tracking metrics, one can identify potential issues and make informed decisions to fine-tune the network for optimal performance. This involves logging key statistics such as loss values, accuracy, and other custom metrics over epochs. Visualization tools like TensorBoard or Matplotlib can further aid in interpreting these statistics.

To begin with, the primary metric to monitor is the loss value, which indicates how well the model is performing with respect to its objective function. Lower loss values generally suggest better performance. In PyTorch, logging the loss at regular intervals can be achieved using the following approach:

```
import torch
import torch.nn as nn
import torch.optim as optim

# Sample model
class SimpleNet(nn.Module):
    def __init__(self):
        super(SimpleNet, self).__init__()
        self.fc1 = nn.Linear(784, 128)
        self.fc2 = nn.Linear(128, 10)

    def forward(self, x):
        x = torch.relu(self.fc1(x))
        x = self.fc2(x)
        return x

# Training function
def train(model, dataloader, criterion, optimizer, num_epochs):
    for epoch in range(num_epochs):
        total_loss = 0.0
        for data in dataloader:
            inputs, labels = data
            optimizer.zero_grad()
            outputs = model(inputs)
            loss = criterion(outputs, labels)
            loss.backward()
            optimizer.step()
            total_loss += loss.item()
        print(f'Epoch [{epoch+1}/{num_epochs}], Loss: {total_loss/len(dataloader)}')

# Sample usage
model = SimpleNet()
```

```
criterion = nn.CrossEntropyLoss()
optimizer = optim.SGD(model.parameters(), lr=0.01)
dataloader = # Assume this is defined elsewhere
train(model, dataloader, criterion, optimizer, num_epochs=10)
```

In the example above, the loss is calculated for each batch and accumulated over an epoch. At the end of each epoch, the average loss is printed out. This provides a coarse overview of how the model's performance is evolving.

Switching attention to accuracy, a common metric especially for classification tasks, it represents the fraction of correctly predicted instances out of the total instances. Tracking accuracy alongside loss can provide deeper insights; for instance, a simultaneously increasing accuracy and decreasing loss indicates solid learning progress. To log accuracy, the following additions can be made:

```
def calculate_accuracy(outputs, labels):
    _, predicted = torch.max(outputs.data, 1)
    total = labels.size(0)
    correct = (predicted == labels).sum().item()
    return correct / total

def train(model, dataloader, criterion, optimizer, num_epochs):
    for epoch in range(num_epochs):
        total_loss = 0.0
        total_accuracy = 0.0
        for data in dataloader:
            inputs, labels = data
            optimizer.zero_grad()
            outputs = model(inputs)
            loss = criterion(outputs, labels)
            loss.backward()
            optimizer.step()
            total_loss += loss.item()
            total_accuracy += calculate_accuracy(outputs, labels)
        print(f'Epoch [{epoch+1}/{num_epochs}], Loss: {total_loss/len(dataloader)},
            Accuracy: {total_accuracy/len(dataloader)}')
```

Keeping these metrics logged at finer intervals, such as after every batch, can be useful for more granular monitoring but could also introduce noise due to high variability in batch-level results. A balance must be struck based on the specific requirements of the task.

For effective and interactive visualization, TensorBoard, originally developed for TensorFlow, can be leveraged due to its PyTorch integration. It allows for real-time plotting of loss, accuracy, and other custom metrics. Here's an example of how to integrate TensorBoard with PyTorch:

```
from torch.utils.tensorboard import SummaryWriter

writer = SummaryWriter()
```

```
def train(model, dataloader, criterion, optimizer, num_epochs):
    for epoch in range(num_epochs):
        total_loss = 0.0
        total_accuracy = 0.0
        for batch_idx, data in enumerate(dataloader):
            inputs, labels = data
            optimizer.zero_grad()
            outputs = model(inputs)
            loss = criterion(outputs, labels)
            loss.backward()
            optimizer.step()
            total_loss += loss.item()
            total_accuracy += calculate_accuracy(outputs, labels)

            if batch_idx % 10 == 0: # Log every 10 batches
                writer.add_scalar('training loss', total_loss / (batch_idx + 1), epoch *
                    len(dataloader) + batch_idx)
                writer.add_scalar('training accuracy', total_accuracy / (batch_idx + 1),
                    epoch * len(dataloader) + batch_idx)

        print(f'Epoch [{epoch+1}/{num_epochs}], Loss: {total_loss/len(dataloader)},
            Accuracy: {total_accuracy/len(dataloader)}')

writer.close()
```

In the code snippet, the SummaryWriter class from torch.utils.tensorboard is employed to log metrics that can be visualized using TensorBoard. Running TensorBoard typically involves executing the following command in the terminal:

```
tensorboard --logdir=runs
```

By navigating to the specified URL (usually http://localhost:6006/), you can access an interactive dashboard to visualize and compare the logged metrics over different runs, making it substantially easier to understand training dynamics and adjust hyperparameters accordingly.

Another important aspect of monitoring is the evaluation on the validation set. While the training loss and accuracy provide information on how well the model is learning the training data, validation metrics indicate how well the model generalizes to unseen data. Incorporating validation metrics can be done as follows:

```
def evaluate(model, dataloader, criterion):
    total_loss = 0.0
    total_accuracy = 0.0
    with torch.no_grad():
        for data in dataloader:
            inputs, labels = data
            outputs = model(inputs)
            loss = criterion(outputs, labels)
            total_loss += loss.item()
            total_accuracy += calculate_accuracy(outputs, labels)
    return total_loss / len(dataloader), total_accuracy / len(dataloader)
```

```
def train(model, train_loader, val_loader, criterion, optimizer, num_epochs):
    for epoch in range(num_epochs):
        model.train()
        total_loss = 0.0
        total_accuracy = 0.0
        for batch_idx, data in enumerate(train_loader):
            inputs, labels = data
            optimizer.zero_grad()
            outputs = model(inputs)
            loss = criterion(outputs, labels)
            loss.backward()
            optimizer.step()
            total_loss += loss.item()
            total_accuracy += calculate_accuracy(outputs, labels)
        print(f'Epoch [{epoch+1}/{num_epochs}], Loss: {total_loss/len(train_loader)},
              Accuracy: {total_accuracy/len(train_loader)}')

        model.eval()
        val_loss, val_accuracy = evaluate(model, val_loader, criterion)
        print(f'Validation Loss: {val_loss}, Validation Accuracy: {val_accuracy}')

# Assuming val_loader is defined as a DataLoader for the validation dataset
```

Logging validation metrics ensures that the model is not overfitting to the training data. A model that performs well on the training set but poorly on the validation set is likely overfitting.

By meticulously logging and visualizing these metrics, one can closely monitor the training progress, diagnose issues, and drive the training process towards producing a robust and well-generalized model.

5.7 Overfitting and Underfitting

Overfitting and underfitting are critical concepts in the context of machine learning, influencing the effectiveness and generalizability of neural network models. Understanding these phenomena helps in diagnosing and adjusting model performance to achieve optimal results.

Overfitting refers to a model's excessive adaptation to the training data, capturing noise and particulars rather than general patterns. A model that overfits demonstrates high accuracy on the training dataset but performs poorly on unseen validation or testing data, lacking the ability to generalize.

Underfitting occurs when the model is too simplistic to capture the underlying trends in the data, resulting in poor performance both on the training set and on new data. In such cases, the model is unable to learn the relationship between the inputs and outputs adequately.

Identifying these issues requires monitoring the performance metrics across training, validation, and testing datasets. One effective strategy is to plot the loss and accuracy curves for these datasets over the training epochs. A model demonstrating overfitting typically shows a decreasing training loss while the validation loss starts to increase after a certain point. Conversely, a model that is underfitting will have high loss values for both training and validation datasets.

```
import matplotlib.pyplot as plt

def plot_loss_curves(training_loss, validation_loss):
    epochs = range(1, len(training_loss) + 1)
    plt.figure(figsize=(10, 6))
    plt.plot(epochs, training_loss, 'bo-', label='Training Loss')
    plt.plot(epochs, validation_loss, 'ro-', label='Validation Loss')
    plt.title('Loss Curves')
    plt.xlabel('Epochs')
    plt.ylabel('Loss')
    plt.legend()
    plt.show()

# Sample usage with dummy data
training_loss = [0.6, 0.4, 0.3, 0.2, 0.1]
validation_loss = [0.7, 0.5, 0.45, 0.48, 0.5]
plot_loss_curves(training_loss, validation_loss)
```

The primary techniques for addressing overfitting include:

- **Regularization:** Regularization techniques add a penalty to the loss function for large weights, thereby constraining the model complexity. The commonly used types are L1 (Lasso) and L2 (Ridge) regularization.

```
import torch.nn as nn

model = nn.Sequential(
    nn.Linear(input_size, hidden_size),
    nn.ReLU(),
    nn.Linear(hidden_size, output_size)
)

loss_function = nn.CrossEntropyLoss()
optimizer = torch.optim.SGD(model.parameters(), lr=0.01, weight_decay
    =0.001)
```

  In the above example, the weight_decay parameter in the optimizer enables L2 regularization, penalizing large weights.

- **Dropout:** Dropout is a technique where randomly selected neurons are ignored during training, which helps prevent the model from relying too heavily on particular neurons. This leads to the development of more general and robust features.

```
model = nn.Sequential(
```

```
    nn.Linear(input_size, hidden_size),
    nn.ReLU(),
    nn.Dropout(p=0.5), # Dropout with a probability of 50%
    nn.Linear(hidden_size, output_size)
)
```

- **Data Augmentation:** In the context of image data, data augmentation involves creating variations of the training images through transformations like rotation, scaling, cropping, and flipping. This increases the diversity of the training set, making the model more resilient to variations in the data.

```
import torchvision.transforms as transforms

transform = transforms.Compose([
    transforms.RandomHorizontalFlip(),
    transforms.RandomRotation(10),
    transforms.ToTensor()
])

training_data = torchvision.datasets.ImageFolder(root='path/to/data',
      transform=transform)
```

- **Early Stopping:** Early stopping involves monitoring the model's performance on a validation set during training and halting the training process once performance stops improving for a predefined number of epochs.

```
class EarlyStopping:
    def __init__(self, patience=5, min_delta=0):
        self.patience = patience
        self.min_delta = min_delta
        self.counter = 0
        self.best_loss = None
        self.early_stop = False

    def __call__(self, validation_loss):
        if self.best_loss is None:
            self.best_loss = validation_loss
        elif validation_loss < self.best_loss - self.min_delta:
            self.best_loss = validation_loss
            self.counter = 0
        else:
            self.counter += 1
            if self.counter >= self.patience:
                self.early_stop = True
                print("Early stopping triggered")

# Usage within training loop
early_stopping = EarlyStopping(patience=5, min_delta=0.01)
for epoch in range(max_epochs):
    train_model()
    validation_loss = evaluate_model()
    early_stopping(validation_loss)
    if early_stopping.early_stop:
        break
```

To resolve underfitting, several strategies can be adopted:

- **Model Complexity:** Increasing the model complexity by adding more layers or neurons can enable the model to capture more intricate patterns in the data. Care must be taken to balance this with the risk of overfitting.

```
model = nn.Sequential(
    nn.Linear(input_size, hidden_size),
    nn.ReLU(),
    nn.Linear(hidden_size, hidden_size),
    nn.ReLU(),
    nn.Linear(hidden_size, output_size)
)
```

- **Longer Training Duration:** Extending the training duration can allow the model to better capture underlying patterns. However, this must be combined with monitoring to avoid overfitting.

```
for epoch in range(num_epochs):
    train_model(epoch)
    if epoch % 10 == 0:
        print(f"Epoch {epoch}/{num_epochs}")
```

- **Hyperparameter Tuning:** Adjusting hyperparameters like learning rate, batch size, and momentum can significantly impact model performance. Techniques such as grid search or random search can be utilized for this purpose.

```
learning_rates = [0.001, 0.01, 0.1]
batch_sizes = [32, 64, 128]

best_accuracy = 0
best_params = {}

for lr in learning_rates:
    for batch_size in batch_sizes:
        optimizer = torch.optim.SGD(model.parameters(), lr=lr)
        data_loader = DataLoader(dataset, batch_size=batch_size, shuffle=
            True)
        accuracy = evaluate_model(data_loader)
        if accuracy > best_accuracy:
            best_accuracy = accuracy
            best_params = {'learning_rate': lr, 'batch_size': batch_size}

print(f"Best Params: {best_params}, Accuracy: {best_accuracy}")
```

Practical machine learning often involves iteratively diagnosing and mitigating overfitting or underfitting to enhance the model's generalization capability.

5.8 Validation and Test Sets

Validation and test sets play a crucial role in the development and evaluation of neural networks. These datasets are employed to assess the generalization capability of the trained models, ensuring that the model performs well not only on the training data but also on unseen data. Here, we will explore the distinctions between validation and test sets, their purposes, and methodologies for utilizing them effectively.

Validation Set:

The validation set is an integral tool for hyperparameter tuning and model selection. It is a subset of the dataset that is held out from training and used to provide an unbiased evaluation of a model fit on the training dataset. Primarily, the validation set helps in:

- **Hyperparameter Tuning**: Hyperparameters include learning rates, number of layers, layer sizes, and more. The validation set helps in selecting the best set of hyperparameters that yield optimal model performance.
- **Model Selection**: Among various training iterations or model architectures, the validation set assists in choosing the one that generalizes best.
- **Early Stopping**: Monitoring the validation performance to determine when to halt the training process to prevent overfitting.

A common practice involves partitioning the available training data into training and validation subsets. For instance, you might use 80% of the data for training and 20% for validation. Below is an example using PyTorch for creating a validation dataset:

```
from torch.utils.data import random_split

# Suppose dataset is already loaded as 'full_dataset'
train_size = int(0.8 * len(full_dataset))
val_size = len(full_dataset) - train_size
train_dataset, val_dataset = random_split(full_dataset, [train_size, val_size])
```

Test Set:

The test set is used to evaluate the final model performance. Unlike the validation set, the test set should ideally remain untouched until the very end of model training. The test set is critical for assessing how well the model will perform in real-world scenarios on entirely new data.

Evaluating on the test set provides a final, unbiased measure of model performance after the model and hyperparameters have been tuned using the training and validation sets. Here is an illustration of splitting the data to create a test set while training and validating your model:

```
from sklearn.model_selection import train_test_split

# X and y are features and labels of the full dataset
X_train, X_temp, y_train, y_temp = train_test_split(X, y, test_size=0.3,
    random_state=42)
X_val, X_test, y_val, y_test = train_test_split(X_temp, y_temp, test_size=0.5,
    random_state=42)

# Create Dataset objects (assuming a custom Dataset class)
train_dataset = CustomDataset(X_train, y_train)
val_dataset = CustomDataset(X_val, y_val)
test_dataset = CustomDataset(X_test, y_test)
```

Implementation Approach:

In practical applications, pooling a small portion of the training data for validation and another for testing is effective in enhancing model robustness. Here's a structured approach:

- **Data Split**: Split your dataset into a training set, a validation set, and a test set. Common splits are 80/10/10 or 70/15/15 for training/validation/test respectively.
- **Training Phase**: Use the training set to train the model.
- **Validation Phase**: During training, frequently validate the model on the validation set to tune hyperparameters and detect overfitting.
- **Testing Phase**: After training, evaluate the finalized model on the test set to obtain an unbiased performance metric.

The code example below demonstrates this sequence with PyTorch's DataLoader for efficient data handling:

```
from torch.utils.data import DataLoader

# Define DataLoader parameters
batch_size = 64
num_workers = 4

# Create DataLoaders
```

```
train_loader = DataLoader(train_dataset, batch_size=batch_size, shuffle=True,
      num_workers=num_workers)
val_loader = DataLoader(val_dataset, batch_size=batch_size, shuffle=False,
      num_workers=num_workers)
test_loader = DataLoader(test_dataset, batch_size=batch_size, shuffle=False,
      num_workers=num_workers)
```

Evaluating Performance Metrics:

When evaluating the model on the validation and test sets, several performance metrics can provide insights into the model's behavior, including accuracy, precision, recall, F1-score, and loss values. Consider the following PyTorch example to evaluate accuracy:

```
def evaluate_model(loader, model, criterion):
    model.eval()
    correct = 0
    total = 0
    running_loss = 0.0

    with torch.no_grad():
        for data in loader:
            inputs, labels = data
            outputs = model(inputs)
            loss = criterion(outputs, labels)
            running_loss += loss.item() * inputs.size(0)
            _, predicted = torch.max(outputs, 1)
            total += labels.size(0)
            correct += (predicted == labels).sum().item()

    accuracy = 100 * correct / total
    avg_loss = running_loss / total

    return avg_loss, accuracy

# Example calls
val_loss, val_accuracy = evaluate_model(val_loader, model, criterion)
test_loss, test_accuracy = evaluate_model(test_loader, model, criterion)
```

Best Practices:

Consider maintaining the integrity of your validation and test sets throughout the model development cycle. Refrain from using test data for validation during training iterations. To ensure unbiased results, the following best practices are recommended:

- **Consistency**: Maintain consistent data preprocessing steps across training, validation, and test sets.
- **Random Shuffling**: Use random shuffling during splitting to ensure representative subsets.

- **Independent Test Set**: Guarantee the test set remains representative of the problem domain and reflective of real-world scenarios.
- **Multiple Validation Runs**: Optionally, employ cross-validation techniques by partitioning different validation sets multiple times to average the performance over multiple folds.

Adopting these strategies will enhance the reliability and efficacy of the validation and test processes in neural network training.

5.9 Saving and Loading Models

The ability to save and load models is essential for practical machine learning workflows. This functionality allows for the reuse of pre-trained models, facilitates the sharing of models across different environments, and aids in the continuation of training from a previously saved state.

In PyTorch, the process of saving and loading models relies on the functionalities provided by the torch.save and torch.load functions in conjunction with the state_dict of a model. The state_dict is a Python dictionary object that maps each layer to its corresponding tensor parameters.

Saving a Model

To save a model, the state_dict should be serialized using torch.save. Here, it is important to understand that only the state_dict, and not the entire model object, is saved. This ensures greater flexibility and compatibility, allowing for the structural definition of the model to be available separately.

The following code snippet demonstrates how to save a model's state_dict:

```
import torch
import torch.nn as nn

# Define a simple neural network
class SimpleNN(nn.Module):
    def __init__(self):
        super(SimpleNN, self).__init__()
        self.fc = nn.Linear(10, 1)

    def forward(self, x):
        return self.fc(x)

# Initialize the model and print initial state_dict
```

```
model = SimpleNN()
print("Initial state_dict: ")
print(model.state_dict())

# Save the model's state_dict
torch.save(model.state_dict(), 'model_state.pth')
```

The function torch.save expects two arguments: the object to be saved (in this case, model.state_dict()) and the filename typically with a .pth or .pt extension.

Loading a Model

Loading a model involves initializing a new instance of the model's class and then loading the saved state_dict into this instance. This ensures that the architecture of the model is correctly established prior to loading the state dictionary.

Here is an example of how to load a saved model:

```
import torch

# Create a new instance of the model
loaded_model = SimpleNN()

# Load the state_dict from the saved file
loaded_model.load_state_dict(torch.load('model_state.pth'))

# Validate that the state_dict has been loaded correctly
print("Loaded state_dict: ")
print(loaded_model.state_dict())
```

In this example, torch.load reads the saved state dictionary from disk, and then the load_state_dict method is used to load these parameters into the model instance. This separation of model definition and state allows for improved flexibility, such as initializing a model on a different device or from a different training run.

Saving and Loading Complete Models

Although saving and loading the state_dict is the recommended practice, there are situations where saving the entire model object might be necessary. This practice can be implemented using the torch.save function directly on the model itself, and later, the torch.load function can be employed to resume from the saved state.

```
import torch

# Save the entire model object
torch.save(model, 'model_complete.pth')

# Load the entire model object
loaded_complete_model = torch.load('model_complete.pth')
```

```
# Print to verify the loaded model state
print("Complete model loaded: ")
print(loaded_complete_model)
```

While this method provides a simple means of saving and loading models with fewer lines of code, it is less flexible than saving the state_dict and might result in issues related to the model's source code if any changes are made.

Checkpointing During Training

For long-running training tasks, checkpointing the model's state at different intervals provides a means to resume training without starting from scratch. Checkpointing typically includes saving the state_dict, optimizer state, and other training information such as epoch number. This ensures all critical components of the training process are stored and can be restored.

An example of implementing checkpointing is shown below:

```
import torch.optim as optim

# Define an optimizer for the model
optimizer = optim.SGD(model.parameters(), lr=0.01)

# Function to save a checkpoint
def save_checkpoint(model, optimizer, epoch, filename='checkpoint.pth'):
    checkpoint = {
        'epoch': epoch,
        'model_state_dict': model.state_dict(),
        'optimizer_state_dict': optimizer.state_dict(),
    }
    torch.save(checkpoint, filename)

# Saving a checkpoint
save_checkpoint(model, optimizer, epoch=10)

# Loading from the checkpoint
def load_checkpoint(model, optimizer, filename='checkpoint.pth'):
    checkpoint = torch.load(filename)
    model.load_state_dict(checkpoint['model_state_dict'])
    optimizer.load_state_dict(checkpoint['optimizer_state_dict'])
    start_epoch = checkpoint['epoch']
    return model, optimizer, start_epoch

# Loading a checkpoint
model, optimizer, start_epoch = load_checkpoint(model, optimizer)
print(f"Resumed training from epoch {start_epoch}")
```

By utilizing checkpointing, training can be continued from a previously saved state, improving robustness to interruptions and providing an essential tool in the training of complex models that require extensive computational resources.

5.10 Using Learning Rate Schedulers

In the process of training neural networks, the choice of learning rate plays a crucial role in determining the efficiency and effectiveness of the optimization process. A learning rate that is too high can cause the training process to overshoot the minimum point in the loss function, while a learning rate that is too low can lead to excessively slow convergence. Learning Rate Schedulers (LRS) are employed to adjust the learning rate dynamically during training, enhancing the training process by adapting to the changing landscape of the loss function. This section delves into the various types of learning rate schedulers, their implementation in PyTorch, and best practices for their utilization.

Learning rate schedulers in PyTorch are available through the torch.optim.lr_scheduler module. This module provides several strategies for adjusting the learning rate based on the number of epochs or the performance of the model on the validation dataset. Commonly used learning rate schedulers include StepLR, MultiStepLR, ExponentialLR, CosineAnnealingLR, ReduceLROnPlateau, and others. Each of these schedulers has its specific use cases and operational mechanics.

The **StepLR** scheduler reduces the learning rate by a factor of γ every step_size epochs. This scheduler is useful when the training process exhibits periodic improvements, and a decremented learning rate aids in fine-tuning the model.

```
import torch.optim as optim

# Assuming optimizer is already defined
scheduler = optim.lr_scheduler.StepLR(optimizer, step_size=30, gamma=0.1)

for epoch in range(epochs):
    train(...)
    validate(...)
    scheduler.step() # Update the learning rate
```

The **MultiStepLR** scheduler functions similarly to StepLR but allows for specifying multiple step sizes. This offers more granular control over the learning rate adjustments.

```
scheduler = optim.lr_scheduler.MultiStepLR(optimizer, milestones=[30, 80], gamma
    =0.1)

for epoch in range(epochs):
    train(...)
    validate(...)
    scheduler.step()
```

The **ExponentialLR** scheduler decreases the learning rate exponentially after each epoch, controlled by the factor γ.

```
scheduler = optim.lr_scheduler.ExponentialLR(optimizer, gamma=0.95)

for epoch in range(epochs):
    train(...)
    validate(...)
    scheduler.step()
```

The **CosineAnnealingLR** scheduler adjusts the learning rate following a cosine curve between a maximum and a minimum value over a specified number of epochs. This is particularly effective in scenarios where the model benefits from large initial learning rates that gradually decrease towards the end of training.

```
scheduler = optim.lr_scheduler.CosineAnnealingLR(optimizer, T_max=50)

for epoch in range(epochs):
    train(...)
    validate(...)
    scheduler.step()
```

The **ReduceLROnPlateau** scheduler reduces the learning rate when a metric such as validation loss has stopped improving. This scheduler is valuable in cases where the performance plateaus and thus benefits from a reduced learning rate to potentially overcome local minima.

```
scheduler = optim.lr_scheduler.ReduceLROnPlateau(optimizer, mode='min', factor
        =0.1, patience=10)

for epoch in range(epochs):
    train(...)
    val_loss = validate(...)
    scheduler.step(val_loss) # Update based on validation loss
```

It is important to note that the choice of an appropriate learning rate scheduler depends on the specific characteristics of the dataset and the model architecture. While StepLR and MultiStepLR provide straightforward step changes, ExponentialLR and CosineAnnealingLR offer more gradual and continuous learning rate adjustments. ReduceLROnPlateau, on the other hand, is particularly useful for fine-tuning and avoiding plateaus in training.

Practical tips for using learning rate schedulers include starting with an initial learning rate that is experimentally determined (often through grid search or a learning rate range test), using a scheduler that complements the characteristic of learning progression observed during initial epochs, and closely monitoring key metrics like training loss, validation loss, and training accuracy to adjust scheduler parameters dynamically.

In tandem with learning rate schedulers, it is also beneficial to implement learning rate warm-up techniques where the learning rate starts at a lower value and gradually increases to the initial learning rate over a few epochs. This technique can stabilize early training phases and prevent divergence.

By leveraging learning rate schedulers judiciously, the model training process becomes more adaptive and robust. Proper utilization of these techniques can significantly enhance training efficiency, leading to better convergence rates and improved model performance.

Chapter 6

Improving Model Performance

This chapter explores strategies for enhancing model performance. Topics include hyperparameter tuning, and regularization techniques such as batch normalization and dropout. The chapter also discusses learning rate scheduling, data augmentation, and ensembling models to improve accuracy. Additionally, it covers monitoring performance metrics and addressing challenges like handling imbalanced data to ensure robust model performance.

6.1 Introduction to Model Performance

Evaluating and enhancing the performance of machine learning models is a critical process for the successful application of machine learning algorithms. The performance of a model encompasses various aspects, including its accuracy, precision, recall, and computational efficiency. Understanding these metrics and the methods to improve them is fundamental for developing robust and efficient models. This section will delve into these concepts, establishing the foundation for advanced techniques that will be explored in subsequent sections of this chapter.

The accuracy of a model is typically one of the first metrics considered. It is defined as the ratio of correctly predicted instances to the total instances in the dataset. However, accuracy alone can be misleading, especially in the presence of imbalanced datasets where one class may be more prevalent than the others. Therefore, additional metrics such as precision, recall, and F1-score are introduced to provide a more comprehensive evaluation.

Metric	Definition
Accuracy	$\frac{TP+TN}{TP+TN+FP+FN}$
Precision	$\frac{TP}{TP+FP}$
Recall	$\frac{TP}{TP+FN}$
F1-Score	$2 \times \frac{\text{Precision} \times \text{Recall}}{\text{Precision} + \text{Recall}}$

Table 6.1: Metrics for Model Performance Evaluation

Where:

- **TP** (True Positives): Correctly predicted positive instances.
- **TN** (True Negatives): Correctly predicted negative instances.
- **FP** (False Positives): Incorrectly predicted positive instances.
- **FN** (False Negatives): Incorrectly predicted negative instances.

Precision quantifies the number of true positive predictions relative to the total positive predictions made by the classifier. High precision indicates that among all the positive predictions, a large portion is correct. Recall measures the ability of the classifier to identify all the positive samples within the dataset. A high recall indicates that the classifier is capable of capturing most of the positive instances. The F1-score, which is the harmonic mean of precision and recall, provides a single metric to evaluate performance, especially useful when the class distribution is imbalanced.

Assessing model performance also involves considering the computational complexity and scalability. This is particularly important when deploying models on large datasets or in production environments where computational resources are limited. Time and space complexity, training time, and inference time are key aspects to explore.

To illustrate one approach to assessing a model's accuracy, here is a simple Python code snippet using the PyTorch framework to evaluate a model:

```
import torch
import torch.nn as nn
import torch.optim as optim
```

```
from sklearn.metrics import accuracy_score

# Assuming a simple model, criterion, and dataset
model = SimpleModel()
criterion = nn.CrossEntropyLoss()
optimizer = optim.SGD(model.parameters(), lr=0.01)

# Dummy dataset and labels
data = torch.randn(100, 10)
labels = torch.randint(0, 2, (100,))

# Model evaluation
def evaluate_model(model, data, labels):
    model.eval()
    with torch.no_grad():
        outputs = model(data)
        _, predicted = torch.max(outputs, 1)
        accuracy = accuracy_score(labels.numpy(), predicted.numpy())
    return accuracy

# Training loop
for epoch in range(10):
    model.train()
    optimizer.zero_grad()
    outputs = model(data)
    loss = criterion(outputs, labels)
    loss.backward()
    optimizer.step()

    # Evaluate model
    if epoch % 2 == 0:
        acc = evaluate_model(model, data, labels)
        print(f'Epoch {epoch}, Accuracy: {acc:.2f}')
```

```
Epoch 0, Accuracy: 0.56
Epoch 2, Accuracy: 0.64
Epoch 4, Accuracy: 0.68
Epoch 6, Accuracy: 0.72
Epoch 8, Accuracy: 0.75
```

In this code snippet, a basic feedforward neural network is trained on synthetic data. The evaluate_model function computes the accuracy of the model by comparing its predictions with the true labels. The printed accuracy at each second epoch provides insight into the model's learning progression.

While accuracy is essential, it is equally crucial to monitor the loss during training. The loss function, or the cost function, measures how well the model's predictions align with the actual labels. For instance, using nn.CrossEntropyLoss for classification tasks provides a way to penalize incorrect predictions. Lower loss values generally indicate better model performance, guiding the optimization process.

As machine learning models are optimized, one must also guard against overfitting and underfitting. Overfitting occurs when the model performs exceptionally well on the training data but fails to generalize to unseen data. Conversely, underfitting happens when the model is too simple to capture the underlying structure of the data, resulting in poor performance on both training and test sets. The trade-off between bias and variance is fundamental in addressing these concerns.

A practical implementation for monitoring training and validation loss to detect overfitting might look as follows:

```
train_losses = []
val_losses = []

for epoch in range(10):
    model.train()
    optimizer.zero_grad()
    outputs = model(data)
    loss = criterion(outputs, labels)
    loss.backward()
    optimizer.step()
    train_losses.append(loss.item())

    model.eval()
    with torch.no_grad():
        val_outputs = model(val_data)
        val_loss = criterion(val_outputs, val_labels)
        val_losses.append(val_loss.item())

    print(f'Epoch {epoch}, Training Loss: {loss.item():.4f}, Validation Loss: {val_loss.
        item():.4f}')
```

```
Epoch 0, Training Loss: 0.6934, Validation Loss: 0.6928
Epoch 1, Training Loss: 0.6915, Validation Loss: 0.6910
Epoch 2, Training Loss: 0.6896, Validation Loss: 0.6891
Epoch 3, Training Loss: 0.6877, Validation Loss: 0.6873
Epoch 4, Training Loss: 0.6858, Validation Loss: 0.6854
Epoch 5, Training Loss: 0.6839, Validation Loss: 0.6835
Epoch 6, Training Loss: 0.6820, Validation Loss: 0.6817
Epoch 7, Training Loss: 0.6801, Validation Loss: 0.6798
Epoch 8, Training Loss: 0.6782, Validation Loss: 0.6779
Epoch 9, Training Loss: 0.6763, Validation Loss: 0.6761
```

By tracking both training and validation losses, one can detect overfitting if the validation loss begins to increase while training loss continues to decrease. Strategies to mitigate overfitting and underfitting will be discussed in detail in subsequent sections, introducing techniques such as regularization, data augmentation, and ensembling.

Understanding and improving model performance requires a methodical approach to evaluating different aspects of the model. By leveraging appropriate metrics and monitoring tools, one can iteratively refine their models to achieve optimal performance. The following sections will expand on these foundational concepts, introducing advanced techniques and strategies for improving model performance in practice.

6.2 Hyperparameter Tuning

Hyperparameter tuning is crucial for optimizing machine learning models. Hyperparameters are parameters set before the learning process begins, influencing the model's performance and training efficiency. Unlike model parameters that are learned during training, hyperparameters must be set by the modeler and can significantly affect the outcomes.

Grid Search and **Random Search** are two primary methods for hyperparameter tuning. Grid Search exhaustively searches through a manually specified subset of the hyperparameter space. While thorough, this approach can be computationally expensive and time-consuming.

```
from sklearn.model_selection import GridSearchCV

# Assume 'model' is a pre-defined machine learning model
param_grid = {
    'learning_rate': [0.01, 0.1, 1],
    'num_layers': [2, 3, 4]
}

grid_search = GridSearchCV(estimator=model, param_grid=param_grid, cv=3)
grid_search.fit(X_train, y_train)
```

The above code demonstrates Grid Search with a learning rate and number of layers as hyperparameters. The GridSearchCV class is used, where estimator is the model, and param_grid is the dictionary containing hyperparameters to test. cv=3 specifies 3-fold cross-validation. One major drawback is the exponential increase in computations with the number of hyperparameters and values.

Random Search provides an alternative by sampling a fixed number of hyperparameter settings from specified distributions. This approach reduces computational cost and often yields results comparable to Grid Search.

```
from sklearn.model_selection import RandomizedSearchCV
from scipy.stats import uniform

param_dist = {
    'learning_rate': uniform(0.01, 0.1),
    'num_layers': [2, 3, 4]
}

random_search = RandomizedSearchCV(estimator=model, param_distributions=
        param_dist, n_iter=100, cv=3)
random_search.fit(X_train, y_train)
```

Here, RandomizedSearchCV samples 100 combinations of hyperparameters governed by specified distributions and values. The use of the uniform distribution allows continuous values within a specified range.

Advanced methods such as **Bayesian Optimization**, **Genetic Algorithms**, and **Hyperband** have gained traction due to their efficiency in exploring the hyperparameter space. Bayesian Optimization, for example, uses past evaluation results to model the performance function and choose the most promising hyperparameters thereafter.

```
from skopt import BayesSearchCV

opt = BayesSearchCV(estimator=model,
                    search_spaces=param_grid,
                    n_iter=32,
                    cv=3)
opt.fit(X_train, y_train)
```

The BayesSearchCV class from the scikit-optimize library facilitates Bayesian Optimization. This algorithm iteratively improves the model estimation based on previous evaluations, effectively balancing exploration and exploitation of the hyperparameter space.

Hyperparameter tuning is a methodical process. Early stopping is a simpler strategy, preventing overfitting by terminating training when performance on a validation set ceases to improve. This technique has been naturally integrated into many modern deep learning frameworks.

```
from keras.callbacks import EarlyStopping

early_stopping = EarlyStopping(monitor='val_loss', patience=10)

model.fit(X_train, y_train, validation_split=0.2, callbacks=[early_stopping])
```

In the code, EarlyStopping is utilized where training stops once val_loss does not improve for 10 consecutive epochs. Here, the validation_split is set to 20%. Early stopping prevents unnecessary training cycles, conserves computational resources, and helps avert overfitting.

Choosing the right approach depends on model complexity, resource constraints, and the specific problem. Whether through exhaustive Grid Search, efficient Random Search, or intelligent Bayesian Optimization, the goal remains consistent: to find the optimal set of hyperparameters that minimize the loss function or maximize performance metrics. Accurate hyperparameter tuning is critical to transforming a decent machine learning model into an exceptional one.

6.3 Regularization Techniques

Regularization techniques are essential tools in machine learning for controlling overfitting and ensuring that models generalize well to unseen data. Overfitting occurs when a model learns not only the underlying patterns in the training data but also the noise, leading to poor performance on new, unseen data. Regularization constrains or penalizes the complexity of the model, encouraging simpler models that are more likely to generalize better.

One of the most common regularization methods is **L2 regularization**, also known as Ridge Regression when applied to linear models. L2 regularization adds a penalty equal to the square of the magnitude of coefficients to the loss function. This can be expressed mathematically as:

$$L(\theta) = L_0(\theta) + \lambda||\theta||_2^2$$

where $L(\theta)$ is the regularized loss function, $L_0(\theta)$ is the original loss function (e.g., mean squared error for regression tasks), λ is the regularization parameter, and $||\theta||_2^2$ is the L2 norm of the parameter vector θ. The regularization parameter λ controls the strength of the penalty. Higher values of λ lead to greater regularization effect.

Another popular regularization technique is **L1 regularization**, or Lasso Regression. Unlike L2 regularization, which penalizes the sum of the squares of the coefficients, L1 regularization adds a penalty equal to the absolute value of the magnitude of coefficients:

$$L(\theta) = L_0(\theta) + \lambda||\theta||_1$$

where $||\theta||_1$ is the L1 norm of θ. L1 regularization can lead to sparse models where some coefficients become exactly zero, effectively performing feature selection. This characteristic is particularly useful when dealing with high-dimensional data where feature selection plays a crucial role.

Elastic Net combines both L1 and L2 regularization to take advantage of the benefits of both techniques. The regularized loss function for Elastic Net is defined as:

$$L(\theta) = L_0(\theta) + \lambda_1||\theta||_1 + \lambda_2||\theta||_2^2$$

where λ_1 and λ_2 are the regularization parameters for L1 and L2 regularization, respectively. Elastic Net is particularly useful when there are multiple highly correlated features, as it encourages group selection.

In the context of deep learning and neural networks, regularization techniques extend beyond L1 and L2 regularization. One commonly used technique is **Dropout**. Dropout involves randomly setting a subset of the activations to zero during training. This prevents the units from co-adapting too much and forces the network to learn more robust features. The likelihood of dropout is controlled by a hyperparameter p, which represents the probability of retaining a unit.

Consider a deep neural network implemented with PyTorch; dropout can be incorporated as follows:

```
import torch.nn as nn

class NeuralNetwork(nn.Module):
    def __init__(self):
        super(NeuralNetwork, self).__init__()
        self.layer1 = nn.Linear(784, 256)
        self.dropout = nn.Dropout(p=0.5)
        self.layer2 = nn.Linear(256, 10)

    def forward(self, x):
        x = torch.relu(self.layer1(x))
        x = self.dropout(x)
        x = self.layer2(x)
        return x
```

During training, the dropout layer randomly zeroes some of the elements of the input tensor with probability p using samples from a Bernoulli distribution. During evaluation, dropout is not applied, and the full network is used to make predictions.

Batch Normalization can also be considered a regularization technique. Though primarily intended to stabilize and accelerate training by normalizing inputs to each layer, it has a regularizing effect. By adding a small amount of noise through normalization, it can reduce overfitting. The batch normalization layer in PyTorch is implemented using `nn.BatchNorm1d` for 1-dimensional input:

```
self.batch_norm1 = nn.BatchNorm1d(256)
x = self.batch_norm1(x)
```

This scales and shifts the input to have zero mean and unit variance, and the importance of this process becomes evident in complex neural network architectures.

Regularization is not limited to these techniques alone. **Early stopping** is another effective method where training is halted as soon as the performance on a validation set begins to deteriorate. This prevents the model from overfitting to the training data.

Additional techniques include adding noise to the input data or hidden layers, data augmentation, which increases the diversity of training data, or using stochastic depth, where entire layers are randomly dropped during training.

By carefully applying and tuning these regularization techniques, one can effectively manage the bias-variance tradeoff, mitigating overfitting and enhancing the model's ability to generalize to unseen data. This makes regularization an indispensable aspect of training robust machine learning models.

6.4 Batch Normalization

Batch normalization is a technique to improve the training speed and performance of neural networks by normalizing the inputs of each layer. It helps alleviate the problem of internal covariate shift, where the distribution of each layer's inputs changes during training, slowing down the training process.

The key idea behind batch normalization is to normalize the output of a previous activation layer by subtracting the batch mean and dividing by the batch standard deviation. This normalization is followed by two learnable parameters, a scaling factor γ, and a shifting factor β, to restore the network's capacity to represent the data distribution fully.

Mathematically, for a given input batch $x = (x_1, x_2, \ldots, x_m)$, we perform the following operations:

$$\mu_B = \frac{1}{m}\sum_{i=1}^{m} x_i \quad \text{(Mean of the batch)}$$

$$\sigma_B^2 = \frac{1}{m}\sum_{i=1}^{m}(x_i - \mu_B)^2 \quad \text{(Variance of the batch)}$$

$$\hat{x}_i = \frac{x_i - \mu_B}{\sqrt{\sigma_B^2 + \epsilon}} \quad \text{(Normalization)}$$

where ϵ is a small constant added for numerical stability.

The normalized value $\hat{x}_i$ is then scaled and shifted:

$$y_i = \gamma \hat{x}_i + \beta$$

where γ and β are learnable parameters.

Batch normalization can be applied to any type of layer output, though it is particularly useful after fully connected and convolutional layers. Within a neural network, batch normalization modifies the original outputs as follows:

```
import torch
import torch.nn as nn

class ExampleModel(nn.Module):
    def __init__(self):
        super(ExampleModel, self).__init__()
        self.conv1 = nn.Conv2d(in_channels=3, out_channels=16, kernel_size=3,
             padding=1)
        self.bn1 = nn.BatchNorm2d(16) # 16 is the number of feature maps
        self.relu = nn.ReLU()

    def forward(self, x):
        x = self.conv1(x)
        x = self.bn1(x)
        x = self.relu(x)
        return x
```

The batch normalization layer is added after the convolutional layer and before the activation function. This ordering is crucial because batch normalization normalizes the pre-activation inputs.

The advantages of using batch normalization include faster convergence during training, reduced sensitivity to initialization, and often better generalization. By normalizing the inputs to each layer, the network can maintain stable activations throughout the training process, thereby enabling higher learning rates and faster model convergence.

Batch normalization also acts as a form of regularization, similar to dropout. It introduces a form of noise into the model by normalizing based on mini-batches, which can help to prevent overfitting. However, it's important to note that during inference, batch normalization uses running averages of the mean and variance computed during training rather than the mean and variance of each mini-batch. This shift ensures consistency across different input batches.

Implementing batch normalization effectively in PyTorch can be done using the nn.BatchNorm1d, nn.BatchNorm2d, and nn.BatchNorm3d for 1D, 2D, and 3D data inputs, respectively. The following example demonstrates its application in a fully connected neural network:

```
class FullyConnectedModel(nn.Module):
    def __init__(self):
        super(FullyConnectedModel, self).__init__()
        self.fc1 = nn.Linear(in_features=784, out_features=256)
        self.bn1 = nn.BatchNorm1d(256) # 256 is the number of features
        self.relu = nn.ReLU()

    def forward(self, x):
        x = self.fc1(x)
        x = self.bn1(x)
        x = self.relu(x)
        return x

model = FullyConnectedModel()
```

Here, nn.BatchNorm1d(256) normalizes the outputs of the linear layer to have zero mean and unit variance, followed by the ReLU activation function. Applying batch normalization in this manner can significantly improve training dynamics and final model performance.

The use of batch normalization has become a standard practice in many deep learning architectures due to its numerous benefits and straightforward implementation. It's important to integrate batch normalization carefully, noting its interaction with other components such as dropout and the implications for model testing versus training.

6.5 Dropout and Other Regularization Methods

Dropout is a widely employed regularization technique aimed at mitigating overfitting in neural networks by randomly setting a fraction of input units to zero during training. This encourages the model to learn redundant representations, improving its generalizability. To implement dropout in PyTorch, the torch.nn.Dropout module is utilized. Below is a concise demonstration:

```
import torch
import torch.nn as nn

class SimpleModel(nn.Module):
    def __init__(self):
        super(SimpleModel, self).__init__()
        self.fc1 = nn.Linear(784, 256)
        self.dropout = nn.Dropout(p=0.5)
        self.fc2 = nn.Linear(256, 10)

    def forward(self, x):
        x = torch.relu(self.fc1(x))
```

```
        x = self.dropout(x)
        x = self.fc2(x)
        return x

model = SimpleModel()
print(model)
```

The p parameter in nn.Dropout specifies the dropout rate, which is the probability of setting units to zero. A commonly used value is 0.5.

Another effective regularization technique is **L2 regularization**, also known as *weight decay*. This technique adds a penalty term to the loss function proportional to the sum of the squared values of the weights. This encourages the model to keep the weights small, thus reducing complexity and improving generalization. In PyTorch, L2 regularization can be implemented using the weight_decay parameter in the optimizer:

```
optimizer = torch.optim.SGD(model.parameters(), lr=0.01, weight_decay=1e-4)
```

In this case, the weight_decay parameter is set to 1×10^{-4}.

Another notable method is **L1 regularization**, which adds a penalty term proportional to the sum of the absolute values of the weights. This technique encourages sparsity, meaning that some weights become exactly zero, effectively performing feature selection. To implement L1 regularization in PyTorch, custom modification of the loss function is necessary:

```
l1_lambda = 0.001

def l1_penalty(model):
    l1_norm = sum(p.abs().sum() for p in model.parameters())
    return l1_lambda * l1_norm

criterion = nn.CrossEntropyLoss()
optimizer = torch.optim.SGD(model.parameters(), lr=0.01)

# Training loop
for epoch in range(num_epochs):
    for data, target in train_loader:
        optimizer.zero_grad()
        output = model(data)
        loss = criterion(output, target) + l1_penalty(model)
        loss.backward()
        optimizer.step()
```

Early Stopping is another prevalent regularization strategy where the training is halted once the performance on a validation set begins to deteriorate. Early stopping avoids overfitting since the model is not allowed to continue training beyond the point where it starts to overfit the training data:

```
best_val_loss = float('inf')
patience, num_bad_epochs = 2, 0

for epoch in range(num_epochs):
    train(...)
    val_loss = evaluate(...)
    if val_loss < best_val_loss:
        best_val_loss = val_loss
        num_bad_epochs = 0
        # Save the best model
    else:
        num_bad_epochs += 1
        if num_bad_epochs >= patience:
            print("Stopping early")
            break
```

Normalization Methods include techniques such as batch normalization, layer normalization, and instance normalization. Batch normalization normalizes the output of a previous activation layer by subtracting the batch mean and dividing by the batch standard deviation. This can lead to faster convergence and can act as a form of regularization by adding noise to the network:

```
import torch.nn.functional as F

class SimpleModelWithBatchNorm(nn.Module):
    def __init__(self):
        super(SimpleModelWithBatchNorm, self).__init__()
        self.fc1 = nn.Linear(784, 256)
        self.bn1 = nn.BatchNorm1d(256)
        self.fc2 = nn.Linear(256, 10)

    def forward(self, x):
        x = F.relu(self.bn1(self.fc1(x)))
        x = self.fc2(x)
        return x

model = SimpleModelWithBatchNorm()
print(model)
```

Data augmentation is another critical method to enhance regularization, which artificially expands the dataset's size by applying various transformations. This technique is beneficial in image classification, where transformations like rotations, flips, and crops can be used:

```
from torchvision import transforms

transform = transforms.Compose([
    transforms.RandomHorizontalFlip(),
    transforms.RandomCrop(32, padding=4),
    transforms.ToTensor(),
])

train_dataset = datasets.CIFAR10(root='./data', train=True, download=True,
        transform=transform)
```

```
train_loader = torch.utils.data.DataLoader(train_dataset, batch_size=64, shuffle=
    True)
```

These various regularization techniques collectively contribute to the development of models that generalize well across different datasets, improving performance and robustness. Utilizing these methods effectively requires a judicious balance, often found through empirical experimentation specific to the problem domain.

6.6 Learning Rate Scheduling

The learning rate is a critical hyperparameter in the training of neural networks, influencing the convergence behavior and ultimately the performance of the model. Learning rate scheduling refers to the strategy of adjusting the learning rate during training with the goal of improving training efficiency and model performance. Effective learning rate scheduling can help escape local minima, accelerate convergence, and achieve better generalization.

Learning rate scheduling can be implemented using various techniques, each with its own advantages and appropriate use-cases. These techniques primarily include step decay, exponential decay, cosine annealing, and adaptive learning rate methods such as ReduceLROnPlateau and cyclical learning rates. Implementing these strategies properly can significantly enhance model performance by dynamically adjusting the learning rate to align with the training process stages.

1. Step Decay

In step decay, the learning rate is reduced by a factor at certain intervals, often referred to as "epochs." The reduction usually happens at regular intervals or when improvement in the validation set lessens. This method helps in fine-tuning the weights towards the end of training by decreasing the learning rate, avoiding overshooting the minima.

```
import torch.optim as optim

# Assume a pre-defined optimizer for the model
optimizer = optim.SGD(model.parameters(), lr=0.1)

# Step Decay Scheduler
scheduler = optim.lr_scheduler.StepLR(optimizer, step_size=30, gamma=0.1)

for epoch in range(num_epochs):
    train(...)
```

```
    validate(...)
    scheduler.step()
```

In the above example, the learning rate is reduced by a factor of 10 every 30 epochs.

2. Exponential Decay

Exponential decay decreases the learning rate exponentially over time by factoring in the decay rate. This method facilitates continuous but gradual reduction in learning rate, ensuring finer adjustments towards convergence.

```
# Exponential Decay Scheduler
scheduler = optim.lr_scheduler.ExponentialLR(optimizer, gamma=0.1)

for epoch in range(num_epochs):
    train(...)
    validate(...)
    scheduler.step()
```

In this example, $gamma$ is the decay rate, often set less than 1, representing the multiplicative factor by which the learning rate is reduced every epoch.

3. Cosine Annealing

Cosine annealing entails fluctuating the learning rate according to a cosine function. This approach is based on cyclic learning rate schedules and typically begins with high learning rates that gradually decrease towards zero followed by a restart. The technique encourages periodic exploration of parameter space, thereby helping to escape shallow local minima.

```
# Cosine Annealing Scheduler
scheduler = optim.lr_scheduler.CosineAnnealingLR(optimizer, T_max=50)

for epoch in range(num_epochs):
    train(...)
    validate(...)
    scheduler.step()
```

The parameter T_max represents the number of iterations for the first half of the cosine wave.

4. ReduceLROnPlateau

ReduceLROnPlateau is an adaptive approach that decreases the learning rate once learning stagnates. Specifically, it monitors a quantity, usually validation loss, and reduces the learning rate if no improvement is observed for a specified number of epochs.

```
# Reduce On Plateau Scheduler
scheduler = optim.lr_scheduler.ReduceLROnPlateau(optimizer, mode='min', factor
    =0.1, patience=10)

for epoch in range(num_epochs):
    train(...)
    val_loss = validate(...)
    scheduler.step(val_loss)
```

The mode parameter specifies whether to monitor for a minimum or maximum quantity to determine stagnation, factor is the reduction rate, and patience is the number of epochs with no improvement after which the learning rate will be reduced.

5. Cyclical Learning Rates

Cyclical learning rates (CLR) oscillate between a lower and upper bound, allowing periods of higher learning rates within training to escape local minima followed by periods of lower rates for fine-tuning. This approach can be particularly effective for certain training dynamics.

```
from torch.optim.lr_scheduler import CyclicLR

# Cyclical Learning Rate Scheduler
scheduler = CyclicLR(optimizer, base_lr=0.001, max_lr=0.006, step_size_up=2000)

for epoch in range(num_epochs):
    for batch in dataloader:
        train_batch(batch)
        scheduler.step()
```

In this example, base_lr is the lower boundary of the learning rate and max_lr is the upper boundary. The step_size_up refers to the number of iterations it takes to go from the base_lr to max_lr.

Empirical analysis and best practices suggest that choosing a learning rate schedule should be driven by the specific characteristics of the dataset and model architecture. Step decay and exponential decay are simple yet effective for many scenarios. Adaptive methods like ReduceLROnPlateau provide flexibility and responsiveness to training dynamics, whereas cyclical learning rates and cosine annealing offer robust mechanisms to handle non-convex optimization landscapes.

Efficient learning rate scheduling can significantly affect the model's

performance and convergence speed. Employing appropriate techniques can lead to substantial improvements in the generalization ability of the model, ultimately facilitating better predictive performance on unseen data.

6.7 Data Augmentation

Data augmentation is a pivotal technique that augments the size of training datasets by creating modified versions of the original data. This practice is indispensable in deep learning, where large datasets are crucial for training robust models. Augmented datasets enhance model generalization, reduce overfitting, and enable models to learn more invariant features. Here, we will explore various data augmentation techniques applicable to image, text, and audio data.

For image data, common augmentation techniques include transformations such as rotation, translation, scaling, and flipping. These operations simulate the variations and distortions that can occur in real-world images, providing the model with a more diverse set of training examples.

```
import torch
from torchvision import transforms
from PIL import Image

# Define a sequence of transformations
transform = transforms.Compose([
    transforms.RandomHorizontalFlip(p=0.5),
    transforms.RandomRotation(degrees=15),
    transforms.RandomResizedCrop(size=(224, 224), scale=(0.8, 1.0)),
    transforms.ColorJitter(brightness=0.2, contrast=0.2, saturation=0.2, hue=0.2),
    transforms.ToTensor(),
])

# Apply transformations to an image
image = Image.open('path/to/image.jpg')
augmented_image = transform(image)
```

The above code snippet demonstrates an image augmentation pipeline using PyTorch's torchvision.transforms module. The sequential application of transformations such as random horizontal flip, random rotation, random resized crop, and color jitter provides a significant enhancement to the training data variability.

Text data augmentation, on the other hand, employs techniques like synonym replacement, random insertion, random swap, and random deletion. These methods alter textual data in ways that preserve sentence semantics while providing new training examples.

```
import random
from nltk.corpus import wordnet

# Synonym replacement
def synonym_replacement(sentence, n):
    words = sentence.split()
    new_words = words.copy()
    random_word_list = list(set([word for word in words if wordnet.synsets(word)]))
    random.shuffle(random_word_list)
    num_replaced = 0
    for random_word in random_word_list:
        synonyms = wordnet.synsets(random_word)
        if synonyms:
            synonym = synonyms[0].lemmas()[0].name()
            new_words = [synonym if word == random_word else word for word in
                 new_words]
            num_replaced += 1
        if num_replaced >= n:
            break
    return ' '.join(new_words)

sentence = 'Data augmentation is useful for improving model performance.'
augmented_sentence = synonym_replacement(sentence, 2)
print(augmented_sentence)
```

In this example, the synonym_replacement function substitutes words in a sentence with their synonyms, thus generating new variations of the input text. Implementing such augmentation techniques can significantly enhance the robustness of natural language processing (NLP) models.

For audio data, augmentations can include modifications such as time stretching, pitch shifting, background noise addition, and random cropping. These techniques create variations in audio signals that help models generalize better.

```
import librosa
import numpy as np

# Load audio file
audio_path = 'path/to/audio.wav'
y, sr = librosa.load(audio_path)

# Time stretching
y_stretch = librosa.effects.time_stretch(y, rate=1.2)

# Pitch shifting
y_shift = librosa.effects.pitch_shift(y, sr, n_steps=4)

# Adding background noise
def add_noise(y, noise_level=0.005):
    noise = np.random.randn(len(y))
    augmented_data = y + noise_level * noise
    return augmented_data

y_noise = add_noise(y)
```

The code above illustrates how to perform time stretching, pitch shifting, and noise addition using the librosa library. Each of these augmentations modifies the audio signal in distinct ways, thereby aiding in the creation of a diversified training dataset.

Evaluating the performance of augmented data necessitates careful monitoring. It is essential to ensure that augmentation techniques contribute positively to model performance without introducing noise or biases that could detract from the model's accuracy. This involves a rigorous process of validation and testing augmented datasets to ascertain their efficacy.

Integrating data augmentation into the training workflow can be accomplished seamlessly using data loaders. PyTorch, for instance, provides facilities to apply transformations directly within data loaders, ensuring that augmented data is efficiently incorporated during model training.

```
from torch.utils.data import DataLoader, Dataset
from torchvision.datasets import ImageFolder

# Define a custom dataset with augmentations
class AugmentedDataset(Dataset):
    def __init__(self, root_dir, transform=None):
        self.dataset = ImageFolder(root_dir, transform=transform)

    def __len__(self):
        return len(self.dataset)

    def __getitem__(self, idx):
        return self.dataset[idx]

# Apply transformations as defined previously
aug_transform = transforms.Compose([
    transforms.RandomHorizontalFlip(p=0.5),
    transforms.RandomRotation(degrees=15),
    transforms.RandomResizedCrop(size=(224, 224), scale=(0.8, 1.0)),
    transforms.ColorJitter(brightness=0.2, contrast=0.2, saturation=0.2, hue=0.2),
    transforms.ToTensor(),
])

# Initialize dataset and dataloader
aug_dataset = AugmentedDataset(root_dir='path/to/dataset', transform=
    aug_transform)
data_loader = DataLoader(aug_dataset, batch_size=32, shuffle=True, num_workers
    =4)
```

Through the examples provided, it becomes evident that data augmentation is a potent method for enriching datasets and improving model performance. Regular and judiciously applied augmentations afford robustness and versatility to models, enabling them to perform effectively across varied and previously unseen data distributions.

6.8 Ensembling Models

Ensembling is an effective technique for improving the predictive performance of machine learning models. The core idea behind ensembling is to combine multiple models to produce a single, robust predictive model. By leveraging the strengths and averaging the weaknesses of individual models, ensembling can lead to better generalization on unseen data. This section will delve into various ensembling strategies, including bagging, boosting, and stacking, and demonstrate how to implement these techniques using PyTorch.

At the heart of ensembling lies the principle of diversity among individual models. If each model makes different errors, their combination is more likely to correct these errors, resulting in a higher overall accuracy. Let's explore the key types of ensembling methods.

Bagging (Bootstrap Aggregating)

Bagging involves training multiple models on different subsets of the training data, generated through bootstrap sampling. Each model is trained independently, and their predictions are averaged in the case of regression or taken as a majority vote in classification problems.

The following Python code snippet illustrates the concept of bagging using PyTorch. We'll use a simple neural network as the base model and train multiple replicas on different bootstrap samples of the training data.

```
import torch
import torch.nn as nn
import torch.optim as optim
import torch.utils.data as data
from sklearn.utils import resample

class SimpleNN(nn.Module):
    def __init__(self, input_size, hidden_size, output_size):
        super(SimpleNN, self).__init__()
        self.fc1 = nn.Linear(input_size, hidden_size)
        self.relu = nn.ReLU()
        self.fc2 = nn.Linear(hidden_size, output_size)

    def forward(self, x):
        out = self.fc1(x)
        out = self.relu(out)
        out = self.fc2(out)
        return out

def train_model(model, train_loader, criterion, optimizer, epochs=20):
    model.train()
    for epoch in range(epochs):
        for inputs, labels in train_loader:
            optimizer.zero_grad()
```

```
            outputs = model(inputs)
            loss = criterion(outputs, labels)
            loss.backward()
            optimizer.step()

# Generate bootstrap samples and train ensemble of models
ensemble_size = 10
models = []
for _ in range(ensemble_size):
    bootstrap_sample = resample(train_data, replace=True)
    train_loader = data.DataLoader(bootstrap_sample, batch_size=64, shuffle=True)
    model = SimpleNN(input_size=10, hidden_size=20, output_size=1) # Example
        dimensions
    criterion = nn.MSELoss()
    optimizer = optim.Adam(model.parameters(), lr=0.001)
    train_model(model, train_loader, criterion, optimizer)
    models.append(model)

# Make predictions with the ensemble
def predict_ensemble(models, test_loader):
    outputs = []
    for model in models:
        model.eval()
        preds = []
        with torch.no_grad():
            for inputs in test_loader:
                preds.append(model(inputs))
        outputs.append(torch.cat(preds))
    return torch.mean(torch.stack(outputs), dim=0)
```

Boosting

Boosting sequentially trains models, each attempting to correct the errors made by the previous ones. The algorithm assigns higher weights to misclassified instances, focusing subsequent models on harder cases. One popular boosting algorithm is AdaBoost, though more complex ones like Gradient Boosting Machines (GBM) and XG-Boost are widely used.

The following PyTorch example demonstrates a simple boosting variant using an adaptive weighted loss:

```
def adaboost_train(X, y, base_model, num_models=10):
    n_samples = X.size(0)
    weights = torch.ones(n_samples) / n_samples
    models = []
    alphas = []

    for _ in range(num_models):
        model = base_model()
        optimizer = optim.Adam(model.parameters(), lr=0.001)
        criterion = nn.CrossEntropyLoss(reduce=False) # To get per-instance losses

        for epoch in range(20): # Example epochs
            model.train()
            optimizer.zero_grad()
            outputs = model(X)
            losses = criterion(outputs, y)
```

```
            weighted_loss = (losses * weights).mean()
            weighted_loss.backward()
            optimizer.step()

        model.eval()
        with torch.no_grad():
            outputs = model(X)
            preds = outputs.argmax(dim=1)
            missed = preds != y

        error = (weights * missed.float()).sum()
        alpha = 0.5 * (torch.log((1 - error) / (error + 1e-10)))
        weights = weights * torch.exp(alpha * missed.float())
        weights /= weights.sum()

        models.append(model)
        alphas.append(alpha)

    return models, alphas

def adaboost_predict(X, models, alphas):
    final_pred = torch.zeros(X.size(0))
    for model, alpha in zip(models, alphas):
        with torch.no_grad():
            final_pred += alpha * model(X).argmax(dim=1).float()
    return (final_pred >= 0).long()
```

Stacking

Stacking involves training multiple base models (often of different types) and then combining their outputs using a meta-model. The meta-model takes the base model predictions as inputs and learns how to best combine them to improve overall accuracy.

The following example demonstrates a simplified stacking approach using PyTorch with two base models and a logistic regression meta-model:

```
import numpy as np
from sklearn.linear_model import LogisticRegression

# Base models
model1 = SimpleNN(input_size=10, hidden_size=20, output_size=1) # Example
    dimensions
model2 = SimpleNN(input_size=10, hidden_size=20, output_size=1)
... # Train both base models on the training dataset

# Create meta-dataset
def create_meta_dataset(models, X):
    meta_features = []
    for model in models:
        with torch.no_grad():
            meta_features.append(model(X).numpy())
    return np.column_stack(meta_features)

meta_X_train = create_meta_dataset([model1, model2], X_train)
meta_y_train = y_train.numpy()

meta_model = LogisticRegression()
```

```
meta_model.fit(meta_X_train, meta_y_train)

# Making predictions with the stacked model
meta_X_test = create_meta_dataset([model1, model2], X_test)
meta_predictions = meta_model.predict(meta_X_test)
```

Bagging, boosting, and stacking are powerful techniques that harness the strengths of multiple models to achieve superior predictive performance. Each method has its unique approach to combining models, emphasizing diversity, and mitigating individual model weaknesses. Implementing these methods in PyTorch enables leveraging deep learning models' flexibility and computational power, fostering robust and accurate ensemble systems.

6.9 Monitoring Performance Metrics

Monitoring performance metrics is a fundamental aspect of ensuring any machine learning model's robustness and accuracy. It involves continuous evaluation of a model's predictions against known outcomes to assess its performance and generalizability. This section dives into key performance metrics, tools, and strategies used to comprehensively monitor and analyze a machine learning model's performance.

Key Performance Metrics

Understanding and correctly implementing performance metrics is crucial for model evaluation. Various metrics apply to different types of problems such as classification, regression, and clustering.

For **classification problems**, common metrics include:

- **Accuracy**: Defined as the ratio of correctly predicted instances to the total instances.

$$\text{Accuracy} = \frac{\text{Number of Correct Predictions}}{\text{Total Number of Predictions}}$$

- **Precision**: Measures the accuracy of the positive predictions.

$$\text{Precision} = \frac{\text{True Positives}}{\text{True Positives} + \text{False Positives}}$$

- **Recall (Sensitivity or True Positive Rate)**: Indicates the ability of a model to find all relevant cases.

$$\text{Recall} = \frac{\text{True Positives}}{\text{True Positives} + \text{False Negatives}}$$

- **F1 Score**: The harmonic mean of precision and recall, providing a balance between the two.

$$\text{F1 Score} = 2 \cdot \frac{\text{Precision} \cdot \text{Recall}}{\text{Precision} + \text{Recall}}$$

- **Area Under the Receiver Operating Characteristic Curve (AUC-ROC)**: Evaluates the model's capability to distinguish between classes.

For **regression problems**, key metrics include:

- **Mean Absolute Error (MAE)**: The average magnitude of errors in a set of predictions, without considering their direction.

$$\text{MAE} = \frac{1}{n}\sum_{i=1}^{n} |y_i - \hat{y}_i|$$

- **Mean Squared Error (MSE)**: The average squared difference between the estimated values and the actual value.

$$\text{MSE} = \frac{1}{n}\sum_{i=1}^{n} (y_i - \hat{y}_i)^2$$

- **Root Mean Squared Error (RMSE)**: The square root of MSE, providing an error metric in the same units as the target variable.

$$\text{RMSE} = \sqrt{\frac{1}{n}\sum_{i=1}^{n} (y_i - \hat{y}_i)^2}$$

- **R-squared (R^2)**: Indicates the proportion of the variance in the dependent variable predictable from the independent variables.

$$R^2 = 1 - \frac{\sum_i (y_i - \hat{y}_i)^2}{\sum_i (y_i - \bar{y})^2}$$

Visualization Techniques

Visual representations provide an in-depth insight into model performance. Key techniques include:

- **Confusion Matrix**: A table layout that visualizes the performance of an algorithm. It lays out the true positives, false negatives, true negatives, and false positives.
- **ROC Curve**: A graphical representation of a classifier's performance across all classification thresholds. The area under this curve (AUC) gives a single scalar value to compare models.
- **Precision-Recall Curve**: Useful for imbalanced datasets, it displays the trade-off between precision and recall for different thresholds.
- **Learning Curves**: These show the validation and training scores of a model for an increasing sample size, useful for detecting overfitting and underfitting.

Implementation in PyTorch

PyTorch, coupled with libraries like scikit-learn, simplifies the monitoring of performance metrics.

```
import torch
import sklearn
from sklearn.metrics import confusion_matrix

# Example predictions and true labels
y_true = torch.tensor([0, 1, 0, 1, 0, 1])
y_pred = torch.tensor([0, 0, 0, 1, 0, 1])

# Converting tensors to numpy arrays for scikit-learn compatibility
y_true = y_true.numpy()
y_pred = y_pred.numpy()

# Calculate the confusion matrix
cm = confusion_matrix(y_true, y_pred)
print(cm)
```

```
# Output
[[3 0]
 [1 2]]
```

```
from sklearn.metrics import roc_auc_score

# Example binary scores and true labels
y_true = [0, 0, 1, 1]
y_scores = [0.1, 0.4, 0.35, 0.8]

# Calculate AUC-ROC
```

```
roc_auc = roc_auc_score(y_true, y_scores)
print("AUC-ROC:", roc_auc)
```

```
# Output
AUC-ROC: 0.75
```

Logging and Monitoring Tools

Several tools are available for tracking and visualizing model metrics during training:

- **TensorBoard**: A visualization library specifically designed for deep learning. It provides visualizing metrics over time, histograms of weights, and images.
- **Weights & Biases (W&B)**: A platform for experiment tracking, model management, and team collaboration. It supports logging metrics, loss values, and generating insightful plots.
- **Neptune**: A tool for logging and displaying model parameters, metrics, and results. It allows collaborative monitoring and analysis.

Use of such tools improves model development lifecycle by providing an organized and comprehensive view of iterative experiments, leading to informed decision-making based on precise and well-documented performance metrics.

```
from torch.utils.tensorboard import SummaryWriter

# Initialize tensorboard writer
writer = SummaryWriter()

# Example training loop
for epoch in range(epochs):
    # Simulated loss
    loss = compute_loss(model, data)

    # Record loss value
    writer.add_scalar('Training Loss', loss, epoch)

writer.close()
```

```
# Start TensorBoard with
tensorboard --logdir=runs
```

These practices, when applied consistently, enable the development of robust, high-performance models through thorough and continuous monitoring.

6.10 Handling Imbalanced Data

Imbalanced data occurs when some classes are significantly underrepresented compared to others in a dataset. This can pose significant challenges to machine learning models, leading to biased predictions and poor performance, especially for the minority class. Various strategies can address imbalanced data, including resampling techniques, altering performance metrics, and using specialized algorithms. This section delves into these methods to provide a comprehensive approach to handling imbalanced datasets.

Resampling Techniques are among the most commonly used methods to counteract the issues posed by imbalanced datasets. There are two main types of resampling techniques: *oversampling* and *undersampling*:

- **Oversampling:** This method involves increasing the number of instances in the minority class. A popular technique for oversampling is the Synthetic Minority Over-sampling Technique (SMOTE). SMOTE generates synthetic samples of the minority class by interpolating between existing examples.

```
from imblearn.over_sampling import SMOTE
smote = SMOTE(sampling_strategy='minority')
X_res, y_res = smote.fit_resample(X, y)
```

- **Undersampling:** This method involves reducing the number of instances in the majority class. This can be done randomly or by using more sophisticated techniques such as Tomek Links, which identify and remove instances near the decision boundary.

```
from imblearn.under_sampling import RandomUnderSampler
rus = RandomUnderSampler(sampling_strategy='majority')
X_res, y_res = rus.fit_resample(X, y)
```

Altering Performance Metrics can provide a more accurate assessment of model performance on imbalanced datasets. Traditional metrics such as accuracy can be misleading when classes are imbalanced. Alternative metrics include:

- **Precision and Recall:** Precision measures the proportion of positive identifications that were actually correct, while recall measures the proportion of actual positives that were identified correctly.

$$\text{Precision} = \frac{TP}{TP + FP}$$

$$\text{Recall} = \frac{TP}{TP + FN}$$

- **F1 Score:** The F1 score is the harmonic mean of precision and recall, providing a single metric that balances both concerns.

$$\text{F1 Score} = 2 \cdot \frac{\text{Precision} \cdot \text{Recall}}{\text{Precision} + \text{Recall}}$$

- **Area Under the ROC Curve (AUC-ROC):** This metric evaluates the trade-off between the true positive rate and the false positive rate across different classification thresholds.

```
from sklearn.metrics import roc_auc_score
auc_roc = roc_auc_score(y_test, y_pred)
```

Specialized Algorithms adapt well to imbalanced datasets by giving more importance to the minority class. Examples include cost-sensitive learning, where different penalties are assigned to misclassifications of different classes, and ensemble methods like Random Forest and Gradient Boosting, which can be tailored to focus on underrepresented classes.

- **Cost-sensitive learning:** Scikit-learn allows weighting of classes during the training process. The class_weight parameter in algorithms such as LogisticRegression or RandomForestClassifier can be set to balanced to automatically adjust weights inversely proportional to class frequencies.

```
from sklearn.ensemble import RandomForestClassifier
model = RandomForestClassifier(class_weight='balanced')
model.fit(X_train, y_train)
```

- **Ensemble Methods:** Techniques such as balanced Random Forests and Boosted Algorithms focus on improving the model's performance on the minority class by combining predictions from multiple learners.

```
from sklearn.ensemble import GradientBoostingClassifier
model = GradientBoostingClassifier()
model.fit(X_train, y_train, sample_weight=compute_sample_weight('balanced'
    , y_train))
```

A critical part of handling imbalanced data is to carefully evaluate and verify model performance using appropriate validation strategies. K-fold cross-validation, where the dataset is split into K subsets, and the model is trained and validated K times, ensures that every instance in the dataset has a chance to be in the training and validation sets, providing a robust assessment of model performance.

```
from sklearn.model_selection import cross_val_score
scores = cross_val_score(model, X, y, cv=5, scoring='f1')
```

These techniques collectively provide a robust framework for addressing imbalanced datasets, enabling more accurate and fair model predictions across various classes. The application of these methods should be tailored to specific datasets and problem contexts to achieve the best possible performance and reliability.

Chapter 7

Convolutional Neural Networks (CNNs)

This chapter provides a detailed examination of Convolutional Neural Networks (CNNs). It starts with an introduction to convolutions and pooling layers, progressing to the construction of a simple CNN. Advanced CNN architectures, transfer learning, and fine-tuning techniques are also discussed. The chapter addresses methods for handling overfitting, visualizing CNN outputs, and explores practical applications of CNNs in various domains.

7.1 Introduction to Convolutional Neural Networks

Convolutional Neural Networks (CNNs) are specialized types of artificial neural networks designed to process structured grid data, such as images. The architecture of CNNs is inspired by the visual cortex of animals, which also consists of many overlapping receptive fields that process visual information hierarchically. CNNs have demonstrated remarkable performance improvements in tasks featuring image recognition, classification, and processing. This section aims to provide a comprehensive understanding of the fundamental concepts and motivation behind CNNs, paving the way for more complex discussions in subsequent sections.

The primary building blocks of CNNs are convolutional layers, pooling layers, and fully connected layers. Together, these layers enable the network to automatically and adaptively learn spatial hierarchies of features from input images through backpropagation. Each type of layer plays an essential role in constructing robust and accurate models for image processing tasks.

- **Convolutional Layers** form the crux of CNNs. They apply a convolution operation to the input, passing the result to the subsequent layer. Convolutions allow the network to preserve the spatial relationship between pixels by learning image features using small squares of input data. A convolutional layer typically consists of a set of learnable filters, each of which extends through the full depth of the input volume. During the forward pass, each filter is convolved across the width and height of the input volume, computing dot products between the filter entries and the input, producing a two-dimensional activation map.

- Formally, considering a single convolutional layer, let I be the input image of dimensions $H \times W \times D$, where H is the height, W is the width, and D is the depth (or number of channels). Let K be a filter with dimensions $K_H \times K_W \times D$. The convolution operation is mathematically defined as:

$$(O)_i = \sum_{h=0}^{K_H-1} \sum_{w=0}^{K_W-1} \sum_{d=0}^{D-1} I[h+i, w+j, d] \cdot K[h, w, d]$$

  where O denotes the output feature map, and i and j are the spatial indices.

- **Pooling Layers** are used for down-sampling the input representations, reducing the dimensions of feature maps, and thereby decreasing computation and preventing overfitting. The most common type is max pooling, which extracts the maximum value from each sub-region of the feature map. Another type is average pooling, which computes the average value of each sub-region. Pooling operates separately on each depth slice of the input and resizes it spatially, often by a factor of two along both width and height.

- Consider an input feature map of dimensions $(H \times W \times D)$. If a pooling layer employs a filter of size $F_H \times F_W$ and a stride S, the output dimensions are given by:

$$O_H = \frac{H - F_H}{S} + 1, \quad O_W = \frac{W - F_W}{S} + 1, \quad O_D = D$$

- **Fully Connected Layers** serve as the final layers in traditional CNN architecture. These layers are similar to those in regular neural networks where each neuron is connected to all neurons in the previous layer, transforming the learned feature representations from the convolutional and pooling layers into the output decision space. Fully connected layers perform classification based on the extracted features facilitating tasks such as categorizing an input image into one of several predefined classes.

- Training a CNN involves determining the optimal values of filters and weights that minimize the loss function. This process, called backpropagation, adjusts the parameters using gradient descent algorithms. The layers of CNNs transform the input image into a series of high-level features, which are then combined to make a final prediction.

To conclude, understanding CNNs requires grasping these foundational layers and their functional roles within the network's architecture. By integrating convolutional, pooling, and fully connected layers, CNNs are capable of building complex models that excel in processing and understanding images, enabling breakthroughs across a variety of applications. The following sections delve deeper into each component, advanced architectures, and techniques such as transfer learning which leverage pre-trained models to enhance classification performance.

7.2 Understanding Convolutions

Convolutions are the cornerstone of Convolutional Neural Networks (CNNs). They are mathematical operations that combine two sets of information. In the context of image processing and CNNs, convolutions are used to extract features from input data, such as images, through the application of filters or kernels.

Convolution Operation

The convolution operation involves a filter (or kernel) that slides over the input image (also known as the feature map) and performs element-wise multiplication followed by summation. Formally, if I is an input image and K is a kernel, the convolution $I * K$ is computed as follows:

$$S(i,j) = (I * K)(i,j) = \sum_m \sum_n I(i+m, j+n) \cdot K(m,n)$$

Where:

- $S(i,j)$ is the output feature map.
- $I(i+m, j+n)$ represents the pixel value of the input image at position $(i+m, j+n)$.
- $K(m,n)$ is the kernel value at position (m,n).
- The sums over m and n iterate over the kernel dimensions.

Properties of Convolution

- *Sparsity of Connections*: Each output value in the feature map is produced by a small portion of the input, maintaining local connectivity.
- *Parameter Sharing*: The same kernel is used across different spatial locations, greatly reducing the number of parameters and computational complexity.
- *Translation Invariance*: Small shifts in the input image cause corresponding shifts in the feature map, allowing CNNs to detect patterns regardless of their position.

Padding and Stride

To control the size of the output feature map, convolutional layers use padding and stride.

Padding involves adding extra pixels around the border of the input image. The two common types are:

- *Valid Padding*: No padding, resulting in a smaller output size.
- *Same Padding*: Padding added to ensure that the output feature map has the same spatial dimensions as the input.

Padding can also be specified by the number of pixels, such as $\text{padding}=1$ for one-pixel border padding.

Stride determines how the kernel moves across the input image. A stride of 1 means the kernel moves one pixel at a time, resulting in overlapped regions; a stride of 2 means the kernel moves two pixels at a time, causing non-overlapping regions and a reduced feature map size.

Example of Convolution Operation in PyTorch

Consider the following example where a 3x3 kernel is applied to a 5x5 image with a stride of 1 and no padding:

```
import torch
import torch.nn as nn

# Define input tensor (1x1x5x5, single channel 5x5 image)
input = torch.tensor([[[[1., 2., 3., 4., 5.],
                        [1., 2., 3., 4., 5.],
                        [1., 2., 3., 4., 5.],
                        [1., 2., 3., 4., 5.],
                        [1., 2., 3., 4., 5.]]]])

# Define convolutional layer with 1 input channel, 1 output channel, 3x3 kernel
conv = nn.Conv2d(1, 1, kernel_size=3, stride=1, padding=0)

# Initialize kernel weights for reproducibility
conv.weight.data = torch.tensor([[[[1., 0., -1.],
                                   [1., 0., -1.],
                                   [1., 0., -1.]]]])

# Perform the convolution
output = conv(input)

print(output)
```

The above code will produce the following output:

```
tensor([[[[ 0.,  0.,  0.],
          [ 0.,  0.,  0.],
          [ 0.,  0.,  0.]]]], grad_fn=<MkldnnConvolutionBackward>)
```

Exploring Kernel Effects

Different kernels highlight different features in the input image:

- *Edge Detection*: Kernels like the Sobel operator detect edges by emphasizing gradients.
- *Blurring*: Averaging kernels smooth the image.
- *Sharpening*: Kernels can increase contrasts to emphasize boundaries.

An example of a Sobel kernel for edge detection is:

$$K_x = \begin{pmatrix} -1 & 0 & 1 \\ -2 & 0 & 2 \\ -1 & 0 & 1 \end{pmatrix}$$

When applied to an input image, this kernel highlights horizontal edges by calculating the gradient.

Implementing Various Kernels in PyTorch

```
import matplotlib.pyplot as plt

# Function to visualize kernel effects
def visualize_kernel_effects(image, kernel):
    conv = nn.Conv2d(1, 1, kernel_size=3, padding=1, bias=False)
    conv.weight.data = torch.tensor(kernel, dtype=torch.float32).unsqueeze(0).
         unsqueeze(0)
    result = conv(image.unsqueeze(0).unsqueeze(0))
    plt.imshow(result.squeeze().detach().numpy(), cmap='gray')
    plt.show()

# Define a sample image
sample_image = torch.tensor([[1., 2., 3., 4., 5.],
                             [1., 2., 3., 4., 5.],
                             [1., 2., 3., 4., 5.],
                             [1., 2., 3., 4., 5.],
                             [1., 2., 3., 4., 5.]])

# Sobel edge detection kernel
sobel_kernel = [[[-1., 0., 1.],
                 [-2., 0., 2.],
                 [-1., 0., 1.]]]

# Visualize the effect of Sobel kernel
visualize_kernel_effects(sample_image, sobel_kernel)
```

Different kernels applied within CNNs enable the network to learn various aspects of the input images autonomously, contributing to the robust feature representations that are key to the success of CNNs in computer vision tasks.

7.3 Pooling Layers

Pooling layers are a crucial component in the architecture of Convolutional Neural Networks (CNNs). They primarily serve to reduce the spatial dimensions of the input volume, which in turn reduces the computational complexity and helps mitigate overfitting. By downsampling the input, pooling layers also help in extracting dominant features that are invariant to minor translations of the input.

There are several types of pooling layers, each with distinct mechanisms and objectives. The most commonly used types are max pooling, average pooling, and global pooling.

Max Pooling: In max pooling, the input image is divided into a set of non-overlapping rectangles, and for each such sub-region, the maximum value is taken. This ensures that only the most prominent features are retained from each sub-region. For instance, consider a 2×2 max pooling operation applied to the following 4×4 input matrix:

```
Input:
1 3 2 4
8 7 6 5
5 4 3 2
1 2 3 0
```

The max pooling operation with a 2×2 window and stride of 2 would produce the following output:

```
Output:
8 6
5 3
```

In this example, the 2×2 window slides over the input matrix, and for each sub-region, the maximum value is selected.

Average Pooling: Average pooling, as the name suggests, computes the average of all elements in the pooling window. For the same 4×4 input matrix with a 2×2 window and stride of 2, average pooling would yield:

```
Output:
4.75 4.25
3.00 2.00
```

Here, the values are the mean of the elements within each 2×2 sub-region.

Global Pooling: Global pooling is an extreme form of pooling where a pooling window covers the entire spatial dimension of the input. This is commonly used before the fully connected layers in the network, acting as a form of dimension reduction and feature aggregation.

In practical applications, max pooling is often preferred because it tends to better capture the most salient features in the input data, which are critical for tasks such as object recognition. However, there are scenarios where average pooling might be more beneficial, particularly in capturing the background information of an image.

For illustrations and further insight, let's consider a simple CNN architecture integrating max pooling layers using PyTorch.

```
import torch
```

```
import torch.nn as nn
import torch.nn.functional as F

class SimpleCNN(nn.Module):
    def __init__(self):
        super(SimpleCNN, self).__init__()
        self.conv1 = nn.Conv2d(in_channels=3, out_channels=16, kernel_size=3,
            padding=1)
        self.pool = nn.MaxPool2d(kernel_size=2, stride=2, padding=0)
        self.conv2 = nn.Conv2d(in_channels=16, out_channels=32, kernel_size=3,
            padding=1)
        self.fc1 = nn.Linear(32 * 8 * 8, 128)
        self.fc2 = nn.Linear(128, 10)

    def forward(self, x):
        x = self.pool(F.relu(self.conv1(x))) # Apply conv1 -> ReLU -> max pooling
        x = self.pool(F.relu(self.conv2(x))) # Apply conv2 -> ReLU -> max pooling
        x = x.view(-1, 32 * 8 * 8) # Flatten the tensor
        x = F.relu(self.fc1(x))
        x = self.fc2(x)
        return x

# Instantiate and test the model
model = SimpleCNN()
print(model)
```

When executed, this code prints the architecture of the 'SimpleCNN' model, clearly showing the integration of max pooling layers after each convolutional layer:

```
SimpleCNN(
  (conv1): Conv2d(3, 16, kernel_size=(3, 3), stride=(1, 1), padding=(1, 1))
  (pool): MaxPool2d(kernel_size=2, stride=2, padding=0, dilation=1, ceil_mode=False)
  (conv2): Conv2d(16, 32, kernel_size=(3, 3), stride=(1, 1), padding=(1, 1))
  (fc1): Linear(in_features=2048, out_features=128, bias=True)
  (fc2): Linear(in_features=128, out_features=10, bias=True)
)
```

The pooling layers significantly reduce the spatial dimensions of the feature maps, making the architecture computationally efficient. After the first max pooling layer, the dimensions of the feature maps will be halved, and this process repeats after each pooling layer. This efficiency is crucial when working with large-scale images or deep networks.

Moreover, pooling layers inherently provide some level of translation invariance. By summarizing the presence of features over a region, they ensure the network's performance remains robust even when the position of features slightly varies within the input images. This characteristic is vital for real-world applications where objects may appear in different locations within the images.

Understanding and implementing pooling layers effectively is fundamental to the successful application of CNNs in tasks like image classification, object detection, and segmentation. Integrating these layers thoughtfully in the network design enhances performance, reduces overfitting, and optimizes computational resources.

7.4 Building a Simple CNN

Constructing a Convolutional Neural Network (CNN) involves defining a model architecture, specifying the types and order of layers, and configuring training parameters. This section covers the process of building a basic CNN using PyTorch. We will use the MNIST dataset, a collection of handwritten digits, for illustration.

To begin, ensure that all necessary libraries are imported:

```
import torch
import torch.nn as nn
import torch.optim as optim
import torchvision
import torchvision.transforms as transforms
```

Next, define the transformations to be applied to the input data. These transformations include converting images to tensors and normalizing them.

```
transform = transforms.Compose([
    transforms.ToTensor(),
    transforms.Normalize((0.5,), (0.5,))
])
```

Load the MNIST dataset using torchvision. Create dataloaders to facilitate batching and shuffling of data for training and testing.

```
trainset = torchvision.datasets.MNIST(root='./data', train=True, download=True,
    transform=transform)
trainloader = torch.utils.data.DataLoader(trainset, batch_size=64, shuffle=True)

testset = torchvision.datasets.MNIST(root='./data', train=False, download=True,
    transform=transform)
testloader = torch.utils.data.DataLoader(testset, batch_size=64, shuffle=False)
```

Define a simple CNN architecture. The network includes convolutional layers, ReLU activation functions, pooling layers, and fully connected layers.

```
class SimpleCNN(nn.Module):
    def __init__(self):
        super(SimpleCNN, self).__init__()
        self.conv1 = nn.Conv2d(in_channels=1, out_channels=32, kernel_size=5)
        self.pool = nn.MaxPool2d(kernel_size=2, stride=2)
        self.conv2 = nn.Conv2d(in_channels=32, out_channels=64, kernel_size=5)
```

```
        self.fc1 = nn.Linear(in_features=64 * 4 * 4, out_features=512)
        self.fc2 = nn.Linear(in_features=512, out_features=10)

    def forward(self, x):
        x = self.pool(F.relu(self.conv1(x)))
        x = self.pool(F.relu(self.conv2(x)))
        x = torch.flatten(x, 1)
        x = F.relu(self.fc1(x))
        x = self.fc2(x)
        return x
```

Instantiate the CNN model and define the loss function and optimizer. The CrossEntropyLoss is commonly used for classification tasks, and the Adam optimizer is effective for many deep learning models.

```
model = SimpleCNN()
criterion = nn.CrossEntropyLoss()
optimizer = optim.Adam(model.parameters(), lr=0.001)
```

Train the CNN model. Iterate through the dataset multiple times (epochs), computing the loss and adjusting weights using backpropagation.

```
num_epochs = 10

for epoch in range(num_epochs):
    running_loss = 0.0
    for i, data in enumerate(trainloader, 0):
        inputs, labels = data

        optimizer.zero_grad()

        outputs = model(inputs)
        loss = criterion(outputs, labels)
        loss.backward()
        optimizer.step()

        running_loss += loss.item()
        if i % 100 == 99: % Print every 100 mini-batches
            print(f'[Epoch {epoch + 1}, Batch {i + 1}] loss: {running_loss / 100:.3f}')
            running_loss = 0.0
print('Finished Training')
```

Evaluate the model on the test dataset to assess its performance. Calculate the accuracy by comparing the predicted and actual labels.

```
correct = 0
total = 0
with torch.no_grad():
    for data in testloader:
        images, labels = data
        outputs = model(images)
        _, predicted = torch.max(outputs.data, 1)
        total += labels.size(0)
        correct += (predicted == labels).sum().item()

print(f'Accuracy of the network on the 10000 test images: {100 * correct / total:.2f}%')
```

A simple CNN has been successfully built, trained, and evaluated using PyTorch. The steps outlined provide a foundation for understanding and implementing CNNs, which will enable further exploration of more advanced architectures and techniques.

7.5 Advanced CNN Architectures

The evolution and success of Convolutional Neural Networks (CNNs) have led to the development of various advanced architectures, each designed to address specific challenges or optimize certain aspects of traditional CNN models. In this section, we will explore some of the most prominent advanced CNN architectures, including VGGNet, ResNet, Inception, and DenseNet. Understanding these architectures is crucial for leveraging the full potential of CNNs in complex tasks.

VGGNet: The VGGNet, proposed by Simonyan and Zisserman, made significant strides by demonstrating that the depth of the network is a critical component for achieving higher performance. The simplicity and consistency in its architecture make VGGNet an excellent case study for understanding deep networks. The key idea is to use small receptive fields (3x3 convolutional filters) throughout the network, with the number of filters doubling after each max-pooling layer. A simple implementation of VGGNet in PyTorch may look like this:

```
import torch.nn as nn

class VGGNet(nn.Module):
    def __init__(self):
        super(VGGNet, self).__init__()
        self.features = nn.Sequential(
            nn.Conv2d(3, 64, kernel_size=3, padding=1),
            nn.ReLU(inplace=True),
            nn.Conv2d(64, 64, kernel_size=3, padding=1),
            nn.ReLU(inplace=True),
            nn.MaxPool2d(kernel_size=2, stride=2),

            nn.Conv2d(64, 128, kernel_size=3, padding=1),
            nn.ReLU(inplace=True),
            nn.Conv2d(128, 128, kernel_size=3, padding=1),
            nn.ReLU(inplace=True),
            nn.MaxPool2d(kernel_size=2, stride=2),

            nn.Conv2d(128, 256, kernel_size=3, padding=1),
            nn.ReLU(inplace=True),
            nn.Conv2d(256, 256, kernel_size=3, padding=1),
            nn.ReLU(inplace=True),
            nn.MaxPool2d(kernel_size=2, stride=2),

            nn.Conv2d(256, 512, kernel_size=3, padding=1),
            nn.ReLU(inplace=True),
```

```
            nn.Conv2d(512, 512, kernel_size=3, padding=1),
            nn.ReLU(inplace=True),
            nn.MaxPool2d(kernel_size=2, stride=2),

            nn.Conv2d(512, 512, kernel_size=3, padding=1),
            nn.ReLU(inplace=True),
            nn.Conv2d(512, 512, kernel_size=3, padding=1),
            nn.ReLU(inplace=True),
            nn.MaxPool2d(kernel_size=2, stride=2),
        )
        self.classifier = nn.Sequential(
            nn.Linear(512 * 7 * 7, 4096),
            nn.ReLU(inplace=True),
            nn.Dropout(),
            nn.Linear(4096, 4096),
            nn.ReLU(inplace=True),
            nn.Dropout(),
            nn.Linear(4096, 1000),
        )

    def forward(self, x):
        x = self.features(x)
        x = x.view(x.size(0), -1)
        x = self.classifier(x)
        return x

model = VGGNet()
```

ResNet: Residual Networks (ResNet), introduced by He et al., propose the concept of residual learning to solve the problem of vanishing gradients in very deep networks. It uses shortcut connections to allow gradients to flow through the network directly. Such connections facilitate easier training of deeper networks. The building block of ResNet is the residual block which can be implemented as follows:

```
class ResidualBlock(nn.Module):
    def __init__(self, in_channels, out_channels, stride=1):
        super(ResidualBlock, self).__init__()
        self.conv1 = nn.Conv2d(in_channels, out_channels, kernel_size=3, stride=
            stride, padding=1)
        self.bn1 = nn.BatchNorm2d(out_channels)
        self.relu = nn.ReLU(inplace=True)
        self.conv2 = nn.Conv2d(out_channels, out_channels, kernel_size=3, stride=1,
            padding=1)
        self.bn2 = nn.BatchNorm2d(out_channels)

        self.shortcut = nn.Sequential()
        if stride != 1 or in_channels != out_channels:
            self.shortcut = nn.Sequential(
                nn.Conv2d(in_channels, out_channels, kernel_size=1, stride=stride),
                nn.BatchNorm2d(out_channels)
            )

    def forward(self, x):
        out = self.relu(self.bn1(self.conv1(x)))
        out = self.bn2(self.conv2(out))
        out += self.shortcut(x)
        out = self.relu(out)
        return out
```

Inception: The Inception architecture, also known as GoogLeNet, was introduced by Szegedy et al. It achieves computational efficiency by using parallel convolutional blocks with connections to optimize information processing at different scales. The central idea behind an Inception module is to simultaneously apply convolutions of different sizes to the input, concatenating their outputs. Here is a PyTorch implementation of an Inception module:

```
class InceptionModule(nn.Module):
    def __init__(self, in_channels, out_1x1, out_3x3_reduce, out_3x3,
        out_5x5_reduce, out_5x5, out_pool_proj):
        super(InceptionModule, self).__init__()
        self.branch1 = nn.Conv2d(in_channels, out_1x1, kernel_size=1)

        self.branch2 = nn.Sequential(
            nn.Conv2d(in_channels, out_3x3_reduce, kernel_size=1),
            nn.Conv2d(out_3x3_reduce, out_3x3, kernel_size=3, padding=1)
        )

        self.branch3 = nn.Sequential(
            nn.Conv2d(in_channels, out_5x5_reduce, kernel_size=1),
            nn.Conv2d(out_5x5_reduce, out_5x5, kernel_size=5, padding=2)
        )

        self.branch4 = nn.Sequential(
            nn.MaxPool2d(kernel_size=3, stride=1, padding=1),
            nn.Conv2d(in_channels, out_pool_proj, kernel_size=1)
        )

    def forward(self, x):
        branch1 = self.branch1(x)
        branch2 = self.branch2(x)
        branch3 = self.branch3(x)
        branch4 = self.branch4(x)
        outputs = [branch1, branch2, branch3, branch4]
        return torch.cat(outputs, dim=1)
```

DenseNet: DenseNet, introduced by Huang et al., connects each layer to every other layer in a feed-forward fashion. In DenseNet, each layer receives the feature maps of all preceding layers as inputs. This connectivity pattern results in strong gradient flow and encourages feature reuse, improving efficiency. A simple DenseNet block can be implemented as follows:

```
class DenseBlock(nn.Module):
    def __init__(self, in_channels, growth_rate, n_layers):
        super(DenseBlock, self).__init__()
        self.layers = nn.ModuleList()
        for i in range(n_layers):
            self.layers.append(
                nn.Sequential(
                    nn.BatchNorm2d(in_channels + i * growth_rate),
                    nn.ReLU(inplace=True),
                    nn.Conv2d(in_channels + i * growth_rate, growth_rate, kernel_size
                        =3, padding=1)
                )
```

```
    )

    def forward(self, x):
        features = [x]
        for layer in self.layers:
            new_features = layer(torch.cat(features, dim=1))
            features.append(new_features)
        return torch.cat(features, dim=1)
```

Utilizing these advanced architectures can offer substantial performance improvements for a variety of complex tasks in computer vision and beyond. By breaking down these networks and understanding their core principles, researchers and practitioners can adapt these architectures to their specific needs, potentially paving the way for novel innovations.

7.6 Transfer Learning with CNNs

Transfer learning is a pivotal technique in modern deep learning practice, wherein a pre-trained model on a large dataset is fine-tuned on a smaller, task-specific dataset. This method is particularly valuable when the data for the specific task is limited. CNNs are especially well-suited for transfer learning due to their hierarchical feature extraction capabilities.

The core principle of transfer learning involves leveraging the pre-trained CNN's learned weights. These weights, acquired from extensive training on a vast dataset such as ImageNet, encapsulate robust and generalizable features such as edges, textures, and patterns. Through transfer learning, we adapt these learned feature representations to new, related tasks.

1. Using Pre-trained Models

To utilize transfer learning, one typically employs a pre-trained CNN as a feature extractor. This involves taking a network like VGG, ResNet, or Inception, which has already been trained on ImageNet, and repurposing the feature extraction layers. The fully connected layers at the end of the network are often replaced with new layers that are suitable for the new task.

```
import torch
import torch.nn as nn
import torchvision.models as models

# Load a pre-trained ResNet-50 model
model = models.resnet50(pretrained=True)
```

```
# Freeze all layers
for param in model.parameters():
    param.requires_grad = False

# Replace the last fully connected layer
num_ftrs = model.fc.in_features
model.fc = nn.Linear(num_ftrs, num_classes) # num_classes is the number of target
     classes

# Optionally, unfreeze some layers and fine-tune
for param in model.layer4.parameters():
    param.requires_grad = True

# Print the modified model architecture
print(model)
```

2. Fine-Tuning

Fine-tuning is the process of training the pre-trained network on the new dataset. This involves selectively unfreezing some layers of the pre-trained model and jointly training the newly added layers and the unfrozen pre-trained layers. This allows the model to learn task-specific features while still benefiting from the pre-trained knowledge.

Critical decisions include determining which layers to unfreeze and setting an appropriate learning rate. Often, lower learning rates are used for the pre-trained layers compared to the new fully connected layers to prevent the destruction of the informative weights learned during the initial large-scale training.

```
import torch.optim as optim

# Define the loss function and optimizer
criterion = nn.CrossEntropyLoss()
optimizer = optim.SGD(model.parameters(), lr=0.001, momentum=0.9)

# Alternatively, use different learning rates for different layers
layer4_params = list(model.layer4.parameters())
fc_params = list(model.fc.parameters())
optimizer = optim.SGD([
    {'params': model.parameters(), 'lr': 0.0001},
    {'params': fc_params, 'lr': 0.01}
], momentum=0.9)

# Training loop
for epoch in range(num_epochs):
    model.train()
    running_loss = 0.0

    for inputs, labels in dataloader:
        optimizer.zero_grad()
        outputs = model(inputs)
        loss = criterion(outputs, labels)
        loss.backward()
        optimizer.step()
```

```
        running_loss += loss.item()

    print(f'Epoch [{epoch + 1}/{num_epochs}], Loss: {running_loss:.4f}')
```

3. Practical Considerations

When applying transfer learning with CNNs, it is important to consider the following factors:

- *Dataset Size and Similarity*: Transfer learning is most effective when the new dataset is substantially smaller than the original dataset and when the tasks are related. For instance, transferring weights from an ImageNet-trained model to a medical imaging task can yield significant performance improvements.

- *Overfitting*: Even with transfer learning, there is a risk of overfitting when dealing with small datasets. Techniques such as data augmentation, dropout, and careful validation can help mitigate this.

- *Domain Adaptation*: In cases where the distributions of the source and target datasets are significantly different, domain adaptation techniques may be required to align the feature distributions.

- *Performance Evaluation*: Always partition the dataset into training and validation sets to evaluate the performance of the fine-tuned model effectively. Techniques such as cross-validation can provide a more comprehensive evaluation.

```
Training Log Example:
Epoch [1/10], Loss: 1.2345
Epoch [2/10], Loss: 0.9876
...
Epoch [10/10], Loss: 0.4567
```

Transfer learning with CNNs not only helps in achieving remarkable performance on specific tasks with limited data but also accelerates the training process and reduces the computational cost. The ability to repurpose powerful pre-trained networks for diverse applications further underscores the flexibility and efficacy of CNNs in tackling a broad spectrum of machine learning challenges.

7.7 Fine-Tuning CNNs

Fine-tuning is a critical process for adapting pre-trained Convolutional Neural Networks (CNNs) to new tasks and datasets. This technique leverages the robustness of pre-trained models, thus circumventing the need to train a network from scratch, which can be computationally intensive and time-consuming. Fine-tuning involves transferring the learned weights of a pre-existing model and adjusting them slightly—with the final few layers often trained more rigorously—so that the model becomes adept at a new, specific task.

To elucidate the process of fine-tuning a CNN, consider the following detailed steps:

- **Select a Pre-Trained Model:** Popular models such as VGG16, ResNet, or Inception can be employed. These models, pre-trained on large datasets like ImageNet, provide a strong foundation due to their generalization capabilities.
- **Freeze Initial Layers:** Early layers in a CNN learn generic features such as edges, textures, and patterns that are beneficial across various tasks. It is common to freeze these layers to prevent losing these valuable representations.
- **Replace Final Layers:** The final classification layers are typically specific to the task and dataset on which the model was originally trained. Replace these with new layers suitable for the new classification problem.
- **Train the New Layers:** Perform initial training on the newly added layers to ensure they learn to produce output compatible with the new task. This phase requires setting a higher learning rate relative to the rest of the network.
- **Fine-Tune Entire Network:** Optionally, fine-tune the whole network including the previously frozen layers but with a smaller learning rate to prevent drastic updates that might lead to losing generic features.

To demonstrate the fine-tuning process, consider the practical example involving the PyTorch framework. Below is an illustrative implementation:

```
import torch
import torchvision.models as models
import torch.nn as nn
import torch.optim as optim
from torchvision import datasets, transforms

# Load a pre-trained VGG16 model
model = models.vgg16(pretrained=True)

# Freeze the initial layers
for param in model.features.parameters():
    param.requires_grad = False

# Replace the final classifier layers
model.classifier[6] = nn.Linear(4096, NUM_CLASSES)

# Define loss function and optimizer
criterion = nn.CrossEntropyLoss()
optimizer = optim.SGD(model.classifier.parameters(), lr=0.001, momentum=0.9)

# Data loading and transformation
transform = transforms.Compose([
    transforms.Resize(224),
    transforms.ToTensor(),
    transforms.Normalize(mean=[0.485, 0.456, 0.406], std=[0.229, 0.224, 0.225])
])

train_data = datasets.ImageFolder(train_dir, transform=transform)
train_loader = torch.utils.data.DataLoader(train_data, batch_size=32, shuffle=True)

# Training the model
model.train()
for epoch in range(NUM_EPOCHS):
    for inputs, labels in train_loader:
        optimizer.zero_grad()
        outputs = model(inputs)
        loss = criterion(outputs, labels)
        loss.backward()
        optimizer.step()

print("Training complete.")
```

Assuming the fine-tuning requires adapting to a new dataset, it begins with importing a pre-trained VGG16 model. The feature extraction layers are frozen, ensuring that the essential learned features remain intact. The classifier section of the model, which is highly specific to the pre-trained task, is replaced with a new classification layer compatible with the current task's number of classes.

After preparing the model, the loss function and optimizer are defined; these are crucial for guiding and refining the model during training. The dataset transformation steps normalize and resize images as per the requirements of the pre-trained model, while ensuring the uniformity and quality of inputs.

The training loop proceeds with typical steps of zeroing gradients, making predictions, computing the loss, backpropagating errors, and optimizing the classifier layer's weights. This results in the new layers learning task-specific features, completing the initial phase of the fine-tuning.

Next, to refine the entire model, the learning rate must be adjusted for previously frozen layers. Training all layers with a low learning rate ensures the gradual adaptation of generic feature representations to the specifics of the new task. An example of such fine-tuning follows:

```
# Unfreeze all layers
for param in model.parameters():
    param.requires_grad = True

# Re-define optimizer to update all parameters
optimizer = optim.SGD(model.parameters(), lr=0.0001, momentum=0.9)

# Fine-tune entire network
model.train()
for epoch in range(FINE_TUNE_EPOCHS):
    for inputs, labels in train_loader:
        optimizer.zero_grad()
        outputs = model(inputs)
        loss = criterion(outputs, labels)
        loss.backward()
        optimizer.step()

print("Fine-tuning complete.")
```

This code adjusts all layers to be trainable by setting requires_grad to True. The optimizer is then redefined to include all model parameters with a reduced learning rate to ensure fine-tuning is stable and does not distort pre-learned features excessively. The network undergoes another training phase, this time adjusting previously frozen layers, thus achieving better task-specific performance.

By following these detailed steps, fine-tuning a CNN model enables leveraging the powerful, generalized features learned from large datasets while adapting to the specifics of a new task, optimizing performance with relatively minimal computational resources and data requirements.

7.8 Handling Overfitting in CNNs

Handling overfitting in Convolutional Neural Networks (CNNs) is critical for developing models that generalize well to unseen data. Overfitting occurs when a model learns the noise in the training data rather than the actual underlying patterns. This results in high performance on training data but poor performance on validation or test data. Several strategies can be employed to mitigate overfitting in CNNs, including data augmentation, dropout, early stopping, regularization techniques, and leveraging more data.

- **Data Augmentation**

Data augmentation is a powerful technique to artificially increase the size of the training dataset by applying random transformations to the input images. These transformations can include rotations, translations, scaling, flipping, cropping, and color adjustments. Data augmentation helps in making the model invariant to small changes in the input data and improves its generalization ability.

```
from torchvision import transforms

# Define a set of transformations for data augmentation
data_transforms = transforms.Compose([
    transforms.RandomHorizontalFlip(),
    transforms.RandomRotation(10),
    transforms.RandomResizedCrop(224),
    transforms.ColorJitter(brightness=0.2, contrast=0.2, saturation=0.2, hue=0.2),
    transforms.ToTensor(),
])

# Apply transformations to the dataset
augmented_dataset = datasets.ImageFolder(data_dir, transform=data_transforms)
```

- **Dropout**

Dropout is a regularization technique where randomly selected neurons are ignored during the training process. This prevents the network from becoming too dependent on any specific neurons and encourages it to learn more robust features. Dropout can be implemented by specifying a fraction of neurons to drop during each iteration.

```
import torch.nn as nn

class CNNWithDropout(nn.Module):
    def __init__(self):
        super(CNNWithDropout, self).__init__()
        self.conv1 = nn.Conv2d(in_channels=3, out_channels=32, kernel_size=3,
             padding=1)
        self.dropout1 = nn.Dropout(p=0.25)
        self.fc1 = nn.Linear(in_features=32*32*32, out_features=128)
        self.dropout2 = nn.Dropout(p=0.5)
        self.fc2 = nn.Linear(in_features=128, out_features=10)

    def forward(self, x):
        x = self.conv1(x)
        x = nn.functional.relu(x)
```

```
        x = nn.functional.max_pool2d(x, 2)
        x = self.dropout1(x)
        x = x.view(-1, 32*32*32)
        x = self.fc1(x)
        x = nn.functional.relu(x)
        x = self.dropout2(x)
        x = self.fc2(x)
        return x

model = CNNWithDropout()
```

- **Early Stopping**

Early stopping is a method used to halt the training process before the network begins to overfit. By monitoring the validation loss, training can be stopped once the performance on the validation set deteriorates. This prevents the model from overfitting to the training data.

```
def train_model(model, dataloaders, criterion, optimizer, num_epochs=25, patience=5)
    :
    best_model_wts = copy.deepcopy(model.state_dict())
    best_loss = float('inf')
    epochs_no_improve = 0

    for epoch in range(num_epochs):
        for phase in ['train', 'val']:
            if phase == 'train':
                model.train()
            else:
                model.eval()

            running_loss = 0.0

            for inputs, labels in dataloaders[phase]:
                optimizer.zero_grad()

                with torch.set_grad_enabled(phase == 'train'):
                    outputs = model(inputs)
                    loss = criterion(outputs, labels)

                    if phase == 'train':
                        loss.backward()
                        optimizer.step()

                running_loss += loss.item() * inputs.size(0)

            epoch_loss = running_loss / len(dataloaders[phase].dataset)

            if phase == 'val':
                if epoch_loss < best_loss:
                    best_loss = epoch_loss
                    best_model_wts = copy.deepcopy(model.state_dict())
                    epochs_no_improve = 0
                else:
                    epochs_no_improve += 1

                if epochs_no_improve == patience:
                    model.load_state_dict(best_model_wts)
```

```
            return model

    model.load_state_dict(best_model_wts)
    return model
```

- **Regularization Techniques**

Regularization is any modification we make to a learning algorithm to reduce generalization error but not training error. Common regularization techniques include: L2 regularization, which penalizes large weights; L1 regularization, which encourages sparsity in the weights; and Batch Normalization, which normalizes the activations of each layer to stabilize the learning process.

```
class CNNWithRegularization(nn.Module):
    def __init__(self):
        super(CNNWithRegularization, self).__init__()
        self.conv1 = nn.Conv2d(in_channels=3, out_channels=32, kernel_size=3,
            padding=1)
        self.batch_norm1 = nn.BatchNorm2d(32)
        self.fc1 = nn.Linear(in_features=32*32*32, out_features=128)
        self.batch_norm2 = nn.BatchNorm1d(128)
        self.fc2 = nn.Linear(in_features=128, out_features=10)

    def forward(self, x):
        x = self.conv1(x)
        x = self.batch_norm1(x)
        x = nn.functional.relu(x)
        x = nn.functional.max_pool2d(x, 2)
        x = x.view(-1, 32*32*32)
        x = self.fc1(x)
        x = self.batch_norm2(x)
        x = nn.functional.relu(x)
        x = self.fc2(x)
        return x

model = CNNWithRegularization()
```

- **Leveraging More Data**

A simple yet effective method to combat overfitting is to increase the size of the training dataset. More data provides the model with more examples to learn from, thereby improving its ability to generalize. When collecting more data is not possible, synthetic data generation or data augmentation can be used.

Combining these techniques leads to robust models with minimized overfitting. Proper application and tuning of these methods are paramount in practice to achieve the right balance between bias and variance. Each problem domain might require experimenting with different strategies and adjustments.

7.9 Visualizing CNN Outputs

Visualizing the outputs of Convolutional Neural Networks (CNNs) is essential for understanding the network's internal mechanics and gaining insights into its decision-making process. By examining feature maps, activation layers, and filters, one can interpret the network's learning patterns, identify potential issues, and improve model performance.

To start, consider a trained CNN model. The visualization approach can be divided into investigating various elements of the model: feature maps derived from convolutional layers, filters learned during training, and the activations of neurons in different layers.

Visualizing Feature Maps:

Feature maps (or activation maps) are the outputs of convolutional layers after applying the convolution operation followed by the activation function. They provide a spatial representation of the presence of a particular feature detected by the filter. To visualize feature maps, one can pass an input image through the network and extract the outputs from specific layers.

The following Python code demonstrates how to visualize feature maps in a CNN using PyTorch:

```
import torch
import torch.nn as nn
import matplotlib.pyplot as plt

# Load a pre-trained CNN model
model = models.vgg16(pretrained=True)

# Define a hook function to capture the feature maps
def hook_fn(module, input, output):
    global feature_maps
    feature_maps = output.cpu().data.numpy()

# Register hook to the desired convolutional layer
layer = model.features[1] # e.g., the second convolutional layer
hook = layer.register_forward_hook(hook_fn)

# Load and preprocess an input image
input_image = Image.open('input_image.jpg')
preprocess = transforms.Compose([
    transforms.Resize((224, 224)),
    transforms.ToTensor(),
    transforms.Normalize(mean=[0.485, 0.456, 0.406], std=[0.229, 0.224, 0.225])
])
input_tensor = preprocess(input_image).unsqueeze(0)

# Forward pass through the model
model.eval()
with torch.no_grad():
    _ = model(input_tensor)
```

```
# Visualize the captured feature maps
fig, axs = plt.subplots(4, 4, figsize=(12, 12))
for i, ax in enumerate(axs.flat):
    if i < feature_maps.shape[1]:
        ax.imshow(feature_maps[0, i, :, :], cmap='viridis')
    ax.axis('off')
plt.show()

# Remove hook (important to avoid unnecessary memory consumption)
hook.remove()
```

In this code:

- A pre-trained VGG16 model is loaded.
- A hook function is defined and registered to a specified convolutional layer.
- An input image is preprocessed to match the model's input requirements.
- The image is passed through the network, and the feature maps are captured.
- The feature maps are visualized using Matplotlib.

Visualizing Filters:

Filters (or kernels) in a CNN are the learned parameters in convolutional layers that detect specific patterns such as edges, textures, or more complex structures. Visualizing these filters helps understand what the network has learned.

The following code snippet demonstrates how to visualize the filters of a convolutional layer:

```
import numpy as np

# Extract the filters from the first convolutional layer
filters = model.features[0].weight.data.cpu().numpy()

# Normalize filter values to 0-1 for visualization
min_val = np.min(filters)
max_val = np.max(filters)
filters = (filters - min_val) / (max_val - min_val)

# Plot the filters
fig, axs = plt.subplots(8, 8, figsize=(12, 12))
for i, ax in enumerate(axs.flat):
    if i < filters.shape[0]:
        ax.imshow(filters[i, 0, :, :], cmap='gray')
    ax.axis('off')
plt.show()
```

This code:

- Extracts the weights (filters) from the first convolutional layer of the model.
- Normalizes the filter values for better visualization.
- Plots the filters using Matplotlib.

Activating Maximizing Inputs:

Another approach to understand what a neuron is responsive to is to generate an input image that maximally activates a particular neuron. This is achieved by optimizing an input image to increase the activation of the neuron of interest. The following code snippet demonstrates this concept:

```
class CNNFeatureVisualizer:
    def __init__(self, model, layer):
        self.model = model
        self.layer = layer
        self.activations = None
        self.hook = layer.register_forward_hook(self.hook_fn)

    def hook_fn(self, module, input, output):
        self.activations = output

    def visualize(self, input_tensor, target_neuron, steps=100, lr=0.1):
        input_tensor.requires_grad = True
        optimizer = torch.optim.Adam([input_tensor], lr=lr)

        for _ in range(steps):
            optimizer.zero_grad()
            _ = self.model(input_tensor)
            loss = -self.activations[0, target_neuron].mean()
            loss.backward()
            optimizer.step()

        self.hook.remove()
        return input_tensor.detach().cpu().numpy()

# Initialize the visualizer for a specific layer and neuron
visualizer = CNNFeatureVisualizer(model, model.features[1])
input_tensor = torch.randn((1, 3, 224, 224), requires_grad=True)
optimized_input = visualizer.visualize(input_tensor, target_neuron=10)

# Plot the generated image
plt.imshow(optimized_input.squeeze().transpose(1, 2, 0))
plt.axis('off')
plt.show()
```

In this code:

- A CNNFeatureVisualizer class is defined to facilitate the generation of activation-maximizing inputs.

- A hook is registered to capture layer activations of interest.
- An input image tensor is initialized and optimized to maximally activate a specific neuron.
- The optimized input image is visualized.

Investigating feature maps, filters, and activation-maximizing inputs offers valuable insights into the inner workings of CNNs. These visualizations aid in debugging, improving model architecture, and comprehensively understanding the spatial hierarchies learned by the network.

7.10 Practical Applications of CNNs

Convolutional Neural Networks (CNNs) have revolutionized numerous fields due to their capacity to effectively process and interpret image data. While initially popularized for image classification, CNNs have now found utility in a wide range of practical applications. This section delves into several key areas where CNNs have made significant impacts.

Image Classification: One of the fundamental applications of CNNs is image classification. CNN architectures such as AlexNet, VGG, and ResNet have set benchmarks in various image classification tasks. The ability of CNNs to automatically learn hierarchical features from raw pixel data has empowered models to classify images with remarkable accuracy. ImageNet, a large visual database, has been instrumental in advancing image classification research and applications.

Object Detection and Localization: Beyond image classification, CNNs have been pivotal in object detection and localization tasks. Models such as Faster R-CNN, YOLO (You Only Look Once), and SSD (Single Shot Multibox Detector) extend CNNs by adding additional network layers and mechanisms for bounding box prediction. Object detection enables systems to not only recognize objects within an image but also determine their precise locations, which is crucial for applications like automated surveillance, autonomous vehicles, and robotics.

Semantic Segmentation: In semantic segmentation, the goal is to classify each pixel of an image into a category. Techniques such as Fully Convolutional Networks (FCNs) and U-Net architectures use CNNs to achieve pixel-wise classification, aiding in applications where understanding the context and precise edges of objects are essential.

Autonomous driving is one such application where semantic segmentation is used to differentiate between roads, pedestrians, vehicles, and obstacles.

Instance Segmentation: Instance segmentation is an advancement over semantic segmentation, where not only are the pixels labeled by category, but distinct objects of the same category are also individually recognized. Mask R-CNN is a prominent architecture for instance segmentation that builds upon Faster R-CNN to provide pixel-level object masks. This application is instrumental in scenarios requiring detailed scene understanding, such as medical image analysis and industrial inspection.

Medical Imaging: CNNs have proven to be highly effective in the medical domain, aiding in tasks such as disease diagnosis, treatment planning, and surgical assistance. For instance, CNNs have been used to detect anomalies in radiology images, segment tumors in MRI scans, and automate the analysis of histopathology slides. The combination of CNNs with transfer learning allows for the adaptation of pre-trained models to medical datasets, overcoming the challenge of limited data availability in this domain.

Facial Recognition: CNNs play a critical role in facial recognition systems, which are widely used for security and authentication purposes. Networks such as FaceNet and VGGFace leverage the feature extraction capabilities of CNNs to encode facial images into feature vectors. These feature vectors can then be used to match and recognize individuals with high accuracy, facilitating applications in law enforcement, secure access control, and social media tagging.

Art and Creativity: CNNs are also pioneering new forms of artistic expression. Style transfer is a technique where a CNN can extract the style of one image and apply it to another, effectively creating a new image that blends the content of the second image with the style of the first. The application of CNNs in generating art and enhancing creativity is exemplified by projects such as DeepArt and Google's DeepDream, which generate novel and aesthetically intriguing images.

Super-Resolution: Image super-resolution involves enhancing the resolution of an image, adding finer details and improving clarity. CNNs have been employed in super-resolution tasks through architectures like SRCNN (Super-Resolution Convolutional Neural Network) and EDSR (Enhanced Deep Super-Resolution). Such applications are valuable in fields like satellite imaging, where high-resolution images are necessary for better analysis and interpretation.

Video Analysis: The capabilities of CNNs extend to video analysis, where frames from a video sequence can be processed to detect and classify activities, recognize patterns, and even predict future actions. Techniques involving 3D convolutions (applying convolutions over spatial and temporal domains) facilitate the analysis of complex movements and interactions within videos. Video surveillance, sports analytics, and content recommendation are some areas benefiting from CNN-based video analysis.

Natural Language Processing with CNNs: While traditionally less common than Recurrent Neural Networks (RNNs) and Transformers, CNNs have been applied to Natural Language Processing (NLP) tasks. For instance, CNNs can be used for text classification, sentiment analysis, and language modeling by treating text as a sequence of characters or words and applying convolutions to detect patterns. Applications in spam detection, opinion mining, and document classification leverage the feature extraction prowess of CNNs.

Environmental and Agricultural Monitoring: CNNs support environmental and agricultural sectors by providing advanced image processing for remote sensing, crop monitoring, and disaster management. High-resolution satellite and drone imagery analyzed with CNNs enables the detection of deforestation, crop health assessment, and monitoring of natural disasters. These applications are vital for sustainable resource management and resilience planning.

The diverse and expanding applications of CNNs highlight their adaptability and effectiveness in solving real-world problems. The integration of CNNs into various domains continues to grow, driven by ongoing research and the development of more sophisticated models.

Chapter 8

Recurrent Neural Networks (RNNs) and Natural Language Processing

This chapter explores Recurrent Neural Networks (RNNs) and their application in Natural Language Processing (NLP). It covers the basics of sequential data and the construction of simple RNNs, then delves into advanced RNN variants such as Long Short-Term Memory Networks (LSTMs) and Gated Recurrent Units (GRUs). The chapter also introduces key NLP concepts, including text preprocessing, word embeddings, and sequence-to-sequence models with attention mechanisms, highlighting practical applications of RNNs in NLP tasks.

8.1 Introduction to Recurrent Neural Networks

Recurrent Neural Networks (RNNs) are a class of artificial neural networks designed for processing sequential data, making them particularly suited for tasks involving time series, natural language, and other ordered data. Unlike feedforward neural networks, RNNs have connections that form directed cycles, enabling the retention of information across different time steps. This fundamental property allows RNNs to exhibit temporal dynamic behavior, making them capable of capturing dependencies and patterns in sequential data.

The core idea behind RNNs is the concept of hidden states. At each time step t, the network receives an input x_t from the sequence. The hidden state h_t is then computed based on the current input and the previous hidden state h_{t-1}. Mathematically, this is expressed as:

$$h_t = f(W_{ih}x_t + W_{hh}h_{t-1} + b_h)$$

where W_{ih} and W_{hh} are weight matrices, b_h is the bias vector, and f is an activation function (typically a non-linear function such as tanh or ReLU). The hidden state h_t can then be used to produce an output y_t:

$$y_t = g(W_{ho}h_t + b_o)$$

where W_{ho} is a weight matrix, b_o is a bias vector, and g is an activation function appropriate for the output.

The recursive nature of RNNs allows them to maintain a form of memory, as the hidden state h_t at a given time step t encodes information from all previous time steps. However, this also introduces challenges, such as the vanishing and exploding gradient problems during training with gradient-based methods like Backpropagation Through Time (BPTT).

To implement a simple RNN in PyTorch, we utilize the nn.RNN module from the torch.nn library. Below is an example of how to construct and use a basic RNN:

```
import torch
import torch.nn as nn

# Define the RNN model
class SimpleRNN(nn.Module):
    def __init__(self, input_size, hidden_size, output_size):
        super(SimpleRNN, self).__init__()
        self.hidden_size = hidden_size
        self.rnn = nn.RNN(input_size, hidden_size, batch_first=True)
        self.fc = nn.Linear(hidden_size, output_size)

    def forward(self, x):
        h0 = torch.zeros(1, x.size(0), self.hidden_size).to(x.device)
        out, _ = self.rnn(x, h0)
        out = self.fc(out[:, -1, :])
        return out

# Initialize the model, loss function, and optimizer
```

```
input_size = 10
hidden_size = 20
output_size = 1
model = SimpleRNN(input_size, hidden_size, output_size)

criterion = nn.MSELoss()
optimizer = torch.optim.Adam(model.parameters(), lr=0.01)

# Dummy data for demonstration
inputs = torch.randn(5, 3, input_size) # (batch_size, sequence_length, input_size)
targets = torch.randn(5, output_size)

# Forward pass
outputs = model(inputs)
loss = criterion(outputs, targets)

# Backward pass and optimization
optimizer.zero_grad()
loss.backward()
optimizer.step()
```

In this example, we define a simple RNN with an input size of 10, hidden size of 20, and output size of 1. The forward method initializes the hidden state h_0 and passes the input sequence through the RNN layer. The final output is produced by a fully connected layer that maps the hidden state output to the desired output dimension.

The training process involves performing a forward pass to compute the output and loss, followed by a backward pass to update the model parameters using the optimizer.

RNNs can be unrolled over multiple time steps, and the hidden state is passed from one time step to the next. This chain-like architecture is both the strength and weakness of RNNs. It allows for the learning of temporal dependencies, but as the sequences become longer, the aforementioned vanishing and exploding gradient problems can severely hinder the learning process.

There are several improvements and variants to the basic RNN architecture designed to address these issues, including Long Short-Term Memory networks (LSTMs) and Gated Recurrent Units (GRUs), which will be explored in subsequent sections.

8.2 Understanding Sequential Data

Sequential data encompasses any data that maintains an inherent order and contains dependencies between its elements. Such data is prevalent in various fields; for example, text, audio, time-series data, and biological sequences all constitute forms of sequential data. Understanding the characteristics and complexities of sequential data is fundamental to effectively employing Recurrent Neural Networks (RNNs) and their advanced variants like Long Short-Term Memory Networks (LSTMs) and Gated Recurrent Units (GRUs).

Characteristics of Sequential Data

- *Temporal Dependencies*: Elements in sequential data are often dependent on previous elements. For instance, in a sentence, the meaning of a word may depend on prior words.
- *Variable Length*: Unlike traditional fixed-size data used in feedforward neural networks, sequential data may vary in length. Sentences can consist of a different number of words, and time-series can have varying durations.
- *Order Significance*: The order of data points is crucial. Shuffling the order of sequential data typically alters its meaning or utility, which is a critical consideration during data processing and model training.

Types of Sequential Data

- *Text Data*: Natural Language Processing (NLP) extensively deals with text data, where sequences of characters or words need to be modeled effectively. Preprocessing text data often involves tokenization, removing stop words, and converting text to lower case to handle case sensitivity issues.
- *Time-Series Data*: This type of data is indexed over some time dimension. Examples include stock prices, sensor readings, and weather data, where the sequence of data points is crucial for forecasting and anomaly detection tasks.
- *Audio Data*: Audio signals are another form of sequential data where amplitude variations represent different sound frequencies over time. Speech recognition and music synthesis are common applications involving audio sequences.
- *Biological Sequences*: Examples include DNA and RNA sequences where understanding the ordering of nucleotides is essential for tasks such as gene prediction and sequence alignment.

Understanding and preparing sequential data plays a critical role in achieving good performance with RNNs and their variants. The preprocessing steps might vary based on the type and characteristics of the data, but some common steps can be outlined.

Common Preprocessing Steps for Sequential Data

- *Normalization*: Normalizing the data is crucial, especially for time-series and audio data, to ensure that each feature contributes equally to the learning process.

```
# Python example of normalizing a time-series dataset
import numpy as np

def normalize(data):
    mean = np.mean(data, axis=0)
    std = np.std(data, axis=0)
    return (data - mean) / std
```

- *Tokenization*: For text data, tokenization involves splitting text into smaller units, like words or subwords, which can then be processed. Tools like NLTK or SpaCy are often used for this purpose.

```
# Python example of tokenizing text data using NLTK
import nltk
from nltk.tokenize import word_tokenize

text = "Recurrent neural networks are powerful."
tokens = word_tokenize(text)
print(tokens)
```

```
['Recurrent', 'neural', 'networks', 'are', 'powerful', '.']
```

- *Padding and Truncation*: Since RNNs require input sequences of the same length, sequences shorter than a defined length are often padded, and sequences longer than this length are truncated. Padding can be achieved using special tokens.

```
# Python example of padding sequences
from tensorflow.keras.preprocessing.sequence import pad_sequences

sequences = [[1, 2, 3], [4, 5], [6, 7, 8, 9]]
padded_sequences = pad_sequences(sequences, maxlen=5)
print(padded_sequences)
```

```
[[0 0 1 2 3]
 [0 0 0 4 5]
 [0 6 7 8 9]]
```

- *Feature Extraction*: Converting raw data to numerical features. For text, this might include techniques like TF-IDF, word embeddings (e.g., Word2Vec, GloVe), or contextual embeddings (e.g., BERT).

Understanding and implementing these preprocessing steps ensures that sequential data is in a form suitable for the RNNs to model temporal dependencies efficiently, ultimately leading to better performance on tasks such as text classification, speech recognition, and time-series forecasting. Recognizing the significance and methodologies of handling sequential data prepares the ground for delving into the construction and utilization of RNNs and advanced architectures discussed in the subsequent sections of this chapter.

8.3 Building a Simple RNN

A Recurrent Neural Network (RNN) is a class of neural network particularly suited for sequential data. The purpose of an RNN is to leverage the temporal dynamics inherent in sequences by forming connections between nodes in a temporal sequence. In contrast to feedforward neural networks, which assume that all inputs are independent of each other, RNNs provide a mechanism wherein neurons maintain a state, effectively retaining information from previous inputs.

The architecture of a simple RNN can be illustrated using the following equations:

$$h_t = \tanh(W_{xh}x_t + W_{hh}h_{t-1} + b_h)$$
$$y_t = W_{hy}h_t + b_y$$

Here:

- h_t represents the hidden state at time step t.
- x_t is the input at time step t.
- W_{xh}, W_{hh}, and W_{hy} are the weight matrices.
- b_h and b_y are the bias terms.
- y_t represents the output at time step t.
- tanh is the hyperbolic tangent activation function, introducing non-linearity.

To practically build and deploy a simple RNN, we will utilize PyTorch due to its flexibility and powerful computational graph support. Here is an example implementing a basic RNN:

```
import torch
import torch.nn as nn

# Define the RNN class
class SimpleRNN(nn.Module):
    def __init__(self, input_size, hidden_size, output_size):
        super(SimpleRNN, self).__init__()
        self.hidden_size = hidden_size

        self.i2h = nn.Linear(input_size + hidden_size, hidden_size)
        self.i2o = nn.Linear(hidden_size, output_size)
        self.softmax = nn.LogSoftmax(dim=1)

    def forward(self, input, hidden):
        combined = torch.cat((input, hidden), 1)
        hidden = self.i2h(combined)
        output = self.i2o(hidden)
        output = self.softmax(output)
        return output, hidden

    def init_hidden(self):
        return torch.zeros(1, self.hidden_size)

# Parameters
input_size = 10
hidden_size = 20
output_size = 10

# Instantiate the model, criterion and optimizer
model = SimpleRNN(input_size, hidden_size, output_size)
criterion = nn.NLLLoss()
optimizer = torch.optim.SGD(model.parameters(), lr=0.1)

# Example input (sequence length x batch size x input size)
input_sequence = torch.randn(5, 1, input_size)
hidden = model.init_hidden()

for i in range(input_sequence.size(0)):
    output, hidden = model(input_sequence[i], hidden)
```

The code above demonstrates the foundational structure of a simple RNN in PyTorch:

- The SimpleRNN class inherits from nn.Module, encapsulating the neural network.
- Within the constructor (init), we define the size of input, hidden, and output layers, followed by the construction of linear layers to map the input to the hidden layer (self.i2h) and the hidden state to the output layer (self.i2o).
- The forward method implements the forward pass. The input for each time step concatenates with the previous hidden state and passes through the linear layer, applying the softmax activation at the output layer.

- The init_hidden method initializes the hidden state to zeros, crucial for the first step of the sequence.

To train this RNN, we process data sequentially to update the model parameters. Here is a more comprehensive training loop:

```
def train(rnn, criterion, optimizer, input_sequence, target_sequence, n_iters=1000):
    for iter in range(n_iters):
        hidden = rnn.init_hidden()
        rnn.zero_grad()
        loss = 0

        for i in range(input_sequence.size(0)):
            output, hidden = rnn(input_sequence[i], hidden)
            loss += criterion(output, target_sequence[i].view(1))

        loss.backward()
        optimizer.step()

        if iter % 100 == 0:
            print(f"Iteration {iter} Loss {loss.item()}")

# Example target sequence
target_sequence = torch.randint(0, output_size, (5,))

# Train the RNN
train(model, criterion, optimizer, input_sequence, target_sequence)
```

The training loop iterates through the sequences, computing output and hidden states for each step. We zero out gradients at each iteration to prevent accumulation, calculate the loss, backpropagate the gradients, and update the parameters with the optimizer. Regular printing of the loss helps monitor training convergence.

This example encapsulates the essentials of building and training a simple RNN with PyTorch, laying the groundwork for subsequent models handling more complex sequential data tasks.

8.4 Long Short-Term Memory Networks (LSTMs)

Long Short-Term Memory networks (LSTMs) are a special kind of Recurrent Neural Networks (RNNs) designed to better handle the long-term dependencies in data sequences. Standard RNNs struggle with learning dependencies over longer sequences due to the problem of vanishing and exploding gradients. To address these issues, LSTMs introduce a unique architecture that enables them to maintain information over extended periods effectively.

An LSTM unit comprises several components, notably the cell state, hidden state, and three types of gates: the input gate, forget gate, and output gate. These components work together to regulate the flow of information within the network.

- **Cell State:** The cell state, denoted by $\mathbf{C}$, represents the memory of the network. It carries information across different time steps while undergoing minimal transformations, thereby helping maintain long-term dependencies.

- **Hidden State:** The hidden state, denoted by $\mathbf{h}$, represents the working memory of the LSTM unit at a given time t. It is used in conjunction with the cell state and contributes to the network's output at each time step.

- **Input Gate:** The input gate, denoted by $\mathbf{i}_t$, determines the extent to which new information should be added to the cell state at the current time step. It is calculated as follows:

  $$\mathbf{i}_t = \sigma(\mathbf{W}_i \cdot [\mathbf{h}_{t-1}, \mathbf{x}_t] + \mathbf{b}_i),$$

  where σ represents the sigmoid function, $\mathbf{W}_i$ is the weight matrix for the input gate, $\mathbf{h}_{t-1}$ is the hidden state from the previous time step, $\mathbf{x}_t$ is the current input vector, and $\mathbf{b}_i$ is the bias term.

- **Forget Gate:** The forget gate, denoted by $\mathbf{f}_t$, controls which information from the cell state should be discarded. It can be expressed as:

  $$\mathbf{f}_t = \sigma(\mathbf{W}_f \cdot [\mathbf{h}_{t-1}, \mathbf{x}_t] + \mathbf{b}_f),$$

  where $\mathbf{W}_f$ is the weight matrix for the forget gate, and $\mathbf{b}_f$ is the corresponding bias term.

- **Output Gate:** The output gate, denoted by $\mathbf{o}_t$, decides the extent of the cell state that should be exposed as the hidden state at the next time step. This is given by:

  $$\mathbf{o}_t = \sigma(\mathbf{W}_o \cdot [\mathbf{h}_{t-1}, \mathbf{x}_t] + \mathbf{b}_o),$$

  where $\mathbf{W}_o$ is the weight matrix for the output gate, and $\mathbf{b}_o$ is the associated bias term.

The LSTM unit updates the cell state and hidden state as follows:

$$\tilde{\mathbf{C}}_t = \tanh(\mathbf{W}_C \cdot [\mathbf{h}_{t-1}, \mathbf{x}_t] + \mathbf{b}_C),$$

$$\mathbf{C}_t = \mathbf{f}_t \odot \mathbf{C}_{t-1} + \mathbf{i}_t \odot \tilde{\mathbf{C}}_t,$$

$$\mathbf{h}_t = \mathbf{o}_t \odot \tanh(\mathbf{C}_t),$$

where $\tilde{\mathbf{C}}_t$ represents the candidate cell state, $\mathbf{W}_C$ is the weight matrix for the candidate cell state, $\mathbf{b}_C$ is the corresponding bias term, and $\odot$ denotes element-wise multiplication.

The gradient flow within LSTMs is regulated by these gates, alleviating the issues of vanishing and exploding gradients. This allows them to remember patterns in data over much longer sequences compared to traditional RNNs.

The implementation of an LSTM network in PyTorch can be demonstrated with a straightforward example. Below is a sample code to define and initialize an LSTM network:

```
import torch
import torch.nn as nn
import torch.optim as optim

class LSTMNetwork(nn.Module):
    def __init__(self, input_size, hidden_size, num_layers, output_size):
        super(LSTMNetwork, self).__init__()
        self.hidden_size = hidden_size
        self.num_layers = num_layers

        self.lstm = nn.LSTM(input_size, hidden_size, num_layers, batch_first=True)
        self.fc = nn.Linear(hidden_size, output_size)

    def forward(self, x):
        h0 = torch.zeros(self.num_layers, x.size(0), self.hidden_size).to(x.device)
        c0 = torch.zeros(self.num_layers, x.size(0), self.hidden_size).to(x.device)

        out, _ = self.lstm(x, (h0, c0))
        out = self.fc(out[:, -1, :])

        return out

input_size = 10
hidden_size = 20
num_layers = 2
output_size = 1
model = LSTMNetwork(input_size, hidden_size, num_layers, output_size)
print(model)
```

Executing this code will produce the following model structure:

```
LSTMNetwork(
  (lstm): LSTM(10, 20, num_layers=2, batch_first=True)
  (fc): Linear(in_features=20, out_features=1, bias=True)
)
```

An LSTM network processes sequences step-by-step, maintaining information across time steps through its memory cells. The interplay between cell state and hidden state, controlled by the gates, enables LSTMs to capture long-term dependencies effectively. Thus, LSTM networks are particularly well-suited for tasks involving sequential data, such as text classification, language modeling, and machine translation. The practicality and relative ease of implementation of LSTMs in modern deep learning frameworks reinforce their wide usage and continued relevance in NLP and other domains.

8.5 Gated Recurrent Units (GRUs)

Gated Recurrent Units (GRUs) are a type of Recurrent Neural Network (RNN) architecture introduced to address some of the limitations associated with traditional RNNs, particularly the challenges related to the vanishing gradient problem. GRUs, like Long Short-Term Memory networks (LSTMs), employ gate mechanisms to control the flow of information, making it easier to capture long-range dependencies in sequential data.

A GRU is defined using two primary gates: the reset gate and the update gate. These gates enable the GRU to selectively update its state and manage the information passing through the cell.

The update gate z_t determines the extent to which the unit updates its activation or content. It plays a similar role to the forget gate in LSTMs, merging both the forget and input operations into a single gate.

The reset gate r_t controls the combination of the new input with the previous memory or hidden state, enabling the model to forget past activations selectively.

Given an input sequence $x = \{x_1, x_2, \ldots, x_T\}$, the GRU cell computations for time step t are as follows:

- Update Gate: The update gate z_t is computed as:

$$z_t = \sigma(W_z \cdot x_t + U_z \cdot h_{t-1} + b_z)$$

  where W_z and U_z are the weight matrices for the input and the recurrent terms, respectively, b_z is the bias term, and σ denotes the sigmoid activation function.

- Reset Gate: The reset gate r_t is determined by:

$$r_t = \sigma(W_r \cdot x_t + U_r \cdot h_{t-1} + b_r)$$

where W_r and U_r are the weight matrices for the input and the recurrent terms, respectively, and b_r is the bias term.

- Current Memory Content: The candidate activation $\tilde{h}_t$ is then computed as:

$$\tilde{h}_t = \text{tanh}(W \cdot x_t + U \cdot (r_t \odot h_{t-1}) + b)$$

where $\odot$ denotes element-wise multiplication, and tanh is the hyperbolic tangent activation function.

- Final Memory at Current Time Step: The final output or hidden state h_t is obtained as:

$$h_t = (1 - z_t) \odot h_{t-1} + z_t \odot \tilde{h}_t$$

The update gate z_t balances between the previous hidden state h_{t-1} and the candidate hidden state $\tilde{h}_t$, effectively allowing the model to regulate its memory. The reset gate r_t enables the model to reset its memory when needed, which is useful for tasks requiring shorter-term dependencies.

To implement a GRU in PyTorch, the 'torch.nn' module provides the 'GRU' class, streamlining the creation and training of GRUs. Below is an example of how to define and use a GRU layer in a PyTorch-based neural network:

```
import torch
import torch.nn as nn

class GRUNet(nn.Module):
    def __init__(self, input_size, hidden_size, num_layers, output_size):
        super(GRUNet, self).__init__()
        self.hidden_size = hidden_size
        self.num_layers = num_layers
        self.gru = nn.GRU(input_size, hidden_size, num_layers, batch_first=True)
        self.fc = nn.Linear(hidden_size, output_size)

    def forward(self, x):
        h0 = torch.zeros(self.num_layers, x.size(0), self.hidden_size).to(x.device)
        out, hn = self.gru(x, h0)
        out = self.fc(out[:, -1, :])
        return out
```

```
# Example usage:
input_size = 10
hidden_size = 20
num_layers = 2
output_size = 1

model = GRUNet(input_size, hidden_size, num_layers, output_size)
x = torch.randn(5, 10, input_size) # batch_size=5, sequence_length=10
output = model(x)
print(output.shape)
```

The GRU layer in PyTorch simplifies managing the gates and the computations described earlier. The ‘GRU‘ class parameters include the input size, hidden size, number of layers, and an optional batch normalization flag.

To visualize and understand how GRUs improve on traditional RNNs and LSTMs, it is helpful to experiment with different configurations and datasets. Utilizing real-world NLP tasks, such as sentiment analysis or language modeling, reveals the GRU's efficiency in handling long-term dependencies without the complexity of LSTM cells. Direct application examples provide practical insights into GRU's performance and adaptability across various sequences and learning tasks.

8.6 Introduction to Natural Language Processing

Natural Language Processing (NLP) is a subfield of artificial intelligence (AI) that focuses on enabling computers to understand, interpret, and generate human languages. NLP combines computational linguistics—rule-based modeling of human language—with machine learning, deep learning, and statistical models. Accurate NLP techniques have become increasingly significant as they enable the development of applications such as chatbots, sentiment analysis systems, machine translation, information retrieval, and more.

Tokenization is one of the fundamental steps in any NLP task. It involves dividing a piece of text into smaller units called tokens. Tokens can be words, subwords, or characters, depending on the application. Word-level tokenization, where the text is split into individual words, is commonly used. Below is an example of how to perform word-level tokenization using Python:

```
import nltk
nltk.download('punkt')
```

```
from nltk.tokenize import word_tokenize

text = "Natural language processing enables computers to understand human languages
    ."
tokens = word_tokenize(text)
print(tokens)
```

The output of running this code will be:

```
['Natural', 'language', 'processing', 'enables', 'computers', 'to', 'understand', 'human', 'languages', '.']
```

Text normalization is another essential aspect of NLP, involving the transformation of text into a consistent format. Text normalization usually includes converting text to lowercase, stemming, lemmatization, and removing punctuation and stop words. Below is an example to illustrate these concepts:

- **Lowercasing**: Converting all characters in the text to lowercase.
- **Stemming**: Reducing words to their root form. For example, "running" becomes "run".
- **Lemmatization**: Similar to stemming but reduces words to their base or dictionary form, considering the context. For example, "better" becomes "good".
- **Removing punctuation and stop words**: Removing unnecessary symbols and frequently used words that do not contribute much to the meaning of the text, like "and", "the".

Consider the following Python code that performs text normalization:

```
from nltk.corpus import stopwords
from nltk.stem import PorterStemmer, WordNetLemmatizer
import string

nltk.download('stopwords')
nltk.download('wordnet')

text = "Running fast is better than standing still."
tokens = word_tokenize(text)

# Lowercasing
tokens = [word.lower() for word in tokens]

# Removing punctuation
tokens = [word for word in tokens if word.isalnum()]

# Removing stop words
stop_words = set(stopwords.words('english'))
tokens = [word for word in tokens if word not in stop_words]

# Stemming
```

```
stemmer = PorterStemmer()
stemmed_tokens = [stemmer.stem(word) for word in tokens]

# Lemmatization
lemmatizer = WordNetLemmatizer()
lemmatized_tokens = [lemmatizer.lemmatize(word) for word in tokens]

print("Stemmed Tokens: ", stemmed_tokens)
print("Lemmatized Tokens: ", lemmatized_tokens)
```

The output of running this code will be:

```
Stemmed Tokens: ['run', 'fast', 'better', 'stand', 'still']
Lemmatized Tokens: ['running', 'fast', 'better', 'standing', 'still']
```

Part-of-Speech (POS) tagging is a technique for assigning parts of speech to each word (such as nouns, verbs, adjectives) in a sentence. This tagging enriches the understanding of the text's grammatical structure. Python's NLTK library provides functionalities for POS tagging, demonstrated below:

```
nltk.download('averaged_perceptron_tagger')
tokens = word_tokenize("Natural language processing enables computers to understand
    human languages.")
pos_tags = nltk.pos_tag(tokens)
print(pos_tags)
```

The output of running this code will be:

```
[('Natural', 'JJ'), ('language', 'NN'), ('processing', 'NN'), ('enables', 'VBZ'),
 ('computers', 'NNS'), ('to', 'TO'), ('understand', 'VB'),
 ('human', 'JJ'), ('languages', 'NNS'), ('.', '.')]
```

Named Entity Recognition (NER) involves locating and classifying named entities in text into predefined categories like names of persons, organizations, locations, expressions of times, etc. Below is an example using the Python library spaCy for NER:

```
import spacy
nlp = spacy.load('en_core_web_sm')

text = "Apple is looking at buying U.K. startup for $1 billion."
doc = nlp(text)

for entity in doc.ents:
    print(f"Text: {entity.text}, Label: {entity.label_}")
```

The output of running this code will be:

```
Text: Apple, Label: ORG
Text: U.K., Label: GPE
Text: $1 billion, Label: MONEY
```

Dependency parsing provides a deeper understanding of grammatical relationships within a sentence. It aims to establish syntactic dependencies between words, describing the grammatical structure. spaCy also offers functionality for dependency parsing:

```
for token in doc:
    print(f"Text: {token.text}, Dep: {token.dep_}, Head: {token.head.text}")
```

The output of running this code will be:

```
Text: Apple, Dep: nsubj, Head: is
Text: is, Dep: ROOT, Head: is
Text: looking, Dep: acl, Head: is
Text: at, Dep: prep, Head: looking
Text: buying, Dep: pcomp, Head: at
Text: U.K., Dep: compound, Head: startup
Text: startup, Dep: dobj, Head: buying
Text: for, Dep: prep, Head: buying
Text: $, Dep: quantmod, Head: billion
Text: 1, Dep: compound, Head: billion
Text: billion, Dep: pobj, Head: for
Text: ., Dep: punct, Head: is
```

This section focuses on foundational NLP techniques that serve as building blocks for more advanced topics covered later. Developing an understanding of these techniques provides a solid base for applying RNNs and other deep learning models to complex NLP tasks.

8.7 Text Preprocessing Techniques

Text preprocessing is a critical step in preparing textual data for input into machine learning models, especially in the context of Natural Language Processing (NLP). Proper preprocessing ensures that the raw text is transformed into a clean and meaningful format that can be effectively processed by algorithms. Several preprocessing techniques are widely used to handle the complexities and nuances of human language.

Tokenization refers to the process of splitting text into smaller units called tokens. Tokens can be words, subwords, or characters depending on the granularity required. Tokenization helps convert a continuous sequence of text into discrete elements, which can be more easily analyzed and processed.

```
from nltk.tokenize import word_tokenize

text = "Natural Language Processing with PyTorch is exciting!"
tokens = word_tokenize(text)
print(tokens)
```

```
['Natural', 'Language', 'Processing', 'with', 'PyTorch', 'is', 'exciting', '!']
```

Lowercasing involves converting all characters in the text to lowercase.

This step helps in reducing the complexity of the text by treating words like "Apple" and "apple" as the same word.

```
lowercase_tokens = [token.lower() for token in tokens]
print(lowercase_tokens)
```

['natural', 'language', 'processing', 'with', 'pytorch', 'is', 'exciting', '!']

Removing Punctuation is another essential preprocessing step. Punctuation marks generally do not contribute to the semantic content of the text and can be safely removed, although there are exceptions depending on the specific application.

```
import string

tokens_without_punctuation = [token for token in lowercase_tokens if token not in
    string.punctuation]
print(tokens_without_punctuation)
```

['natural', 'language', 'processing', 'with', 'pytorch', 'is', 'exciting']

Stop Words Removal eliminates common words that add little informational value to the text, such as "is", "and", "the". These words are known as stop words. By removing them, the focus is placed on the more meaningful words.

```
from nltk.corpus import stopwords

stop_words = set(stopwords.words('english'))
filtered_tokens = [token for token in tokens_without_punctuation if token not in
    stop_words]
print(filtered_tokens)
```

['natural', 'language', 'processing', 'pytorch', 'exciting']

Stemming reduces words to their root forms. For instance, "running" and "runner" would both be reduced to "run". Stemming helps in unifying various word forms into a single representation.

```
from nltk.stem import PorterStemmer

stemmer = PorterStemmer()
stemmed_tokens = [stemmer.stem(token) for token in filtered_tokens]
print(stemmed_tokens)
```

['natur', 'languag', 'process', 'pytorch', 'excit']

Lemmatization, alternatively, reduces words to their base or dictionary form, known as lemma. Unlike stemming, lemmatization considers the context and converts the word to its meaningful base form.

```
from nltk.stem import WordNetLemmatizer
```

```
lemmatizer = WordNetLemmatizer()
lemmatized_tokens = [lemmatizer.lemmatize(token) for token in filtered_tokens]
print(lemmatized_tokens)
```

```
['natural', 'language', 'processing', 'pytorch', 'exciting']
```

Part-of-Speech Tagging involves labeling each token in a text with its corresponding part of speech, such as noun, verb, adjective, etc. This information can be crucial for various NLP tasks where context inference is required.

```
import nltk

nltk.download('averaged_perceptron_tagger')
pos_tags = nltk.pos_tag(lemmatized_tokens)
print(pos_tags)
```

```
[('natural', 'JJ'), ('language', 'NN'), ('processing', 'NN'), ('pytorch', 'NN'), ('exciting', 'JJ')]
```

Named Entity Recognition (NER) identifies and classifies named entities in text into predefined categories such as the names of persons, organizations, locations, dates, etc. NER helps in extracting structured information from unstructured text.

```
nltk.download('maxent_ne_chunker')
nltk.download('words')
ner_entities = nltk.ne_chunk(nltk.pos_tag(tokens_without_punctuation))
print(ner_entities)
```

```
(S
  (GPE Natural/NNP)
  (GPE Language/NNP)
  (ORGANIZATION Processing/NNP)
  with/IN
  (ORGANIZATION PyTorch/NNP)
  is/VBZ
  exciting/JJ)
```

Text Normalization ensures uniformity in the text by handling different variations of text such as spelling corrections, expanding contractions (e.g., "don't" to "do not"), and removing special characters.

```
from contractions import fix

text_with_contractions = "We're going to learn NLP."
normalized_text = fix(text_with_contractions)
print(normalized_text)
```

```
We are going to learn NLP.
```

Text preprocessing involves multiple steps that enhance the quality and usability of text data. The application of these techniques results in a clean and structured set of tokens that can be fed into machine learning algorithms for further analysis and model building. This cohesive process ensures that the complexities of text data are managed efficiently, enabling more accurate and meaningful insights through subsequent NLP tasks.

8.8 Word Embeddings and Representations

Word embeddings are a form of word representation that enable words to be represented as vectors in a continuous vector space. This representation is essential for many natural language processing (NLP) tasks, as it allows machine learning models to understand and process textual data in a quantitative manner. Traditional methods, such as one-hot encoding, are limited in their ability to capture the semantic relationships and similarities between words; word embeddings address these limitations effectively.

One-Hot Encoding. One-hot encoding is a basic method for representing words as vectors. In this approach, each word in the vocabulary is represented by a vector that has a length equal to the size of the vocabulary. This vector is composed of all zeros except for a single one at the index corresponding to the word. For example, if our vocabulary consists of the words ["apple", "banana", "cherry"]:

```
vocabulary = ["apple", "banana", "cherry"]
one_hot_apple = [1, 0, 0]
one_hot_banana = [0, 1, 0]
one_hot_cherry = [0, 0, 1]
```

While simple to implement, one-hot encoding has significant drawbacks. The vectors are sparse, high-dimensional, and do not capture any semantic relationships between words.

Dense Vector Representations. To overcome these limitations, dense vector representations, or embeddings, are utilized. Word embeddings encode words into low-dimensional continuous vector spaces where semantically similar words have similar representations. Popular methods for generating such embeddings include Word2Vec, GloVe (Global Vectors for Word Representation), and FastText.

Word2Vec. Word2Vec is an algorithm developed by Mikolov et al. that utilizes neural networks to produce word embeddings. It comes in two models: Continuous Bag of Words (CBOW) and Skip-gram.

- **CBOW:** The CBOW model predicts the target word from its context words. For example, given the context words ["The", "cat", "on", "the", "mat"], the model tries to predict the center word "sat".

- **Skip-gram:** Conversely, the Skip-gram model predicts the context words from the target word. For example, given the target word "sat", the model tries to predict its context words ["The", "cat", "on", "the", "mat"].

The implementation of a simple Skip-gram model in PyTorch can be illustrated as follows:

```
import torch
import torch.nn as nn
import torch.optim as optim

class SkipGramModel(nn.Module):
    def __init__(self, vocab_size, embed_dim):
        super(SkipGramModel, self).__init__()
        self.embeddings = nn.Embedding(vocab_size, embed_dim)

    def forward(self, target_word, context_word):
        target_vec = self.embeddings(target_word)
        context_vec = self.embeddings(context_word)
        score = torch.sum(target_vec * context_vec, dim=1)
        return score

vocab_size = 10000 # example vocabulary size
embed_dim = 300 # example embedding dimensions
model = SkipGramModel(vocab_size, embed_dim)
```

GloVe. GloVe is another popular word embedding method. Unlike Word2Vec, which relies on local context windows, GloVe uses global word-word co-occurrence statistics from a corpus to learn word embeddings. GloVe constructs a co-occurrence matrix based on the number of times words appear together within a context window, and then applies matrix factorization techniques to produce a vector space where the distance between vectors captures semantic relationships.

The main idea of GloVe can be formulated as follows:

$$J = \sum_{i,j=1}^{V} f(X_{ij})(\vec{w}_i \cdot \vec{\tilde{w}}_j + b_i + \tilde{b}_j - \log(X_{ij}))^2$$

where X_{ij} is the number of times word i appears in the context of word j, $f(X_{ij})$ is a weighting function, $\vec{w}_i$ and $\vec{\tilde{w}}_j$ are word vectors, and b_i and $\tilde{b}_j$ are biases.

FastText. Developed by Facebook, FastText extends Word2Vec by representing words as bags of character n-grams, allowing it to generate embeddings for words that are not in the vocabulary by composing the embeddings of the n-grams. This is particularly useful for morphologically rich languages and enhances the model's ability to handle words with shared roots.

Implementation Considerations. The choice of word embedding method depends on various factors, including the size of the training corpus, the computational resources available, and the specifics of the NLP task at hand. Modern natural language processing frameworks like PyTorch and TensorFlow include extensive support for integrating pre-trained embeddings such as Word2Vec, GloVe, and FastText into neural network models with ease.

For instance, integrating pre-trained GloVe embeddings in a PyTorch model can be achieved as follows:

```
import torch
import torch.nn as nn
import numpy as np

# Assuming the pre-trained GloVe vectors are loaded into a numpy array `
    glove_vectors`
glove_vectors = np.load('glove_vectors.npy')
embed_dim = glove_vectors.shape[1]

embedding_layer = nn.Embedding.from_pretrained(torch.FloatTensor(glove_vectors))

# Example model using the pre-trained GloVe embeddings
class TextClassificationModel(nn.Module):
    def __init__(self, vocab_size, embed_dim):
        super(TextClassificationModel, self).__init__()
        self.embedding = embedding_layer
        self.fc = nn.Linear(embed_dim, 1)

    def forward(self, x):
        embedded = self.embedding(x)
        output = self.fc(embedded.mean(dim=1))
        return output

model = TextClassificationModel(vocab_size=len(glove_vectors), embed_dim=
    embed_dim)
```

Word embeddings provide a foundation for creating sophisticated models capable of understanding and manipulating natural language with improved accuracy and efficiency. By converting words into meaningful vector representations, embeddings allow neural networks to grasp syntactic and semantic nuances, significantly advancing the field of natural language processing.

8.9 Building an RNN for Text Classification

To construct a Recurrent Neural Network (RNN) for text classification, we begin by understanding the fundamental building blocks involved in the architecture. The process encompasses data preparation, model architecture specification, training, and evaluation stages. Each step is essential to ensure the model accurately classifies the text data.

Data preprocessing is the initial step, involving tokenization, padding, and converting tokens to their corresponding indices based on a predefined vocabulary. Tokenization splits the text into words or subwords, while padding ensures uniform input length by adding special tokens to shorter sequences. Conversion to indices transforms tokens into representations that the model can process.

Consider a sample dataset for sentiment analysis, with sentences labeled as positive or negative. The following Python code demonstrates tokenization and padding using the PyTorch library:

```
import torch
from torchtext.legacy import data, datasets

TEXT = data.Field(tokenize='spacy', include_lengths=True)
LABEL = data.LabelField(dtype=torch.float)

train_data, test_data = datasets.IMDB.splits(TEXT, LABEL)

TEXT.build_vocab(train_data, max_size=25000, vectors='glove.6B.100d', unk_init=
        torch.Tensor.normal_)
LABEL.build_vocab(train_data)

train_iterator, test_iterator = data.BucketIterator.splits(
    (train_data, test_data),
    batch_size=64,
    sort_within_batch=True,
    device=device)
```

We use PyTorch's torchtext library for ease of handling text data. The Field class defines how the text and labels are preprocessed. The dataloaders provide batch-wise data feeds during training and testing.

The next step is to define the RNN architecture. A simple RNN consists of Embedding, RNN, and Linear layers. The Embedding layer converts input indices to dense vectors. The RNN layer processes these embeddings sequentially, and the Linear layer maps the RNN's output to the desired number of classes.

Below is the implementation of an RNN model for text classification:

```
import torch.nn as nn
```

```
class RNN(nn.Module):
    def __init__(self, vocab_size, embedding_dim, hidden_dim, output_dim):
        super().__init__()
        self.embedding = nn.Embedding(vocab_size, embedding_dim)
        self.rnn = nn.RNN(embedding_dim, hidden_dim)
        self.fc = nn.Linear(hidden_dim, output_dim)

    def forward(self, text, text_lengths):
        embedded = self.embedding(text)
        packed_embedded = nn.utils.rnn.pack_padded_sequence(embedded,
            text_lengths)
        packed_output, hidden = self.rnn(packed_embedded)
        output, _ = nn.utils.rnn.pad_packed_sequence(packed_output)
        hidden = hidden.squeeze(0)
        return self.fc(hidden)

vocab_size = len(TEXT.vocab)
embedding_dim = 100
hidden_dim = 256
output_dim = 1

model = RNN(vocab_size, embedding_dim, hidden_dim, output_dim)
```

The nn.RNN layer's hidden dimension determines the capacity of the model to capture information from the sequence. The forward function incorporates pack_padded_sequence and pad_packed_sequence for handling variable-length inputs.

Training the RNN involves defining a loss function and an optimizer. For binary classification tasks, Binary Cross Entropy Loss (BCELoss) is commonly used. We utilize the Adam optimizer to update the model parameters.

The following code snippet demonstrates the training loop:

```
import torch.optim as optim

optimizer = optim.Adam(model.parameters())
criterion = nn.BCEWithLogitsLoss()
model = model.to(device)
criterion = criterion.to(device)

def binary_accuracy(preds, y):
    rounded_preds = torch.round(torch.sigmoid(preds))
    correct = (rounded_preds == y).float()
    acc = correct.sum() / len(correct)
    return acc

EPOCHS = 5

for epoch in range(EPOCHS):
    epoch_loss = 0
    epoch_acc = 0

    model.train()

    for batch in train_iterator:
```

```
        optimizer.zero_grad()

        text, text_lengths = batch.text
        predictions = model(text, text_lengths).squeeze(1)
        loss = criterion(predictions, batch.label)
        acc = binary_accuracy(predictions, batch.label)

        loss.backward()
        optimizer.step()

        epoch_loss += loss.item()
        epoch_acc += acc.item()

    print(f'Epoch {epoch+1} | Loss: {epoch_loss/len(train_iterator):.3f} | Accuracy: {
        epoch_acc/len(train_iterator):.3f}')
```

The training loop iterates over the dataset for a specified number of epochs. For each batch, it computes the prediction, loss, gradients, and updates the model parameters. The accuracy metric is computed by rounding the sigmoid activations and comparing with the ground truth labels.

Finally, the model's performance on unseen data is evaluated using the test set:

```
model.eval()
test_loss = 0
test_acc = 0

with torch.no_grad():
    for batch in test_iterator:
        text, text_lengths = batch.text
        predictions = model(text, text_lengths).squeeze(1)
        loss = criterion(predictions, batch.label)
        acc = binary_accuracy(predictions, batch.label)

        test_loss += loss.item()
        test_acc += acc.item()

print(f'Test | Loss: {test_loss/len(test_iterator):.3f} | Accuracy: {test_acc/len(
    test_iterator):.3f}')
```

The eval mode disables dropout and batch normalization, ensuring stable predictions. The evaluation loop accumulates the loss and accuracy, providing a reliable measure of the model's generalization performance.

Building an RNN for text classification requires meticulous preparation, from data preprocessing to model evaluation. Understanding each component's role aids in constructing and optimizing the model effectively. Through careful implementation and iterative enhancements, robust and accurate text classifiers can be developed to tackle various NLP tasks.

8.10 Sequence to Sequence Models

Sequence to Sequence (Seq2Seq) models are a class of Recurrent Neural Network (RNN) architectures designed to map input sequences to output sequences. Commonly used in tasks such as machine translation, text summarization, and speech recognition, Seq2Seq models can handle inputs and outputs of variable lengths, making them highly versatile for a range of sequential data applications.

The architecture of a Seq2Seq model typically consists of two primary components: an encoder and a decoder. Both components are usually implemented as RNNs, but they can also use more advanced variants like Long Short-Term Memory Networks (LSTMs) or Gated Recurrent Units (GRUs) to better capture long-range dependencies.

The encoder processes the input sequence, summarizing it into a context vector (also known as an encoded state or hidden state). This context vector encapsulates all the relevant information from the input sequence and is passed to the decoder, which then generates the output sequence. The decoder predicts each element of the output sequence step by step, conditioning on the context vector and the previously generated elements.

A typical Seq2Seq model training process involves teacher forcing, a technique where the true previous output token is used as the next input to the decoder during training, rather than the token that the decoder previously generated. The use of teacher forcing can speed up convergence and make the training more stable.

To illustrate the construction and functioning of a Seq2Seq model, let us consider a simple example using PyTorch:

```
import torch
import torch.nn as nn
import torch.optim as optim

# Define the Encoder RNN
class EncoderRNN(nn.Module):
    def __init__(self, input_size, hidden_size):
        super(EncoderRNN, self).__init__()
        self.hidden_size = hidden_size
        self.embedding = nn.Embedding(input_size, hidden_size)
        self.gru = nn.GRU(hidden_size, hidden_size)

    def forward(self, input, hidden):
        embedded = self.embedding(input).view(1, 1, -1)
        output, hidden = self.gru(embedded, hidden)
        return output, hidden

    def initHidden(self):
```

```
        return torch.zeros(1, 1, self.hidden_size, device=device)

# Define the Decoder RNN
class DecoderRNN(nn.Module):
    def __init__(self, hidden_size, output_size):
        super(DecoderRNN, self).__init__()
        self.hidden_size = hidden_size
        self.embedding = nn.Embedding(output_size, hidden_size)
        self.gru = nn.GRU(hidden_size, hidden_size)
        self.out = nn.Linear(hidden_size, output_size)
        self.softmax = nn.LogSoftmax(dim=1)

    def forward(self, input, hidden):
        output = self.embedding(input).view(1, 1, -1)
        output, hidden = self.gru(output, hidden)
        output = self.softmax(self.out(output[0]))
        return output, hidden

    def initHidden(self):
        return torch.zeros(1, 1, self.hidden_size, device=device)

# Training loop
def train(input_tensor, target_tensor, encoder, decoder, encoder_optimizer,
      decoder_optimizer, criterion, max_length=MAX_LENGTH):
    encoder_hidden = encoder.initHidden()

    encoder_optimizer.zero_grad()
    decoder_optimizer.zero_grad()

    input_length = input_tensor.size(0)
    target_length = target_tensor.size(0)

    encoder_outputs = torch.zeros(max_length, encoder.hidden_size, device=device)

    loss = 0

    for ei in range(input_length):
        encoder_output, encoder_hidden = encoder(input_tensor[ei], encoder_hidden)
        encoder_outputs[ei] = encoder_output[0, 0]

    decoder_input = torch.tensor([[SOS_token]], device=device)
    decoder_hidden = encoder_hidden

    for di in range(target_length):
        decoder_output, decoder_hidden = decoder(decoder_input, decoder_hidden)
        topv, topi = decoder_output.topk(1)
        decoder_input = topi.squeeze().detach()

        loss += criterion(decoder_output, target_tensor[di])
        if decoder_input.item() == EOS_token:
            break

    loss.backward()
    encoder_optimizer.step()
    decoder_optimizer.step()

    return loss.item() / target_length

# Example execution
device = torch.device("cuda" if torch.cuda.is_available() else "cpu")

# Assuming input_size and output_size are defined, as well as input_tensor and
```

```
    target_tensor
hidden_size = 256
encoder = EncoderRNN(input_size, hidden_size).to(device)
decoder = DecoderRNN(hidden_size, output_size).to(device)
encoder_optimizer = optim.SGD(encoder.parameters(), lr=0.01)
decoder_optimizer = optim.SGD(decoder.parameters(), lr=0.01)
criterion = nn.NLLLoss()

input_tensor = torch.tensor([1, 2, 3, 4, 5], dtype=torch.long, device=device)
target_tensor = torch.tensor([5, 4, 3, 2, 1, 0], dtype=torch.long, device=device)

loss = train(input_tensor, target_tensor, encoder, decoder, encoder_optimizer,
    decoder_optimizer, criterion)

print(f'Training loss: {loss}')
```

```
Training loss: 1.0923
```

One of the significant challenges of Seq2Seq models is the reliance on the context vector to encapsulate all the information of the input sequence, which can lead to information bottlenecks, especially for long sequences. This problem is alleviated by the attention mechanism, which allows the decoder to focus on different parts of the input sequence at each decoding step. We will explore the attention mechanism in the subsequent section.

Building upon the basic Seq2Seq model, attention-based Seq2Seq models achieve superior performance by dynamically attending to different input parts when generating each output, thus addressing the limitations posed by fixed context vectors.

8.11 Attention Mechanisms

Attention mechanisms have revolutionized the field of neural networks, especially in Natural Language Processing (NLP). They enable models to focus on relevant parts of the input sequence when making predictions, improving performance significantly over traditional methods. The core idea behind attention is that at each step of decoding, the model assigns varying levels of importance to different parts of the input data.

To comprehend attention mechanisms, it's essential to understand how they operate. The process can be broken down into several steps: the calculation of attention scores, the application of the softmax function to generate attention weights, and the computation of the context vector.

Assume we have an encoder-decoder architecture where the encoder processes an input sequence of length T_x, generating a sequence of hidden states $(h_1, h_2, \ldots, h_{T_x})$. The decoder generates the output sequence step-by-step. At each decoding step t, the decoder takes the previously generated output and an intermediate representation to produce the next output. Here, attention mechanisms improve the decoding step.

Given the current decoder hidden state s_t and all encoder hidden states $(h_1, h_2, \ldots, h_{T_x})$, the attention score $e_{t,i}$ for each encoder hidden state i at decoding time step t is calculated using an alignment model, typically a feedforward network:

$$e_{t,i} = \text{alignment}(s_t, h_i)$$

A common choice for the alignment model is a simple feedforward network parameterized by a weight matrix W and bias b:

$$e_{t,i} = v^\top \tanh(W[s_t; h_i] + b)$$

Next, the attention weights $\alpha_{t,i}$ are computed by normalizing the attention scores using a softmax function:

$$\alpha_{t,i} = \frac{\exp(e_{t,i})}{\sum_{k=1}^{T_x} \exp(e_{t,k})}$$

These attention weights represent how much importance the model assigns to each encoder hidden state h_i when producing the output at time step t.

The final step is to compute the context vector c_t at time step t as a weighted sum of the encoder hidden states:

$$c_t = \sum_{i=1}^{T_x} \alpha_{t,i} h_i$$

This context vector c_t is then combined with the decoder's hidden state s_t to produce the output at time step t. Specifically, the context vector is concatenated with the decoder hidden state and passed through a dense layer with an activation function to generate the final output.

The following Python code demonstrates how to implement an attention mechanism using PyTorch:

```
import torch
import torch.nn as nn
import torch.nn.functional as F

class Attention(nn.Module):
    def __init__(self, hidden_dim):
        super(Attention, self).__init__()
        self.hidden_dim = hidden_dim
        self.attn = nn.Linear(hidden_dim * 2, hidden_dim)
        self.v = nn.Parameter(torch.rand(hidden_dim))

    def forward(self, hidden, encoder_outputs):
        timestep = encoder_outputs.size(1)
        h = hidden.repeat(timestep, 1, 1).transpose(0, 1)
        energy = torch.tanh(self.attn(torch.cat([h, encoder_outputs], 2)))
        energy = energy.transpose(1, 2)
        v = self.v.repeat(encoder_outputs.size(0), 1).unsqueeze(1)
        attention_weights = torch.bmm(v, energy).squeeze(1)
        return F.softmax(attention_weights, dim=1)

class DecoderRNN(nn.Module):
    def __init__(self, output_dim, hidden_dim, n_layers, attention):
        super(DecoderRNN, self).__init__()
        self.output_dim = output_dim
        self.hidden_dim = hidden_dim
        self.n_layers = n_layers
        self.attention = attention
        self.rnn = nn.GRU(hidden_dim * 2, hidden_dim, n_layers, batch_first=True)
        self.out = nn.Linear(hidden_dim * 2, output_dim)

    def forward(self, input, hidden, encoder_outputs):
        input = input.unsqueeze(1)
        rnn_output, hidden = self.rnn(input, hidden)
        attn_weights = self.attention(hidden[-1], encoder_outputs)
        context = attn_weights.unsqueeze(1).bmm(encoder_outputs)
        rnn_output = rnn_output.squeeze(1)
        context = context.squeeze(1)
        output = self.out(torch.cat([rnn_output, context], 1))
        return output, hidden
```

In the example above, the Attention class computes the attention weights, and the DecoderRNN class uses these weights to modify its hidden state, focusing on the most relevant parts of the encoder outputs.

Attention mechanisms are particularly effective in sequence-to-sequence models, such as those used in machine translation, text summarization, and image captioning. They allow the model to align output sequences with the most relevant portions of the input sequence dynamically, leading to more accurate and contextually aware predictions.

8.12 Practical Applications of RNNs in NLP

Recurrent Neural Networks (RNNs) are extensively utilized in numerous Natural Language Processing (NLP) applications due to their ability to handle sequential data effectively. Their architecture is particularly well-suited to tackling problems where the context and order of words or tokens significantly impact the task at hand.

Among the most prominent practical applications of RNNs in NLP are language modeling, machine translation, text generation, sentiment analysis, named entity recognition (NER), and speech recognition. Each of these applications leverages the sequential nature of RNNs to process and generate human-readable text in intelligent ways, often surpassing traditional methods in performance.

Language modeling involves predicting the next word in a sequence given the previous words. This is foundational for many NLP tasks. Below, we demonstrate a language model using an RNN implemented in PyTorch.

```
import torch
import torch.nn as nn

class RNNLanguageModel(nn.Module):
    def __init__(self, vocab_size, embedding_dim, hidden_dim, n_layers):
        super(RNNLanguageModel, self).__init__()
        self.embedding = nn.Embedding(vocab_size, embedding_dim)
        self.rnn = nn.RNN(embedding_dim, hidden_dim, n_layers, batch_first=True)
        self.fc = nn.Linear(hidden_dim, vocab_size)

    def forward(self, x, hidden):
        x = self.embedding(x)
        out, hidden = self.rnn(x, hidden)
        out = self.fc(out.contiguous().view(-1, out.size(2)))
        return out, hidden

# Define model parameters
vocab_size = 5000 # Example vocabulary size
embedding_dim = 128
hidden_dim = 256
n_layers = 2

# Instantiate the model and print its architecture
model = RNNLanguageModel(vocab_size, embedding_dim, hidden_dim, n_layers)
print(model)
```

```
RNNLanguageModel(
  (embedding): Embedding(5000, 128)
  (rnn): RNN(128, 256, num_layers=2, batch_first=True)
  (fc): Linear(in_features=256, out_features=5000, bias=True)
)
```

Machine translation, another crucial application, involves translating text from one language to another. Sequence-to-sequence (Seq2Seq) models, often incorporating attention mechanisms, excel in this domain. The following is an outline of a Seq2Seq architecture with attention using RNNs in PyTorch.

```
class EncoderRNN(nn.Module):
    def __init__(self, input_dim, embedding_dim, hidden_dim, n_layers):
        super(EncoderRNN, self).__init__()
        self.embedding = nn.Embedding(input_dim, embedding_dim)
        self.rnn = nn.RNN(embedding_dim, hidden_dim, n_layers, batch_first=True)

    def forward(self, x, hidden):
        x = self.embedding(x)
        outputs, hidden = self.rnn(x, hidden)
        return outputs, hidden

class DecoderRNN(nn.Module):
    def __init__(self, output_dim, embedding_dim, hidden_dim, n_layers):
        super(DecoderRNN, self).__init__()
        self.embedding = nn.Embedding(output_dim, embedding_dim)
        self.rnn = nn.RNN(embedding_dim, hidden_dim, n_layers, batch_first=True)
        self.fc = nn.Linear(hidden_dim, output_dim)

    def forward(self, x, hidden, enc_outputs):
        x = self.embedding(x)
        outputs, hidden = self.rnn(x, hidden)
        outputs = self.fc(outputs.squeeze(1))
        return outputs, hidden

class Seq2Seq(nn.Module):
    def __init__(self, encoder, decoder):
        super(Seq2Seq, self).__init__()
        self.encoder = encoder
        self.decoder = decoder

    def forward(self, src, trg):
        encoder_hidden = None
        enc_outputs, encoder_hidden = self.encoder(src, encoder_hidden)
        decoder_hidden = encoder_hidden
        dec_outputs, _ = self.decoder(trg, decoder_hidden, enc_outputs)
        return dec_outputs

# Define model parameters
input_dim = 6000 # Example source vocabulary size
output_dim = 6000 # Example target vocabulary size
embedding_dim = 256
hidden_dim = 512
n_layers = 3

# Instantiate the Seq2Seq model and print its architecture
encoder = EncoderRNN(input_dim, embedding_dim, hidden_dim, n_layers)
decoder = DecoderRNN(output_dim, embedding_dim, hidden_dim, n_layers)
seq2seq = Seq2Seq(encoder, decoder)
print(seq2seq)
```

```
Seq2Seq(
  (encoder): EncoderRNN(
    (embedding): Embedding(6000, 256)
    (rnn): RNN(256, 512, num_layers=3, batch_first=True)
  )
  (decoder): DecoderRNN(
    (embedding): Embedding(6000, 256)
    (rnn): RNN(256, 512, num_layers=3, batch_first=True)
    (fc): Linear(in_features=512, out_features=6000, bias=True)
  )
)
```

Text generation can be harnessed to create human-like text by training on large datasets of text sequences. This text generation capability forms the basis of applications such as chatbots and content creation tools. Here's how an RNN can be leveraged for text generation.

```
def generate_text(model, start_text, gen_length=100):
    model.eval()
    input_text = torch.tensor([char_to_idx[c] for c in start_text]).unsqueeze(0)
    hidden = None

    generated_text = start_text
    for _ in range(gen_length):
        output, hidden = model(input_text, hidden)
        p = torch.nn.functional.softmax(output[-1], dim=0).detach().numpy()
        char_idx = np.random.choice(len(p), p=p)
        char = idx_to_char[char_idx]
        generated_text += char

        input_text = torch.tensor([[char_idx]])

    return generated_text

# Assuming 'model' is already trained and dictionary 'char_to_idx', 'idx_to_char'
    exist
start_text = "Once upon a time, "
generated_text = generate_text(model, start_text)
print(generated_text)
```

In addition, RNNs are pivotal in sentiment analysis, a task where the sentiment of a given text is classified as positive, negative, or neutral. RNNs can capture the contextual information essential for determining sentiment.

```
class SentimentRNN(nn.Module):
    def __init__(self, vocab_size, embedding_dim, hidden_dim, output_dim,
        n_layers, dropout):
        super(SentimentRNN, self).__init__()
        self.embedding = nn.Embedding(vocab_size, embedding_dim)
        self.rnn = nn.RNN(embedding_dim, hidden_dim, n_layers, batch_first=True,
            dropout=dropout)
        self.fc = nn.Linear(hidden_dim, output_dim)
        self.dropout = nn.Dropout(dropout)

    def forward(self, x, hidden):
        x = self.embedding(x)
        x = self.dropout(x)
        out, hidden = self.rnn(x, hidden)
```

```
        out = self.fc(out[:, -1, :])
        return out

# Define model parameters
vocab_size = 10000 # Example vocabulary size
embedding_dim = 128
hidden_dim = 256
output_dim = 1 % Binary classification
n_layers = 2
dropout = 0.5

# Instantiate the SentimentRNN model and print its architecture
model = SentimentRNN(vocab_size, embedding_dim, hidden_dim, output_dim,
     n_layers, dropout)
print(model)
```

```
SentimentRNN(
  (embedding): Embedding(10000, 128)
  (rnn): RNN(128, 256, num_layers=2, batch_first=True, dropout=0.5)
  (fc): Linear(in_features=256, out_features=1, bias=True)
  (dropout): Dropout(p=0.5)
)
```

Named Entity Recognition (NER) involves identifying and classifying key entities within a text into predefined categories such as names, dates, and locations. Here is an illustration of an NER system using RNNs.

```
class NERTaggerRNN(nn.Module):
    def __init__(self, vocab_size, embedding_dim, hidden_dim, tag_size, n_layers):
        super(NERTaggerRNN, self).__init__()
        self.embedding = nn.Embedding(vocab_size, embedding_dim)
        self.rnn = nn.RNN(embedding_dim, hidden_dim, n_layers, batch_first=True)
        self.fc = nn.Linear(hidden_dim, tag_size)

    def forward(self, x, hidden):
        x = self.embedding(x)
        out, hidden = self.rnn(x, hidden)
        out = self.fc(out)
        return out, hidden

# Define model parameters
vocab_size = 5000 # Example vocabulary size
embedding_dim = 128
hidden_dim = 256
tag_size = 10 # Example number of NER tags
n_layers = 2

# Instantiate the NERTaggerRNN model and print its architecture
model = NERTaggerRNN(vocab_size, embedding_dim, hidden_dim, tag_size,
     n_layers)
print(model)
```

```
NERTaggerRNN(
  (embedding): Embedding(5000, 128)
  (rnn): RNN(128, 256, num_layers=2, batch_first=True)
  (fc): Linear(in_features=256, out_features=10, bias=True)
)
```

Speech recognition systems benefit from RNNs' ability to process sequences of sound waves and convert them into text. The interconnected nature of RNN cells makes them apt for capturing temporal dependencies in audio signals.

Thus, the practical applications of RNNs within NLP are vast and transformative, leveraging their sequential data processing capabilities to innovate and enhance the field of language understanding and generation. The versatility and effectiveness of RNNs in handling diverse NLP tasks solidify their role as fundamental tools in modern artificial intelligence.

Chapter 9

Transfer Learning and Pre-trained Models

This chapter focuses on transfer learning and the use of pre-trained models. It outlines the benefits of transfer learning, explores popular pre-trained models, and demonstrates how to use PyTorch for transfer learning tasks. Detailed discussions include fine-tuning pre-trained models, feature extraction, and handling different input sizes. The chapter also covers transfer learning applications in image classification and natural language processing, along with methods for evaluating performance.

9.1 Introduction to Transfer Learning

Transfer learning, a critical concept in modern machine learning, refers to the technique of reusing a pre-trained model on a new, but related task. This approach leverages the knowledge gained during the training of a model on one dataset, enabling it to be repurposed and utilized for another related function. The underlying premise of transfer learning is that some patterns or features learned by a model in one domain can be valuable in another domain. For example, knowledge learned from recognizing vehicles in images could be transferred to the task of recognizing bicycles.

Mathematically, consider two tasks: a source task T_S with dataset

$D_S = \{(x_S^i, y_S^i)\}$ and a target task T_T with dataset $D_T = \{(x_T^i, y_T^i)\}$. Transfer learning aims to improve the learning efficiency and/or accuracy of the target predictive function $f_T(*)$ in T_T using the knowledge K_S obtained from T_S. Here, D_S and D_T can differ in feature space (X_S and X_T) and/or label space (Y_S and Y_T).

A common scenario where transfer learning proves beneficial is when the target task's dataset is small and insufficient for training a robust model from scratch. In such cases, a pre-trained model serves as a starting point, providing a solid foundation based on a larger corpus of data. This drastically reduces the computational resources and time required for training while enhancing the model's performance in the target domain.

Transfer learning methods can be broadly categorized based on the extent and manner of transfer:

- **Instance-based transfer**: This technique reuses a portion of instances from the source domain in the target domain by re-weighting them based on their relevance to the target task.
- **Feature-based transfer**: This method discovers common features between source and target domains, transforming data from both domains into a new feature space that minimizes divergence and maximizes useful feature extraction.
- **Parameter-based transfer**: This approach uses parameters or parts of models (like layers in neural networks) trained on the source task to initialize the model for the target task. Fine-tuning these parameters aligns the model closely with the target task specifics.
- **Relational-knowledge-based transfer**: This technique applies rules or logical representations learned in the source domain to the target domain.

In the context of deep learning and neural networks, transfer learning primarily involves reusing pre-trained models. These models, often trained on large-scale datasets like ImageNet, capture diverse and rich feature representations that can be adapted to various tasks.

Below is an example of transfer learning using PyTorch, where a model pre-trained on ImageNet is reused:

```
import torch
```

```
import torch.nn as nn
import torch.optim as optim
from torchvision import datasets, models, transforms

# Data preprocessing
data_transforms = {
    'train': transforms.Compose([
        transforms.RandomResizedCrop(224),
        transforms.RandomHorizontalFlip(),
        transforms.ToTensor(),
        transforms.Normalize([0.485, 0.456, 0.406], [0.229, 0.224, 0.225])
    ]),
    'val': transforms.Compose([
        transforms.Resize(256),
        transforms.CenterCrop(224),
        transforms.ToTensor(),
        transforms.Normalize([0.485, 0.456, 0.406], [0.229, 0.224, 0.225])
    ]),
}

data_dir = 'data/hymenoptera_data'
image_datasets = {x: datasets.ImageFolder(os.path.join(data_dir, x),
                                          data_transforms[x])
                  for x in ['train', 'val']}
dataloaders = {x: torch.utils.data.DataLoader(image_datasets[x], batch_size=4,
                                              shuffle=True, num_workers=4)
               for x in ['train', 'val']}

# Load a pre-trained ResNet model
model_ft = models.resnet18(pretrained=True)
num_ftrs = model_ft.fc.in_features
# Modify the final layer to match the number of classes in the target task
model_ft.fc = nn.Linear(num_ftrs, 2)

device = torch.device("cuda:0" if torch.cuda.is_available() else "cpu")
model_ft = model_ft.to(device)

# Define loss function and optimizer
criterion = nn.CrossEntropyLoss()
optimizer_ft = optim.SGD(model_ft.parameters(), lr=0.001, momentum=0.9)

# Train and evaluate
num_epochs = 25
for epoch in range(num_epochs):
    # Training phase
    model_ft.train()
    running_loss = 0.0
    running_corrects = 0
    for inputs, labels in dataloaders['train']:
        inputs, labels = inputs.to(device), labels.to(device)
        optimizer_ft.zero_grad()
        outputs = model_ft(inputs)
        _, preds = torch.max(outputs, 1)
        loss = criterion(outputs, labels)
        loss.backward()
        optimizer_ft.step()
        running_loss += loss.item() * inputs.size(0)
        running_corrects += torch.sum(preds == labels.data)

    epoch_loss = running_loss / len(image_datasets['train'])
    epoch_acc = running_corrects.double() / len(image_datasets['train'])
```

```
    print(f'Epoch {epoch}/{num_epochs-1}')
    print(f'Loss: {epoch_loss:.4f} Acc: {epoch_acc:.4f}')

print('Training complete')
```

The pre-trained resnet18 model's last fully connected layer (fc) is modified to fit the number of classes in the target task. This fine-tuning enables the model to adapt its learnt features from the source domain (ImageNet) to the target domain.

Transfer learning offers significant improvements in training efficiency and overall model performance, enabling rapid prototype development. Its application spans numerous fields including computer vision, natural language processing, and bioinformatics, exemplifying its versatility and effectiveness.

9.2 Understanding Pre-trained Models

Pre-trained models are neural network models that have been previously trained on a massive dataset, often for large-scale classification tasks. Utilizing these models can significantly reduce both the time and computational resources required to develop high-performance models for specific tasks. This section delves into the architecture and functionality of pre-trained models, the advantages they offer, and the processes involved in their deployment for various machine learning tasks.

A pre-trained model is primarily stored along with its architecture and learned weights. The architecture specifies the layers and their connections, while the weights represent the learned parameters that are crucial for making predictions. Some of the most commonly used pre-trained models include VGG, ResNet, Inception, BERT, and GPT.

Architectural Overview

In the context of image classification, pre-trained models like VGG and ResNet are often employed. VGG (Visual Geometry Group) models are characterized by their simplicity, using mostly stacked convolutional layers with small receptive fields. For instance, VGG16 consists of 16 layers: 13 convolutional and 3 fully connected layers. Its straightforward design aids in easy interpretability and adaptation to other tasks.

On the other hand, ResNet (Residual Networks) models utilize residual blocks, which help mitigate the vanishing gradient problem by allowing gradients to propagate directly through an identity shortcut. This architecture enables the construction of significantly deeper networks, such as ResNet50 and ResNet101, which include 50 and 101 layers, respectively.

The Inception model is another prominent architecture known for its inception modules, which apply multiple convolutions with different kernel sizes in parallel within the same layer. This design captures multi-scale features, improving the model's ability to recognize objects at varying scales. The most recognized variant is Inception-v3.

In natural language processing (NLP), models like BERT (Bidirectional Encoder Representations from Transformers) and GPT (Generative Pre-training Transformer) have revolutionized various tasks. BERT is designed to understand the context of a word in a sentence by looking at the words before and after it. This bidirectional approach enables BERT to generate more nuanced word embeddings. In contrast, GPT focuses on generating text by predicting the next word in a sequence, exhibiting strong performance in text generation tasks.

Advantages of Pre-trained Models

Utilizing pre-trained models offers several substantial benefits:

- **Reduced Training Time:** Since pre-trained models come with pre-learned weights, they can significantly shorten the training phase. This is particularly beneficial when working with large-scale datasets or complex architectures.
- **Lower Computational Cost:** Training deep neural networks from scratch requires considerable computational power. Pre-trained models have already undergone intensive training processes, thus requiring less computational resources for further fine-tuning.
- **Better Generalization:** Pre-trained models are typically trained on large and diverse datasets, helping them generalize better to various tasks. For example, a model pre-trained on ImageNet can effectively recognize features in completely different image datasets.
- **Easier Convergence:** Fine-tuning pre-trained models generally leads to faster and more stable convergence due to the property of transfer learning, where initial weights are already close to an optimal solution.

Loading and Using Pre-trained Models in PyTorch

In PyTorch, loading pre-trained models is straightforward due to its comprehensive library of model architectures. To demonstrate, consider how to load and utilize the ResNet50 model:

```
import torch
import torchvision.models as models

# Load the pre-trained ResNet50 model
model = models.resnet50(pretrained=True)

# Set the model to evaluation mode
model.eval()
```

In this example, we import the required modules and load the ResNet50 model by setting pretrained=True, which downloads the model's weights trained on ImageNet. The eval() method sets the model to evaluation mode, necessary for making predictions and preventing certain layers (e.g., dropout layers) from behaving differently during inference.

Fine-Tuning and Feature Extraction

Pre-trained models can be employed in two principal modes: fine-tuning and feature extraction.

- **Fine-Tuning:** This involves continuing the training of the pre-trained model on the target dataset. Here, we adjust all the model's weights, providing the flexibility to adapt intricate features to the specific task. This can be achieved by allowing gradient updates to all layers:

```
# We do not freeze any layers, so all weights will be updated
for param in model.parameters():
    param.requires_grad = True
```

- **Feature Extraction:** This approach leverages the pre-trained model as a fixed feature extractor. The model's convolutional base is used to extract meaningful features, which are then fed into new, task-specific layers. Typically, only these new layers are trained, keeping the pre-trained weights fixed:

```
# Freeze all layers except the final fully connected layer
for param in model.parameters():
    param.requires_grad = False

# Replace the final layer with a new one that matches the target number of
    classes
num_ftrs = model.fc.in_features
model.fc = torch.nn.Linear(num_ftrs, num_classes)

# Train the new final layer weights
```

```
for param in model.fc.parameters():
    param.requires_grad = True
```

Applications and Adaptations

Pre-trained models find their utility across numerous domains. In image classification tasks, they can be adapted to identify a different set of classes other than those they were originally trained on. For instance, a pre-trained ResNet50 can be fine-tuned to classify medical images, signifying a drastic domain shift from natural images.

In natural language processing, models like BERT and GPT can be fine-tuned for specific NLP tasks such as sentiment analysis, machine translation, and question answering. By leveraging the pre-trained weights, these models can achieve state-of-the-art performance with comparatively minimal task-specific training.

Model Performance and Evaluation

Evaluating the performance of pre-trained models hinges on the task and the dataset. Standard metrics such as accuracy, precision, recall, and F1-score offer invaluable insights into model performance. Cross-validation and holdout validation techniques further ensure the robustness of model evaluation.

Comparative analysis between training from scratch and fine-tuning pre-trained models substantiates the efficacy of transfer learning. In subsequent sections, we will explore case studies and practical implementations using PyTorch, extending this conceptual understanding to real-world applications.

9.3 Benefits of Transfer Learning

Transfer learning offers a multitude of advantages, particularly in scenarios where training a model from scratch is impractical due to insufficient data or computational resources. The following points elucidate the primary benefits of employing transfer learning techniques in various machine learning tasks.

- **Reduced Training Time:** One of the most significant advantages of transfer learning is the substantial reduction in training time. Instead of initializing a model with random weights, transfer learning utilizes a pre-trained model with learned weights from a large dataset. This initialization allows the model to converge much more quickly during training on the target task. Below is an example demonstrating the shortened training process using PyTorch on the CIFAR-10 dataset with a ResNet-18 model pre-trained on ImageNet.

```
import torch
import torchvision
import torchvision.transforms as transforms
from torchvision.models import resnet18

# Load CIFAR-10 dataset
transform = transforms.Compose([transforms.Resize(224),
                                transforms.ToTensor(),
                                transforms.Normalize((0.485, 0.456, 0.406),
                                                     (0.229, 0.224, 0.225))])

trainset = torchvision.datasets.CIFAR10(root='./data', train=True,
                                        download=True, transform=transform)
trainloader = torch.utils.data.DataLoader(trainset, batch_size=32, shuffle=True)

# Load pre-trained ResNet-18 model
model = resnet18(pretrained=True)

# Modify the final layer to match the number of classes in CIFAR-10
num_ftrs = model.fc.in_features
model.fc = torch.nn.Linear(num_ftrs, 10)

# Define loss function and optimizer
criterion = torch.nn.CrossEntropyLoss()
optimizer = torch.optim.SGD(model.parameters(), lr=0.001, momentum=0.9)

# Training loop
num_epochs = 10
for epoch in range(num_epochs):
    running_loss = 0.0
    for inputs, labels in trainloader:
        optimizer.zero_grad()
        outputs = model(inputs)
        loss = criterion(outputs, labels)
        loss.backward()
        optimizer.step()
        running_loss += loss.item()

    print(f"Epoch [{epoch+1}/{num_epochs}], Loss: {running_loss/len(trainloader)}")
```

Upon execution, this code initializes the ResNet-18 model with pre-trained weights, thereby significantly reducing the required number of training epochs to achieve a comparable level of accuracy.

```
Epoch [1/10], Loss: 1.8764
Epoch [2/10], Loss: 1.3447
Epoch [3/10], Loss: 1.0802
Epoch [4/10], Loss: 0.9225
Epoch [5/10], Loss: 0.8094
Epoch [6/10], Loss: 0.7207
Epoch [7/10], Loss: 0.6477
Epoch [8/10], Loss: 0.5855
Epoch [9/10], Loss: 0.5316
Epoch [10/10], Loss: 0.4852
```

- **Improved Model Performance:** Transfer learning often yields superior model performance as pre-trained models learn features from extensive and diverse datasets. These learned features can be highly robust and generalizable, making them invaluable when dealing with smaller datasets where training a model from scratch would likely lead to overfitting. For instance, fine-tuning a pre-trained convolutional neural network (CNN) on a small medical image dataset can achieve higher accuracy and generalization compared to a CNN trained solely on the small dataset.

- **Decreased Need for Extensive Labelled Data:** A major advantage of transfer learning lies in its ability to leverage existing models trained on large datasets, which mitigates the challenge of obtaining extensive labelled data. In many domains, procuring labelled data is both time-consuming and expensive. Pre-trained models serve as powerful feature extractors or starting points, enabling effective training with a significantly smaller labelled dataset. This is particularly beneficial in specialized fields such as medical imaging where high-quality labelled data is limited.

- **Enhanced Generalization:** Pre-trained models have already been exposed to a wide variety of data, thereby learning a diverse range of features. When adapted to new tasks, these features can help the model generalize better to previously unseen data. This is especially crucial in industrial applications where the ability to generalize across varying conditions and environments can determine the success of deploying machine learning solutions.

- **Facilitation of Knowledge Sharing and Reusability:** Transfer learning promotes the reuse of knowledge across different but related domains. This characteristic aligns well with the collaborative nature of the scientific community, where sharing pre-trained models accelerates research and development. It enables practitioners to focus efforts on specific adaptations required for their tasks rather than starting from scratch. This collaborative approach is exemplified by the widespread availability of pre-trained models in repositories such as PyTorch Hub and TensorFlow Hub.

Overall, transfer learning presents multiple pragmatic and theoretical benefits that enhance the efficiency, effectiveness, and scope of machine learning applications across a burgeoning range of fields and tasks. The systematic leveraging of previously acquired knowledge accelerates advancements and fosters innovation, thereby paving the way for increasingly sophisticated and capable machine learning systems.

9.4 Exploring Popular Pre-trained Models

The field of machine learning has significantly advanced with the advent of pre-trained models. These models, trained on large, diverse datasets, provide a robust starting point for various tasks. Leveraging pre-trained models can save considerable computational resources and time. In this section, we will delve into some of the most prominent and widely-used pre-trained models in both computer vision and natural language processing domains.

1. ResNet

ResNet, short for Residual Network, introduced by He et al. in 2015, addressed the problem of vanishing gradients in deep networks through the use of residual connections. ResNet models range from ResNet-18 to ResNet-152, with the number indicating the depth of the network. These networks are specifically designed for image classification tasks and have achieved remarkable results on benchmarks like ImageNet.

```
from torchvision import models

# Load a pre-trained ResNet model
resnet50 = models.resnet50(pretrained=True)
```

The following sample execution demonstrates loading and using the ResNet model for inference:

```
>>> import torch
>>> from torchvision import transforms
>>> from PIL import Image
>>> model = resnet50
>>> model.eval()
>>> input_image = Image.open("example_image.jpg")
>>> preprocess = transforms.Compose([
>>>     transforms.Resize(256),
>>>     transforms.CenterCrop(224),
>>>     transforms.ToTensor(),
>>>     transforms.Normalize(mean=[0.485, 0.456, 0.406], std=[0.229, 0.224, 0.225]),
>>> ])
>>> input_tensor = preprocess(input_image)
>>> input_batch = input_tensor.unsqueeze(0)
>>> if torch.cuda.is_available():
>>>     input_batch = input_batch.to('cuda')
>>>     model.to('cuda')

>>> with torch.no_grad():
>>>     output = model(input_batch)
>>> print(output[0])
tensor([...])
```

2. VGG

The Visual Geometry Group (VGG) models, created by Simonyan and Zisserman, are characterized primarily by their simplicity and depth. Available versions include VGG-11, VGG-16, and VGG-19. Unlike ResNet, VGG models use repeated blocks of convolutional layers followed by max pooling.

```
# Load a pre-trained VGG model
vgg16 = models.vgg16(pretrained=True)
```

Similar to ResNet, VGG can be employed for a variety of image processing tasks, especially classification. It uses an architecture that is easy to implement, making it a popular choice for transfer learning.

3. Inception

The Inception architecture, also known as GoogLeNet, was developed by Szegedy et al. and introduced in 2014. The key innovation lies in its inception modules, which allow for the employment of multiple convolutional filters in parallel, reducing computational complexity while maintaining accuracy.

```
# Load a pre-trained Inception model
inception_v3 = models.inception_v3(pretrained=True)
```

4. BERT

In the domain of Natural Language Processing (NLP), Bidirectional Encoder Representations from Transformers (BERT) by Devlin et al. has set a new paradigm. BERT can understand the context of a word based on both its previous and subsequent words. Pre-trained BERT models are available for tasks like text classification, named entity recognition, and question answering.

```
from transformers import BertTokenizer, BertModel

# Load pre-trained BERT model and tokenizer
tokenizer = BertTokenizer.from_pretrained('bert-base-uncased')
model = BertModel.from_pretrained('bert-base-uncased')
```

Here is an example of encoding text input and obtaining its representation:

```
>>> text = "Deep learning is revolutionary."
>>> encoded_input = tokenizer(text, return_tensors='pt')
>>> output = model(**encoded_input)
>>> print(output.last_hidden_state)
tensor([...])
```

5. GPT

Generative Pre-trained Transformer (GPT) models, developed by OpenAI, have demonstrated remarkable capabilities in text generation and understanding. The architecture is based on the transformer model, but it is optimally tuned for autoregressive tasks. The GPT-3 model, in particular, with 175 billion parameters, is highly proficient in almost all NLP tasks.

```
from transformers import GPT2Tokenizer, GPT2LMHeadModel

# Load pre-trained GPT model and tokenizer
tokenizer = GPT2Tokenizer.from_pretrained('gpt2')
model = GPT2LMHeadModel.from_pretrained('gpt2')
```

The following example shows how to generate text based on an initial input:

```
>>> initial_input = "Once upon a time"
>>> input_ids = tokenizer.encode(initial_input, return_tensors='pt')
>>> output = model.generate(input_ids, max_length=50, num_return_sequences=1)
>>> print(tokenizer.decode(output[0], skip_special_tokens=True))
"Once upon a time, there was a small village..."
```

These pre-trained models not only encapsulate extensive knowledge but also provide a robust foundation for transfer learning. Using them effectively can accelerate and enhance the performance of a wide range of machine learning tasks.

9.5 Using PyTorch for Transfer Learning

Transfer learning significantly improves the performance and efficiency of machine learning models by leveraging pre-trained models as a starting point. PyTorch offers a flexible and straightforward approach to implement transfer learning, allowing seamless integration of pre-trained models for various tasks. This section details the procedure to use PyTorch for transfer learning, building upon concepts previously introduced in this chapter.

Begin by importing the necessary libraries and modules. Ensure that you have 'torch', 'torchvision', and 'torchvision.models' installed and imported, as these provide essential functions and pre-trained models that facilitate transfer learning.

```
import torch
import torch.nn as nn
import torch.optim as optim
from torch.optim import lr_scheduler
import torchvision
from torchvision import datasets, models, transforms
import time
import os
import copy
```

Data Preparation

Transfer learning typically involves image data, necessitating the organization of data into a specific directory structure. The data should be split into training and validation sets, each containing class-specific subdirectories.

Apply transformations to the images to resize them to a consistent dimension, normalize pixel values, and perform data augmentation where appropriate. PyTorch's 'transforms' module facilitates these operations.

```
data_transforms = {
    'train': transforms.Compose([
        transforms.RandomResizedCrop(224),
        transforms.RandomHorizontalFlip(),
        transforms.ToTensor(),
        transforms.Normalize([0.485, 0.456, 0.406], [0.229, 0.224, 0.225])
    ]),
    'val': transforms.Compose([
        transforms.Resize(256),
        transforms.CenterCrop(224),
        transforms.ToTensor(),
        transforms.Normalize([0.485, 0.456, 0.406], [0.229, 0.224, 0.225])
    ]),
}
```

Create datasets and dataloaders to manage the batches of images and facilitate efficient training and validation.

```
data_dir = 'data/hymenoptera_data'
image_datasets = {x: datasets.ImageFolder(os.path.join(data_dir, x), data_transforms
    [x])
            for x in ['train', 'val']}
dataloaders = {x: torch.utils.data.DataLoader(image_datasets[x], batch_size=4, shuffle
    =True, num_workers=4)
            for x in ['train', 'val']}
dataset_sizes = {x: len(image_datasets[x]) for x in ['train', 'val']}
class_names = image_datasets['train'].classes
device = torch.device("cuda:0" if torch.cuda.is_available() else "cpu")
```

Loading and Modifying Pre-trained Models

PyTorch provides access to a variety of pre-trained models through the 'torchvision.models' module. Select an appropriate pre-trained model for your task. For instance, consider the 'resnet18' model. Modify the final layer to match the number of classes in the target dataset.

```
model_ft = models.resnet18(pretrained=True)
num_ftrs = model_ft.fc.in_features
model_ft.fc = nn.Linear(num_ftrs, len(class_names))
model_ft = model_ft.to(device)
```

Defining Loss Function and Optimizer

Specify a loss function and an optimizer. For classification tasks, the cross-entropy loss ('nn.CrossEntropyLoss') is commonly used. Additionally, define a learning rate scheduler to decrease the learning rate during training.

```
criterion = nn.CrossEntropyLoss()

optimizer_ft = optim.SGD(model_ft.parameters(), lr=0.001, momentum=0.9)

exp_lr_scheduler = lr_scheduler.StepLR(optimizer_ft, step_size=7, gamma=0.1)
```

Training the Model

Implement the training loop, iterating over the dataset for a specified number of epochs. Ensure that the model is in training mode by calling 'model.train()' and switch to evaluation mode with 'model.eval()' during validation.

```
def train_model(model, criterion, optimizer, scheduler, num_epochs=25):
    since = time.time()

    best_model_wts = copy.deepcopy(model.state_dict())
    best_acc = 0.0

    for epoch in range(num_epochs):
        print('Epoch {}/{}'.format(epoch, num_epochs - 1))
```

```
            print('-' * 10)

            for phase in ['train', 'val']:
                if phase == 'train':
                    model.train()
                else:
                    model.eval()

                running_loss = 0.0
                running_corrects = 0

                for inputs, labels in dataloaders[phase]:
                    inputs = inputs.to(device)
                    labels = labels.to(device)

                    optimizer.zero_grad()

                    with torch.set_grad_enabled(phase == 'train'):
                        outputs = model(inputs)
                        _, preds = torch.max(outputs, 1)
                        loss = criterion(outputs, labels)

                        if phase == 'train':
                            loss.backward()
                            optimizer.step()

                    running_loss += loss.item() * inputs.size(0)
                    running_corrects += torch.sum(preds == labels.data)

                if phase == 'train':
                    scheduler.step()

                epoch_loss = running_loss / dataset_sizes[phase]
                epoch_acc = running_corrects.double() / dataset_sizes[phase]

                print('{} Loss: {:.4f} Acc: {:.4f}'.format(phase, epoch_loss, epoch_acc))

                if phase == 'val' and epoch_acc > best_acc:
                    best_acc = epoch_acc
                    best_model_wts = copy.deepcopy(model.state_dict())

            print()

        time_elapsed = time.time() - since
        print('Training complete in {:.0f}m {:.0f}s'.format(time_elapsed // 60,
            time_elapsed % 60))
        print('Best val Acc: {:4f}'.format(best_acc))

        model.load_state_dict(best_model_wts)
        return model

model_ft = train_model(model_ft, criterion, optimizer_ft, exp_lr_scheduler,
    num_epochs=25)
```

Evaluating the Model

After training, it is crucial to evaluate the model's performance on a hold-out test set or the validation set to ensure that it generalizes well to new data. The following code snippet demonstrates how to perform evaluation.

```
def evaluate_model(model, dataloader):
    model.eval()
    corrects = 0

    with torch.no_grad():
        for inputs, labels in dataloader:
            inputs = inputs.to(device)
            labels = labels.to(device)
            outputs = model(inputs)
            _, preds = torch.max(outputs, 1)
            corrects += torch.sum(preds == labels.data)

    accuracy = corrects.double() / len(dataloader.dataset)
    print(f'Accuracy: {accuracy:.4f}')

evaluate_model(model_ft, dataloaders['val'])
```

The integration of these elements provides a comprehensive approach to utilizing transfer learning with PyTorch, allowing for efficient model training and evaluation on new tasks.

9.6 Fine-Tuning Pre-trained Models

Fine-tuning pre-trained models is a technique widely used in transfer learning to adapt an existing model to a slightly different but related task. This section delves into fine-tuning methodologies, explaining both conceptual and practical aspects. Fine-tuning typically involves initializing a model with pre-trained weights and updating these weights through additional training on the target dataset. This reduces the time and computational resources required compared to training a model from scratch.

When fine-tuning a pre-trained model, it is essential to carefully manage which layers of the model are trainable. Layers early in the network often capture more general features, such as edges or textures when dealing with image data, while later layers capture more task-specific features. This distinction guides the decision on which layers to freeze (i.e., keep weights constant) and which to train further.

Step-by-Step Process for Fine-Tuning a Pre-trained Model in PyTorch:

- **Select and Load a Pre-trained Model:** The first step involves choosing a suitable pre-trained model. Popular choices include ResNet, VGG, and BERT, depending on the task. PyTorch provides seamless access to these models via the torchvision.models module for computer vision and transformers library for natural language processing tasks.

- **Freeze Initial Layers:** Depending on the task and dataset size, freezing initial layers can prevent overfitting and retain essential pre-trained features. This can be accomplished by setting the requires_grad attribute of the layers to False.
- **Modify the Output Layer:** The final layer is typically task-specific (e.g., classification layer size). Transfer learning involves modifying this layer to match the number of classes in the new dataset.
- **Compile the Model:** Define the optimizer and loss function. Typically, a lower learning rate is preferred during fine-tuning as it enables more controlled and gradual updates to the weights.
- **Train the Model:** Proceed with training the model on the new dataset. Monitor performance and adjust hyperparameters if necessary.

Illustrative Example: Fine-Tuning ResNet on a Custom Dataset

In this detailed example, we will fine-tune a ResNet model pre-trained on the ImageNet dataset for a custom image classification task.

```
import torch
import torch.nn as nn
import torch.optim as optim
from torchvision import datasets, models, transforms

# Define transformations for the training set
transform_train = transforms.Compose([
    transforms.Resize(256),
    transforms.CenterCrop(224),
    transforms.ToTensor(),
    transforms.Normalize(mean=[0.485, 0.456, 0.406],
                         std=[0.229, 0.224, 0.225]),
])

# Load the training dataset
train_dataset = datasets.ImageFolder(root='path_to_train_data',
                                     transform=transform_train)
train_loader = torch.utils.data.DataLoader(train_dataset,
                                           batch_size=32,
                                           shuffle=True)

# Load a pre-trained ResNet model
model = models.resnet18(pretrained=True)

# Freeze the initial layers
for param in model.parameters():
    param.requires_grad = False

# Modify the output layer to match the number of classes in the new dataset
```

```
num_ftrs = model.fc.in_features
model.fc = nn.Linear(num_ftrs, num_classes)

# Define the optimizer and loss function
optimizer = optim.SGD(model.fc.parameters(), lr=0.001, momentum=0.9)
criterion = nn.CrossEntropyLoss()

# Training loop
num_epochs = 10
for epoch in range(num_epochs):
    model.train()
    running_loss = 0.0
    for inputs, labels in train_loader:
        optimizer.zero_grad()
        outputs = model(inputs)
        loss = criterion(outputs, labels)
        loss.backward()
        optimizer.step()

        running_loss += loss.item()

    print(f'Epoch {epoch+1}/{num_epochs}, Loss: {running_loss/len(train_loader)}')
```

In this code, the initial layers of the ResNet model are frozen to preserve the learned features from the ImageNet dataset. The final fully connected layer is modified to accommodate the number of classes in the new dataset. The optimizer updates only the parameters of the new fully connected layer.

Considerations for Fine-Tuning:

Selecting an appropriate number of layers to freeze and the learning rate are critical for fine-tuning success. Too many trainable parameters with a small dataset can lead to overfitting, while too few may not capture the nuances of the new task. Additionally, employing techniques like data augmentation and regularization can help enhance the model's robustness.

Fine-tuning can be particularly effective in scenarios where the new dataset is small, and acquiring an extensive dataset is impractical. It leverages the rich feature representations learned from vast datasets, thus offering a path to create high-performing models without enormous data and computational resources.

9.7 Feature Extraction

Feature extraction is a significant technique in the practice of transfer learning and utilizing pre-trained models. It involves leveraging the features from a pre-trained network to train a new model. Pre-trained networks, especially those that are complex such as Convolutional Neural Networks (CNNs), have already learned useful features from large datasets. By repurposing these features for different tasks, we can significantly reduce the amount of required training data and computational resources.

In feature extraction, we use the convolutional layers of a pre-trained network to extract feature maps from the input data. These feature maps are then fed into new, task-specific layers, such as fully connected layers, which are trained from scratch. The convolutional layers are typically frozen during this process, meaning their weights are not updated, allowing them to act as a fixed feature extractor.

Consider a pre-trained model like VGG16. This model has distinct layers that extract features of increasing complexity. For example, initial layers may detect edges, mid-level layers may identify textures, and deep layers may recognize high-level structures like objects or even scenes. By extracting features from one of the deep layers of VGG16, we acquire a sophisticated representation of the input data which can be utilized in a new context.

In PyTorch, feature extraction can be implemented straightforwardly. The following example demonstrates how to use a pre-trained ResNet-50 model to extract features for an image classification task:

```
import torch
import torch.nn as nn
from torchvision import models, transforms
from torch.utils.data import DataLoader
from my_dataset import MyDataset # Assuming 'my_dataset' is a custom dataset
    module

# Load a pre-trained ResNet-50 model
model = models.resnet50(pretrained=True)

# Freeze all the parameters in the pre-trained model
for param in model.parameters():
    param.requires_grad = False

# Replace the final classification layer with a new layer that matches the number of
    classes in our new task
num_ftrs = model.fc.in_features
model.fc = nn.Linear(num_ftrs, num_classes)

# Define transformations for the input data
data_transforms = transforms.Compose([
    transforms.Resize((224, 224)),
    transforms.ToTensor(),
    transforms.Normalize([0.485, 0.456, 0.406], [0.229, 0.224, 0.225]),
])

# Load dataset
train_dataset = MyDataset(transform=data_transforms, train=True)
train_loader = DataLoader(train_dataset, batch_size=32, shuffle=True)
```

```
# Define loss function and optimizer
criterion = nn.CrossEntropyLoss()
optimizer = torch.optim.Adam(model.fc.parameters(), lr=0.001)

# Training loop
model.train()
for epoch in range(num_epochs):
    for inputs, labels in train_loader:
        inputs, labels = inputs.to(device), labels.to(device)

        # Zero the parameter gradients
        optimizer.zero_grad()

        # Forward pass
        outputs = model(inputs)
        loss = criterion(outputs, labels)

        # Backward pass and optimize
        loss.backward()
        optimizer.step()

    print(f'Epoch {epoch+1}/{num_epochs}, Loss: {loss.item()}')
```

In this example, the pre-trained ResNet-50 model's parameters are set to require no gradient updates by setting requires_grad to False. Only the final fully connected layer (model.fc) is replaced with a new layer that matches the number of classes in the new task. The optimizer is then configured to update only the parameters of this newly added layer.

Feature extraction is versatile and can be adapted for various data modalities. While the above example focuses on image classification, the same principles apply to other tasks such as object detection, segmentation, and even applications beyond computer vision, like natural language processing (NLP). One can select a pre-trained model appropriate for the specific domain, such as BERT for NLP tasks, and similarly utilize its feature representations.

Using pre-trained networks for feature extraction can lead to superior performance, particularly when the available training data for the new task is limited. The underlying reason is that the pre-trained models have already learned generalized patterns and features from vast amounts of data, which can efficiently transfer to new tasks, enabling the model to converge faster and often achieving higher accuracy.

It is critical to select the correct depth in the network for feature extraction. Shallower layers capture more generic features that are broadly applicable, such as edges and textures, while deeper layers capture more task-specific features. Experimenting with different layers can yield better results depending on the similarity between the source task and the target task.

Deep learning frameworks, especially PyTorch, provide the flexibility to experiment with different models and layers rapidly. Hence, extracting features from pre-trained models is not just powerful but also accessible, making it a key technique in the toolbox of modern deep learning practitioners.

9.8 Handling Different Input Sizes

Handling various input sizes is a crucial aspect of transfer learning, particularly when adapting pre-trained models to new tasks. When working with image data or natural language processing (NLP) applications, the input dimensions of the pre-trained models often differ from those of the new dataset. PyTorch provides several techniques and functionalities to address this discrepancy efficiently.

Image Data:

For image classification tasks, pre-trained models such as VGG, ResNet, and Inception networks expect input images of a specific size, typically 224×224 pixels. Here are the steps to preprocess images to the required input size:

- **Resizing:** Images from different sources may come in various resolutions. First, all images need to be resized to a consistent size, usually 256×256 pixels for rescaling to higher resolution or aspect-ratio retention while ensuring enough information for cropping.

- **Center Cropping:** Once the images are resized, they need to be cropped to the size expected by the model. For most pre-trained models, this means center-cropping them to 224×224 pixels.

- **Normalization:** After resizing and cropping, the pixel values need to be normalized using the mean and standard deviation of the dataset that the pre-trained model was originally trained on. For instance, ImageNet means and standard deviations are used for models trained on the ImageNet dataset.

The following PyTorch code snippet demonstrates these preprocessing steps:

```
from torchvision import transforms
preprocess = transforms.Compose([
    transforms.Resize(256),
    transforms.CenterCrop(224),
    transforms.ToTensor(),
    transforms.Normalize(mean=[0.485, 0.456, 0.406],
                         std=[0.229, 0.224, 0.225])
])

# Applying preprocessing to an example image
from PIL import Image

input_image = Image.open("example.jpg")
input_tensor = preprocess(input_image)
input_batch = input_tensor.unsqueeze(0) # Create a mini-batch as expected by the
    model
```

Natural Language Processing Data:

For NLP tasks, pre-trained models such as BERT, GPT, or RoBERTa expect text input to be tokenized and converted into specific input formats including token IDs, attention masks, and token type IDs. Here's a brief overview of the processing steps:

- **Tokenization:** Text data must be converted into a sequence of tokens using a tokenizer associated with the pre-trained model.
- **Padding and Truncation:** Since different texts have different lengths, they need to be padded and truncated to a uniform length that fits the model's maximum sequence length capacity.
- **Encoding:** The automated conversion of tokens into token IDs compatible with the model.

Here is the PyTorch code to achieve these steps using the HuggingFace Transformers library:

```
from transformers import BertTokenizer

tokenizer = BertTokenizer.from_pretrained('bert-base-uncased')

# Example text input
text = "This is an example sentence to demonstrate preprocessing."

# Tokenize, pad, and encode the text input
encoding = tokenizer.encode_plus(
    text,
    add_special_tokens=True,
    max_length=128,
    padding='max_length',
    return_attention_mask=True,
    return_tensors='pt'
```

```
)

input_ids = encoding['input_ids']
attention_mask = encoding['attention_mask']
token_type_ids = encoding['token_type_ids']
```

Once the images or text data are preprocessed into the required size and format, they are ready to be fed into the pre-trained models for further training or inference.

When handling different input sizes, it is essential to consider the computational resources available. Smaller input sizes reduce the computational burden but may lose important information. Conversely, larger input sizes preserve more details but at the cost of increased computational complexity and memory usage. Balancing these factors is critical for optimizing model performance and resource usage.

For advanced applications, more sophisticated techniques such as adaptive pooling, dynamic padding, or custom resizing strategies may be employed. These methods are particularly useful when dealing with datasets containing highly variable input sizes. PyTorch facilitates these advanced preprocessing techniques through flexible and efficient APIs, allowing for custom solutions tailored to specific datasets and model requirements.

Through meticulous preprocessing and resizing techniques, different input sizes can be effectively handled, ensuring compatibility and optimal performance of pre-trained models across diverse datasets and applications.

9.9 Transfer Learning for Image Classification

Transfer learning has become an essential technique in image classification, allowing models to leverage pre-trained weights on large datasets and adapt them to specific tasks with relatively smaller datasets. The foundational concept in transfer learning for image classification is to start with a pre-trained model that has been trained on a comprehensive dataset such as ImageNet. This section will delve into the steps and methodologies for implementing transfer learning for image classification using PyTorch.

The process typically involves two primary strategies: feature extraction and fine-tuning. Feature extraction uses the convolutional base of the pre-trained model to extract meaningful features from new images, whereas fine-tuning involves unfreezing some of the top layers of the convolutional base and training both the newly added classifier layers and the last few layers of the convolutional base jointly.

Step 1: Selecting a Pre-trained Model

PyTorch provides a variety of pre-trained models through the torchvision.models module. Popular architectures such as VGG, ResNet, and Inception have demonstrated high performance and are widely used.

```
import torch
import torchvision.models as models

# Load a pre-trained ResNet18 model
model = models.resnet18(pretrained=True)
```

Step 2: Modifying the Final Layer

Once the model is selected, the next step is to modify the final layer to match the number of classes in the specific image classification task. For instance, if the task involves classifying between five different types of flowers, the final fully connected layer should output five logits.

```
import torch.nn as nn

# Modify the fully connected layer to match the number of classes (e.g., 5 classes)
num_features = model.fc.in_features
model.fc = nn.Linear(num_features, 5)
```

Step 3: Freezing the Convolutional Base

In feature extraction, the convolutional base is frozen to prevent it from updating its weights during training. This ensures that the feature extraction process utilizes the learned features from the pre-trained model without alteration.

```
# Freeze all the parameters in the convolutional base
for param in model.parameters():
    param.requires_grad = False
```

Step 4: Training the Fully Connected Layers

Only the parameters of the newly added fully connected layer are updated during training. This can be achieved by passing the parameters of the final layer as the argument to the optimizer.

```
import torch.optim as optim

# Only train the parameters of the final layer
optimizer = optim.Adam(model.fc.parameters(), lr=0.001)
```

The training loop for feature extraction will involve the standard training course, ensuring that only the final layer weights are updated:

```
# Define the loss function
criterion = nn.CrossEntropyLoss()

# Training the model
num_epochs = 10
for epoch in range(num_epochs):
    for inputs, labels in dataloaders['train']:
        # Zero the parameter gradients
        optimizer.zero_grad()

        # Forward pass
        outputs = model(inputs)
        loss = criterion(outputs, labels)

        # Backward pass
        loss.backward()
        optimizer.step()

    print(f'Epoch {epoch+1}/{num_epochs}, Loss: {loss.item()}')
```

Step 5: Fine-Tuning the Model

To achieve potentially better performance, fine-tuning can be employed. This process involves unfreezing some of the layers in the convolutional base and jointly training them with the fully connected layers. A common approach includes unfreezing the last two or three convolutional blocks of the model and refining them along with the fully connected layers.

```
# Unfreeze the last convolutional block
for name, param in model.named_parameters():
    if 'layer4' in name:
        param.requires_grad = True
    else:
        param.requires_grad = False

optimizer = optim.Adam(model.parameters(), lr=1e-4)

# Fine-tuning the model
num_epochs = 10
for epoch in range(num_epochs):
    for inputs, labels in dataloaders['train']:
        optimizer.zero_grad()
        outputs = model(inputs)
        loss = criterion(outputs, labels)
        loss.backward()
        optimizer.step()

    print(f'Epoch {epoch+1}/{num_epochs}, Loss: {loss.item()}')
```

Evaluating the Model

Evaluation of the trained model is critical to confirm its performance. This evaluation typically includes assessing the model on a validation or test dataset and calculating metrics such as accuracy, precision, recall, and F1-score.

```
# Set model to evaluation mode
model.eval()

# Initialization of metrics
correct = 0
total = 0

# No gradient computation
with torch.no_grad():
    for inputs, labels in dataloaders['validation']:
        outputs = model(inputs)
        _, predicted = torch.max(outputs, 1)
        total += labels.size(0)
        correct += (predicted == labels).sum().item()

accuracy = correct / total
print(f'Validation Accuracy: {accuracy * 100:.2f}%')
```

Integrating these steps will allow effective implementation of transfer learning techniques in image classification tasks using pre-trained models, leveraging their robustness and efficiency.

9.10 Transfer Learning for NLP Tasks

Transfer learning has significantly advanced the field of Natural Language Processing (NLP), enabling models to achieve high performance with relatively limited labeled data. This section delves into applying transfer learning specifically to NLP tasks like text classification, named entity recognition (NER), and machine translation, using PyTorch and pre-trained language models such as BERT, GPT, and others.

In the context of NLP, transfer learning generally involves pre-trained language models that have been initially trained on a large corpus of text data. These pre-trained models can be fine-tuned to specific downstream tasks, leveraging the learned representations of language.

Consider the following example of text classification using BERT (Bidirectional Encoder Representations from Transformers). The first step involves loading a pre-trained BERT model and the tokenizer:

```
from transformers import BertTokenizer, BertForSequenceClassification
import torch

# Load pre-trained BERT tokenizer
tokenizer = BertTokenizer.from_pretrained('bert-base-uncased')

# Load pre-trained BERT model for sequence classification
model = BertForSequenceClassification.from_pretrained('bert-base-uncased')
```

Tokenization is essential as it converts text data into a format that can be processed by the BERT model. The tokenizer handles converting text into tokens, managing special tokens, and padding/truncating sequences to a specified length. Below is an example of tokenizing a batch of text sentences:

```
sentences = ["Example sentence one.", "Another example sentence."]
inputs = tokenizer(sentences, padding=True, truncation=True, return_tensors="pt")
print(inputs)
```

The typical output of the tokenizer includes input IDs and attention masks:

```
{'input_ids': tensor([[  101,  2742, 6254, 7078,  2028,  1012,   102,     0,     0],
                      [  101,  2178,  2742, 6254, 7078,  1012,   102,     0,     0]]),
 'attention_mask': tensor([[1, 1, 1, 1, 1, 1, 1, 0, 0],
                          [1, 1, 1, 1, 1, 1, 1, 0, 0]])}
```

Fine-tuning a pre-trained model for a specific NLP task involves updating the model's weights using labeled data. This is typically done using a training loop. Here is an illustrative example:

```
from torch.utils.data import DataLoader, TensorDataset, RandomSampler
from transformers import AdamW

# Create Dataset and DataLoader
train_data = TensorDataset(inputs["input_ids"], inputs["attention_mask"],
    labels_tensor)
train_sampler = RandomSampler(train_data)
train_dataloader = DataLoader(train_data, sampler=train_sampler, batch_size=8)

# Set up the optimizer
optimizer = AdamW(model.parameters(), lr=1e-5)

# Training loop
model.train()
for epoch in range(3): # Number of epochs
    for step, batch in enumerate(train_dataloader):
        b_input_ids, b_input_mask, b_labels = batch
        optimizer.zero_grad()
        outputs = model(b_input_ids, token_type_ids=None,
                        attention_mask=b_input_mask, labels=b_labels)
        loss = outputs.loss
        loss.backward()
        optimizer.step()
        if step % 10 == 0:
            print(f"Epoch: {epoch}, Step: {step}, Loss: {loss.item()}")
```

Named Entity Recognition (NER) can be approached similarly by leveraging pre-trained models like BERT-CRF (Conditional Random Fields). The pre-processing and training steps are analogous, although the output format and evaluation metrics differ.

For machine translation tasks, pre-trained models such as T5 (Text-to-Text Transfer Transformer) and MarianMT can be employed. These models are designed to handle various text generation tasks like translation. Here is a concise implementation using MarianMT:

```
from transformers import MarianMTModel, MarianTokenizer

# Load pre-trained MarianMT model and tokenizer
model_name = 'Helsinki-NLP/opus-mt-en-fr'
tokenizer = MarianTokenizer.from_pretrained(model_name)
model = MarianMTModel.from_pretrained(model_name)

# Example text to translate
text = "Hello, how are you?"

# Tokenize and prepare input for the model
inputs = tokenizer([text], return_tensors="pt", padding=True)

# Perform translation
translated = model.generate(**inputs)
translated_text = [tokenizer.decode(t, skip_special_tokens=True) for t in translated]

print(translated_text)
```

Understanding evaluation metrics and rigorously validating model performance is critical. For instance, in classification tasks, metrics like accuracy, F1-score, precision, and recall are typically employed. For sequence generation tasks, BLEU (Bilingual Evaluation Understudy) score is often used.

```
from sklearn.metrics import accuracy_score, f1_score, precision_score, recall_score

# Assume y_true and y_pred are the ground truth labels and predicted labels,
    respectively

accuracy = accuracy_score(y_true, y_pred)
f1 = f1_score(y_true, y_pred)
precision = precision_score(y_true, y_pred)
recall = recall_score(y_true, y_pred)

print(f"Accuracy: {accuracy}")
print(f"F1 Score: {f1}")
print(f"Precision: {precision}")
print(f"Recall: {recall}")
```

Transfer learning in NLP uses the capabilities of pre-trained language models to achieve superior performance efficiently. The examples provided illustrate the crucial steps involving pre-trained model utilization, fine-tuning, and performance evaluation using PyTorch and the Hugging Face Transformers library.

9.11 Evaluating Transfer Learning Performance

Evaluation of transfer learning performance is a critical step in determining the success of your machine learning models. The process involves the use of various metrics and techniques to understand how well the model has generalized from a source task to a target task. This section delves into the essential methods and metrics utilized to evaluate the efficacy of transfer learning models, particularly in the context of image classification and natural language processing tasks.

In the context of image classification, the primary metrics used include accuracy, precision, recall, F1-score, and confusion matrices. Accuracy is the fraction of correctly predicted instances over the total instances, computed as:

$$Accuracy = \frac{TP + TN}{TP + TN + FP + FN}$$

where TP stands for True Positives, TN for True Negatives, FP for False Positives, and FN for False Negatives.

Precision, which measures the correctness of positive predictions, is given by:

$$Precision = \frac{TP}{TP + FP}$$

Recall, which measures the completeness of positive predictions, is given by:

$$Recall = \frac{TP}{TP + FN}$$

F1-score, the harmonic mean of precision and recall, is useful when the class distribution is imbalanced:

$$F1\text{-}score = 2 \cdot \frac{Precision \cdot Recall}{Precision + Recall}$$

A confusion matrix is a tabular representation of actual vs predicted classifications, helping to visualize the performance across different classes.

Evaluations on natural language processing (NLP) tasks may use similar metrics but often account for aspects unique to language data, such as BLEU score for translation tasks or ROUGE score for summarization tasks. For text classification:

$$Accuracy_{NLP} = \frac{\text{Number of correct predictions}}{\text{Total number of predictions}}$$

$$Precision_{NLP} = \frac{\text{True Positive predictions}}{\text{True Positive predictions + False Positive predictions}}$$

$$Recall_{NLP} = \frac{\text{True Positive predictions}}{\text{True Positive predictions + False Negative predictions}}$$

$$F1\text{-}score_{NLP} = 2 \cdot \frac{\text{Precision} \cdot \text{Recall}}{\text{Precision} + \text{Recall}}$$

When evaluating pre-trained models that have been fine-tuned, it is imperative to split the dataset into training, validation, and test subsets to avoid overfitting and ensure the model's generalizability. Stratified sampling is recommended to maintain the same proportion of each class in all sets.

The performance evaluation of a transfer learning model in PyTorch can be streamlined by leveraging utility functions from libraries such as torchmetrics. Below is an example demonstrating how to compute accuracy, precision, recall, and F1-score using PyTorch for an image classification task.

```
import torch
from torchmetrics import Accuracy, Precision, Recall, F1Score

# Initialize the metrics
accuracy_metric = Accuracy(num_classes=num_classes)
precision_metric = Precision(num_classes=num_classes, average='macro')
recall_metric = Recall(num_classes=num_classes, average='macro')
f1_metric = F1Score(num_classes=num_classes, average='macro')

# Assume y_pred and y_true are your model's predictions and the actual labels
y_pred = model(input_data)
y_true = actual_labels

# Compute metrics
accuracy = accuracy_metric(y_pred, y_true)
precision = precision_metric(y_pred, y_true)
recall = recall_metric(y_pred, y_true)
```

```
f1score = f1_metric(y_pred, y_true)

print(f'Accuracy: {accuracy.item()}')
print(f'Precision: {precision.item()}')
print(f'Recall: {recall.item()}')
print(f'F1 Score: {f1score.item()}')
```

Executing this snippet will yield an output similar to the one below, indicating the performance metrics for your model:

```
Accuracy: 0.85
Precision: 0.84
Recall: 0.83
F1 Score: 0.835
```

Additionally, creating and visualizing the confusion matrix provides deeper insights into which classes are most frequently misclassified. Using torchmetrics, this can be achieved as follows:

```
import matplotlib.pyplot as plt
from torchmetrics import ConfusionMatrix
import seaborn as sns

# Initialize ConfusionMatrix metric
confusion_matrix_metric = ConfusionMatrix(num_classes=num_classes)

# Compute the confusion matrix
conf_matrix = confusion_matrix_metric(y_pred, y_true)

# Plot the confusion matrix using seaborn
plt.figure(figsize=(10, 8))
sns.heatmap(conf_matrix.cpu().numpy(), annot=True, fmt='d', cmap='Blues')
plt.xlabel('Predicted Label')
plt.ylabel('True Label')
plt.title('Confusion Matrix')
plt.show()
```

In understanding the confusion matrix, each cell (i, j) represents the number of instances of class i that were predicted as class j. High values on the diagonal indicate good performance, whereas off-diagonal values signify misclassifications.

For NLP tasks, computing similar metrics can also be performed using PyTorch utility functions tailored for text data. Ensuring these evaluations accurately reflect your model's performance across all datasets guarantees objective measurements of how well the model has adapted to the new task.

Considering the variation in tasks, domain-specific metrics may sometimes be required. For instance, in object detection, metrics such as mean average precision (mAP) are crucial. Meanwhile, for language translation, BLEU scores are more appropriate.

These strategies furnish a comprehensive understanding of your model's performance, aiding in identifying areas needing improvement and ensuring transfer learning models reliably accomplish the intended tasks.

Chapter 10

Deploying PyTorch Models

This chapter addresses the practical aspects of deploying PyTorch models. It begins with saving and exporting models, followed by serving models using Flask and deploying on cloud platforms. The chapter discusses using TorchServe, optimizing models for inference through quantization and sparsity, and utilizing ONNX for interoperability. It also covers the deployment of models on edge devices and highlights best practices for monitoring and maintaining deployed models.

10.1 Introduction to Model Deployment

Deploying machine learning models, particularly those built with PyTorch, is a critical step in transforming developed models into practical applications. This section delves into the fundamental concepts and practices involved in the deployment of PyTorch models, laying the groundwork for subsequent sections that explore specific deployment methods and platforms.

Model Deployment: An Overview

Model deployment refers to the process of making a machine learning model available for use in a production environment. This involves transferring the model from a development setting, often characterized by experimentation and iteration, to a production environment where it can be consumed by users or other systems. The primary objectives of model deployment include ensuring the model's performance, scalability, reliability, and availability.

Key Phases in Model Deployment

- **Exporting the Model:** The first phase involves exporting the trained model from the development environment (typically in a framework-specific format like PyTorch's .pt or .pth files) to a format suitable for inference. This may involve serializing the model and its parameters for later deserialization.
- **Setting Up the Inference Environment:** This phase sets up the necessary environment where the model will perform inference. It includes configuring hardware resources (e.g., CPU, GPU, edge devices), necessary dependencies, and ensuring that the environment mirrors conditions under which the model was trained.
- **Serving the Model:** Serving involves making the model available for inference, often through a RESTful API or similar service interfaces such as gRPC. This step requires a serving infrastructure like web servers or serving frameworks that can efficiently handle incoming inference requests.
- **Load Testing and Optimization:** Ensuring the model and the serving infrastructure can handle the expected load is critical. This involves performing load testing and optimizing both the model (e.g., through quantization and sparsity) and the infrastructure to meet performance criteria.
- **Monitoring and Maintenance:** Post-deployment, it is essential to continuously monitor the model's performance, address any drift in its performance, and perform maintenance activities such as updating the model with new data and retraining.

Challenges in Model Deployment

- **Scalability:** Ensuring the model can scale to handle many requests per second is paramount. This often requires load balancing and horizontal scaling strategies.
- **Latency:** Minimizing the response time for inference is critical in real-time applications. Latency introduced by model size, data preprocessing, and hardware constraints must be addressed.

- **Reliability:** The deployed model must be robust against failure and should have high availability, demanding strategies like redundancy, checkpointing, and failover mechanisms.
- **Security:** Protecting the model from unauthorized access and ensuring data privacy during inference requires robust security measures, including authentication, encryption, and compliance with data protection regulations.
- **Resource Management:** Efficient utilization of computational resources to ensure cost-effective deployment without compromising on performance is vital.

Selecting the Deployment Approach

Choosing the right deployment strategy depends on several factors:

- **Inference Environment:** Whether deployment is on cloud platforms, edge devices, or on-premises servers significantly influences the deployment strategy.
- **Latency and Throughput Requirements:** These requirements dictate whether local inference, batch processing, or real-time serving is most appropriate.
- **Model Size and Complexity:** More complex and larger models may require specific optimizations or specialized hardware for efficient deployment.
- **Development and Maintenance Overhead:** Simplicity and ease of transitioning models from development to production, and the overhead of maintaining the deployed model, require careful consideration.

Frameworks and Tools for Model Deployment

Several tools and frameworks facilitate the deployment of PyTorch models:

- **TorchServe:** A flexible and easy-to-use tool specifically designed for serving PyTorch models at scale. It includes features like multi-model serving, logging, metrics, and model versioning.
- **Flask:** A lightweight WSGI web application framework in Python that can be used to serve machine learning models via REST APIs.

- **ONNX:** The Open Neural Network Exchange format enables interoperability between various deep learning frameworks, allowing models trained in PyTorch to be exported and deployed across multiple backend environments.

- **Cloud Services:** Platforms like AWS SageMaker, Google AI Platform, and Azure Machine Learning provide managed services for deploying and managing PyTorch models in the cloud.

- **Edge Deployment Tools:** Frameworks such as NVIDIA TensorRT, OpenVINO, and PyTorch Mobile assist in deploying models directly on edge devices like smartphones or embedded systems.

The sections that follow will explore these frameworks, tools, and techniques in greater detail, providing practical guides and examples to effectively deploy PyTorch models across various environments.

10.2 Saving and Exporting PyTorch Models

When working with PyTorch, one critical aspect of machine learning workflows is the ability to save and export models. This functionality enables models to be reused, shared, or deployed in different environments. The process of saving and exporting a model ensures that the learned parameters, architecture, and possibly even the training state can be preserved and replicated.

The primary mechanisms provided by PyTorch for saving and exporting models include the use of the $\mathrm{torch.save()}$ and $\mathrm{torch.load()}$ functions, which leverage the PyTorch serialization format. Models can be saved in two main formats: the entire model (including the architecture and learned parameters) and the state dictionary (which only includes the parameters). For more advanced deployment scenarios, such as integrating with other frameworks or optimizing for various platforms, exporting models to formats like ONNX (Open Neural Network Exchange) becomes essential.

Saving and Loading a Full Model

When saving an entire model, PyTorch serializes not only the model parameters but also the architecture. This approach ensures that the exact model can be reloaded without needing to explicitly define the model class. The typical workflow for saving and loading a full model involves the following steps:

```
import torch
import torch.nn as nn
import torch.optim as optim

# Define a simple neural network
class Net(nn.Module):
    def __init__(self):
        super(Net, self).__init__()
        self.fc1 = nn.Linear(784, 128)
        self.fc2 = nn.Linear(128, 10)

    def forward(self, x):
        x = torch.relu(self.fc1(x))
        x = self.fc2(x)
        return x

# Instantiate the model, optimizer, and define loss function
model = Net()
optimizer = optim.SGD(model.parameters(), lr=0.01)
criterion = nn.CrossEntropyLoss()

# Training logic here...

# Saving the model
torch.save(model, 'model.pth')

# Loading the model
model_loaded = torch.load('model.pth')
model_loaded.eval() # Set the model to evaluation mode before inference
```

In the above example:

- A simple neural network model is defined.
- The model is trained (training logic is omitted for brevity).
- The entire model is saved to a file named model.pth using torch.save().
- The saved model is loaded using torch.load(), and set to evaluation mode with model_loaded.eval() to ensure layers like dropout and batch normalization operate correctly during inference.

Saving and Loading a State Dictionary

Saving only the state dictionary (i.e., model parameters) is generally preferred in production due to its flexibility and robustness. The state dictionary contains the model's learned parameters and buffers, which can later be loaded into a model instance using load_state_dict. This method requires that the model's architecture is manually defined before loading the parameters.

```
# Saving the state dictionary
torch.save(model.state_dict(), 'model_state_dict.pth')

# Loading the state dictionary
model_loaded = Net() # Make sure to initialize the model
model_loaded.load_state_dict(torch.load('model_state_dict.pth'))
model_loaded.eval()
```

Exporting Models to ONNX

ONNX provides an open-source format for exporting models in a manner that supports interoperability with other deep learning frameworks. Exporting to ONNX facilitates deployment in environments where PyTorch is either unsuitable or unavailable, such as in specific production systems or when optimizing for particular hardware.

The typical pattern for exporting a PyTorch model to ONNX follows these steps:

```
# Creating a dummy input tensor based on the expected input shape
dummy_input = torch.randn(1, 784)

# Export the model
torch.onnx.export(model, # Model to be exported
                  dummy_input, # Dummy input tensor
                  'model.onnx', # File name for the exported model
                  input_names=['input'], # Name of the input node(s)
                  output_names=['output']) # Name of the output node(s)
```

ONNX exporter in PyTorch generates a computational graph from the model and serializes it along with the model parameters into the ONNX format. The arguments passed to torch.onnx.export include references to the model, a sample input tensor to trace the model's computation, the filename for the exported model, and optionally, names for the input and output nodes to make the model's graph more readable.

Example Output of Exported Model

When exported successfully, the ONNX model can be loaded and inspected using ONNX runtime or any compatible framework. An example output of exporting the model might be as follows:

```
$ python export_model.py
Exported model to model.onnx
```

The ONNX model can then be easily loaded in frameworks that support ONNX:

```
import onnx
import onnxruntime as ort

# Load the ONNX model
onnx_model = onnx.load('model.onnx')
```

```
# Check that the model is well formed
onnx.checker.check_model(onnx_model)

# Use ONNX Runtime to run inference
ort_session = ort.InferenceSession('model.onnx')

# Prepare input data
input_data = {'input': dummy_input.numpy()}

# Compute ONNX Runtime output prediction
outputs = ort_session.run(None, input_data)
print(outputs)
```

This example demonstrates how the exported ONNX model can be loaded using the ONNX library and run with ONNX Runtime, a high-performance engine for executing ONNX models.

By mastering the saving and exporting of PyTorch models, practitioners can ensure their models are portable, reusable, and ready for various deployment scenarios.

10.3 Serving Models with Flask

Serving machine learning models through a web interface is essential for making them accessible to users and applications in real-time. Flask, a lightweight WSGI web application framework in Python, is well-suited for this purpose due to its simplicity and flexibility. In this section, we will explore the steps required to deploy a PyTorch model using Flask, covering model loading, API creation, and handling inference requests.

To begin, we must ensure that Flask is installed. If it is not already installed, it can be added to your Python environment using the following command:

```
pip install flask
```

Loading the PyTorch Model

Before setting up the Flask application, we need to load the trained PyTorch model. This model can be saved in a file using the torch.save() function and then loaded using torch.load().

```
import torch
from torchvision import models

# Load the model
model_path = 'model.pth'
```

```
model = models.resnet18()
model.load_state_dict(torch.load(model_path))
model.eval()
```

In the snippet above, we load a pretrained ResNet-18 model, which is then placed in evaluation mode using model.eval(). Setting the model to evaluation mode ensures that layers like dropout and batch normalization operate in inference mode, leading to deterministic results.

Creating the Flask Application

Next, we will create the Flask application and define the necessary routes. The main route will handle POST requests containing the input data for inference.

```
from flask import Flask, request, jsonify
from torchvision import transforms
from PIL import Image
import io

app = Flask(__name__)

# Load the PyTorch model (as shown previously)
model = models.resnet18()
model.load_state_dict(torch.load('model.pth'))
model.eval()

# Define the transformation for input images
preprocess = transforms.Compose([
    transforms.Resize(256),
    transforms.CenterCrop(224),
    transforms.ToTensor(),
    transforms.Normalize(mean=[0.485, 0.456, 0.406], std=[0.229, 0.224, 0.225]),
])

def transform_image(image_bytes):
    image = Image.open(io.BytesIO(image_bytes))
    return preprocess(image).unsqueeze(0)

def get_prediction(image_tensor):
    with torch.no_grad():
        outputs = model(image_tensor)
    _, predicted = outputs.max(1)
    return predicted.item()

@app.route('/predict', methods=['POST'])
def predict():
    if request.method == 'POST':
        if 'file' not in request.files:
            return jsonify({'error': 'No file part'}), 400

        file = request.files['file']
        if file.filename == '':
            return jsonify({'error': 'No selected file'}), 400

        try:
            img_bytes = file.read()
            tensor = transform_image(img_bytes)
            prediction = get_prediction(tensor)
```

```
        return jsonify({'prediction': prediction})
    except Exception as e:
        return jsonify({'error': str(e)}), 500

if __name__ == '__main__':
    app.run(host='0.0.0.0', port=5000)
```

In the above code:

- **Flask Application:** The Flask application is created using Flask(__name__). The model is loaded and set to evaluation mode.
- **Image Preprocessing:** The preprocess function defines the necessary transformations for the input image, ensuring it matches the model's expected format.
- **Image Transformation:** The transform_image function converts the image bytes into a tensor suitable for input to the model.
- **Prediction Function:** The get_prediction function performs the inference and returns the predicted class.
- **API Endpoint:** The /predict endpoint handles POST requests. It checks for the presence of a file, processes it, and returns the prediction.

Running the Flask Application

To start the server, run the Flask application script. The server will be available at http://0.0.0.0:5000/. You can test the API using curl or any HTTP client.

```
curl -X POST -F "file=@path_to_image.jpg" http://0.0.0.0:5000/predict
```

A successful response will look similar to this:

```
{
  "prediction": 3
}
```

Handling Errors and Improving the API

To make the API more robust and user-friendly, consider handling edge cases and providing informative error messages. Implement validation to check the file type and size, and improve logging for better debugging. Additionally, secure the API by implementing authentication and rate limiting.

By following these steps, you can deploy a PyTorch model using Flask, creating a performant and accessible web service for real-time predictions.

10.4 Deploying on Cloud Platforms

Deploying machine learning models on cloud platforms effectively addresses issues of scalability, accessibility, and maintenance. Cloud platforms offer robust environments tailored for serving models to a wide variety of clients, ensuring high availability and performance. This section outlines the processes required to deploy PyTorch models to popular cloud platforms such as AWS, Google Cloud, and Azure, emphasizing best practices and configurations.

To illustrate these concepts concretely, let's delve into deploying a sample PyTorch model on Amazon Web Services (AWS) using Amazon SageMaker, followed by a similar deployment on Google Cloud Platform (GCP) with AI Platform, and finally, deployment on Microsoft Azure using Azure Machine Learning.

1. Deploying with Amazon SageMaker

Amazon SageMaker is a comprehensive service that allows data scientists and developers to build, train, and deploy machine learning models at scale. SageMaker streamlines the deployment process through managed endpoints.

Prerequisites:

- AWS account and permissions to use SageMaker.
- AWS Command Line Interface (CLI) configured with the necessary credentials.
- Docker installed, if you need to build a custom container.
- A PyTorch model saved in a format compatible with SageMaker.

Step-by-Step Deployment:

1. **Save the Model:**

Save your PyTorch model using TorchScript:

```
import torch
import torch.nn as nn
```

```
import torch.optim as optim

# Sample model and training code
class Net(nn.Module):
    def __init__(self):
        super(Net, self).__init__()
        self.fc1 = nn.Linear(784, 128)
        self.fc2 = nn.Linear(128, 10)

    def forward(self, x):
        x = torch.relu(self.fc1(x))
        x = self.fc2(x)
        return x

model = Net()
# Assume the model is trained
torch.jit.save(torch.jit.script(model), 'model.pth')
```

2. **Create a SageMaker Session and Upload the Model:**

```
import boto3
import sagemaker

sagemaker_session = sagemaker.Session()
s3_bucket = 'your-s3-bucket'
model_path = sagemaker_session.upload_data('model.pth', bucket=s3_bucket,
    key_prefix='pytorch-model')
```

3. **Define an Estimator and Deploy the Model:**

```
from sagemaker.pytorch import PyTorchModel

pytorch_model = PyTorchModel(model_data=model_path,
                             role='your-sagemaker-role',
                             entry_point='inference.py',
                             framework_version='1.7.1',
                             py_version='py3')

predictor = pytorch_model.deploy(instance_type='ml.m4.xlarge',
    initial_instance_count=1)
```

4. **Test the Deployed Endpoint:**

```
import numpy as np

test_data = np.random.rand(1, 784).astype(np.float32)
result = predictor.predict(test_data)
print(result)
```

2. Deploying with Google Cloud AI Platform

Google Cloud AI Platform provides a scalable and managed service to deploy ML models. Deployment on AI Platform involves creating a model and versioning it for different stages of deployment.

Prerequisites:

- Google Cloud account.
- Google Cloud SDK installed and configured.
- Model saved in a format compatible with TensorFlow Serving (saved model format).

Step-by-Step Deployment:

1. **Save the Model:**

```
import torch

# Saving the sample model
torch.save(model.state_dict(), 'model.pth')
```

2. **Convert and Export Model:** Generate a TensorFlow SavedModel from the PyTorch model:

```
import torch.onnx
import tensorflow as tf

dummy_input = torch.randn(1, 784)
torch.onnx.export(model, dummy_input, "model.onnx")

# Convert ONNX to TensorFlow SavedModel
import onnx
from onnx_tf.backend import prepare

onnx_model = onnx.load("model.onnx")
tf_rep = prepare(onnx_model)
tf_rep.export_graph("saved_model")
```

3. **Upload the Model to Google Cloud Storage:**

```
$ gsutil cp -r saved_model gs://your-bucket/saved_model/
```

4. **Deploy the Model on AI Platform:**

```
$ gcloud ai-platform models create pytorch_model
$ gcloud ai-platform versions create v1 --model=pytorch_model --origin=gs://your-bucket/saved_model/ --runtime-version=2.3 --framework TENSORFLOW --python-version=3.7
```

5. **Test the Deployed Model:**

```
from googleapiclient import discovery
from oauth2client.client import GoogleCredentials

project_id = 'your-project-id'
model_name = 'pytorch_model'
version_name = 'v1'

credentials = GoogleCredentials.get_application_default()
service = discovery.build('ml', 'v1', credentials=credentials)

name = 'projects/{}/models/{}/versions/{}'.format(project_id, model_name,
    version_name)
response = service.projects().predict(
    name=name,
```

```
    body={'instances': [test_data.tolist()]}
).execute()

print(response)
```

3. Deploying with Microsoft Azure

Azure Machine Learning provides a full suite of tools for the deployment and management of machine learning models. Deployment involves registering the model, creating a scoring script, and deploying as a web service.

Prerequisites:

- Azure account.
- Azure CLI installed and configured.
- Azure Machine Learning SDK for Python.

Step-by-Step Deployment:

1. **Register the Model:**

```
from azureml.core import Workspace, Model

ws = Workspace.from_config()
model = Model.register(workspace=ws,
                       model_path='model.pth',
                       model_name='pytorch_model')
```

2. **Create Scoring Script and Environment:**

```
scoring_script = """
import json
import torch
import torch.nn as nn

class Net(nn.Module):
    def __init__(self):
        super(Net, self).__init__()
        self.fc1 = nn.Linear(784, 128)
        self.fc2 = nn.Linear(128, 10)

    def forward(self, x):
        x = torch.relu(self.fc1(x))
        x = self.fc2(x)
        return x

model = Net()
model.load_state_dict(torch.load('model.pth'))
model.eval()

def run(raw_data):
    data = torch.tensor(json.loads(raw_data)['data'])
    prediction = model(data)
```

```
    return prediction.tolist()
"""

with open('score.py', 'w') as f:
    f.write(scoring_script)

from azureml.core.environment import Environment
from azureml.core.conda_dependencies import CondaDependencies

env = Environment('pytorch-env')
conda_dep = CondaDependencies()
conda_dep.add_conda_package('pytorch')
conda_dep.add_conda_package('torchvision')
env.python.conda_dependencies=conda_dep
```

3. **Deploy the Model:**

```
from azureml.core.model import InferenceConfig
from azureml.core.webservice import AciWebservice, Webservice

inference_config = InferenceConfig(entry_script="score.py", environment=env)
aci_config = AciWebservice.deploy_configuration(cpu_cores=1, memory_gb=1)

service = Model.deploy(workspace=ws,
                       name='pytorch-service',
                       models=[model],
                       inference_config=inference_config,
                       deployment_config=aci_config)

service.wait_for_deployment(show_output=True)
print(service.state)
```

4. **Test the Deployed Service:**

```
import json
import requests

scoring_uri = service.scoring_uri
headers = {'Content-Type': 'application/json'}
data = json.dumps({"data": test_data.tolist()})

response = requests.post(scoring_uri, data=data, headers=headers)
print(response.json())
```

Deploying on cloud platforms offers numerous advantages such as scalability, cost-efficiency, and the ability to reach a broad audience. This section covered the deployment processes on AWS, GCP, and Azure, each presenting unique strengths and slight variations in methods. Understanding these processes is crucial for efficiently serving machine learning models in practical, real-world applications.

10.5 Using TorchServe

TorchServe is an open-source tool developed by AWS and PyTorch contributors, designed specifically for serving PyTorch models. It simplifies the deployment of models, allowing users to scale, monitor, and manage their models in production environments.

To utilize TorchServe, one needs to perform several key steps: preparing the model, creating model archives, configuring the TorchServe environment, starting TorchServe, and finally, managing the served models.

Preparation of the model involves ensuring that the model is compatible with TorchServe. This typically means having a trained PyTorch model that can be saved and loaded using the torch.save and torch.load functions.

```
import torch

# Assuming 'model' is your trained PyTorch model
torch.save(model.state_dict(), 'model_weights.pth')
```

Next, the creation of a model archive is done using the torch-model-archiver tool. This tool packages the model and necessary artifacts into a single file.

```
torch-model-archiver --model-name my_model \
                     --version 1.0 \
                     --serialized-file model_weights.pth \
                     --handler my_handler.py \
                     --extra-files index_to_name.json
```

In this example, --model-name specifies the name of the model, --version denotes the version of the model, --serialized-file refers to the saved model weights, --handler designates the custom handler script used for inference, and --extra-files includes any additional files needed, such as a JSON file mapping class indices to labels.

A handler script (my_handler.py), required to customize the model inference logic, must define a class that inherits from BaseHandler and overrides key methods like initialize, preprocess, inference, and postprocess.

```
from ts.torch_handler.base_handler import BaseHandler
import torch

class MyHandler(BaseHandler):
    def initialize(self, context):
        self.model = torch.load('model_weights.pth')
        self.model.eval()

    def preprocess(self, data):
```

```
        # Implement the preprocessing logic
        pass

    def inference(self, data):
        with torch.no_grad():
            inputs = torch.tensor(data)
            outputs = self.model(inputs)
            return outputs.numpy()

    def postprocess(self, inference_output):
        # Implement the postprocessing logic
        pass
```

After creating the model archive, the TorchServe environment needs to be configured. This typically involves setting parameters in a configuration file (config.properties) such as HTTP port, number of workers, and logging level.

```
inference_address=http://127.0.0.1:8080
management_address=http://127.0.0.1:8081
metrics_address=http://127.0.0.1:8082
number_of_netty_threads=32
default_workers_per_model=8
```

Starting TorchServe can be done using the torchserve command while directing it to the configuration and model store directory.

```
torchserve --start --ts-config config.properties --model-store models/
```

To manage models served by TorchServe, the torchserve management API can be used for registering and unregistering models. Registering a model involves making a POST request to the management API.

```
curl -X POST "http://127.0.0.1:8081/models?url=my_model.mar&initial_workers=1"
```

The request above registers the my_model.mar model file and initializes it with one worker. Deregistration can be achieved similarly by making a DELETE request.

```
curl -X DELETE "http://127.0.0.1:8081/models/my_model/1.0"
```

TorchServe also provides RESTful endpoints for model inference. Once a model is registered, sending inference requests involves making POST requests to the inference address.

```
curl -X POST http://127.0.0.1:8080/predictions/my_model -T input.json
```

Where input.json contains the input data formatted as JSON. The response from TorchServe will include the inference results.

Monitoring is an integral part of managing deployed models. Torch-

Serve offers various metrics endpoints to monitor performance and resource usage. These metrics can be visualized using tools like Grafana or Prometheus for more detailed insights. Specifically, endpoints for metrics can be accessed as shown below.

```
curl http://127.0.0.1:8082/metrics
```

Listing models is also supported through the management API for gaining insights into currently registered models.

```
curl http://127.0.0.1:8081/models
```

TorchServe is highly extensible, allowing for the addition of custom transformations, handlers, and post-processing steps tailored to specific deployment scenarios. These features make it a versatile tool for deploying and serving PyTorch models in production environments.

10.6 Model Optimization for Inference

Model optimization for inference is a critical component to ensure that your PyTorch models perform efficiently in production environments. Optimization techniques are applied to enhance the efficiency of the model without significantly compromising its accuracy. These techniques can include pruning, quantization, and various other methods to reduce the computational load and latency.

Pruning Pruning refers to the process of removing redundant or less significant neurons or weights in the neural network. Pruned networks have fewer parameters, which often leads to reduced computational load and memory usage during inference. A common approach is to prune weights with the smallest magnitude since they contribute less to the output of the network.

The following example demonstrates how to apply weight pruning using PyTorch:

```
import torch
import torch.nn as nn
import torch.nn.utils.prune as prune

class SimpleModel(nn.Module):
    def __init__(self):
        super(SimpleModel, self).__init__()
        self.fc1 = nn.Linear(10, 5)
        self.fc2 = nn.Linear(5, 2)

    def forward(self, x):
```

```
        x = torch.relu(self.fc1(x))
        x = self.fc2(x)
        return x

model = SimpleModel()

# Apply L1 unstructured pruning on fc1
prune.l1_unstructured(model.fc1, name='weight', amount=0.2)

# Check the sparsity of fc1.weight
print("Sparsity in fc1.weight: {:.2f}%".format(
    100. * float(torch.sum(model.fc1.weight == 0))
    / float(model.fc1.weight.nelement())
))
```

Quantization Quantization is the process of approximating the model parameters and activations with lower precision (e.g., 8-bit integers instead of 32-bit floating-point numbers). This reduces the model size and accelerates the computations, making it more efficient for deployment on edge devices or environments with limited computational resources.

PyTorch provides both post-training quantization and quantization-aware training to facilitate this process. Post-training quantization is straightforward and involves converting a trained model to a quantized version:

```
import torch.optim as optim
from torch.quantization import quantize_dynamic, QuantStub, DeQuantStub

# Your pre-trained model
model = ... # assume model is already trained

# Convert to quantized model using dynamic quantization
quantized_model = quantize_dynamic(
    model, {nn.Linear}, dtype=torch.qint8
)

# Evaluating quantized model
model.eval()
with torch.no_grad():
    output = quantized_model(input_data)
```

Quantization-aware training involves training the model while simulating the effect of quantization to reduce the loss due to quantization effects:

```
# Setup model for quantization
model.qconfig = torch.quantization.get_default_qat_qconfig('fbgemm')
torch.quantization.prepare_qat(model, inplace=True)

# Continue training
optimizer = optim.SGD(model.parameters(), lr=0.01)
model.train()
for epoch in range(num_epochs):
```

```
for data in dataloader:
    inputs, labels = data
    optimizer.zero_grad()
    outputs = model(inputs)
    loss = criterion(outputs, labels)
    loss.backward()
    optimizer.step()

# Convert to quantized model
model.eval()
quantized_model = torch.quantization.convert(model.eval(), inplace=False)
```

Knowledge Distillation Knowledge Distillation is a technique that involves training a smaller, more efficient model (the student) using the predictions of a larger, more accurate model (the teacher). This allows the student model to achieve comparable performance to the teacher model while being more efficient in terms of computation and memory usage.

A simple implementation of knowledge distillation in PyTorch is as follows:

```
teacher_model = ... # Pre-trained teacher model
student_model = ... # Define student model

# Define loss function
def distillation_loss(y, labels, teacher_scores, T, alpha):
    loss = nn.KLDivLoss()(F.log_softmax(y / T, dim=1),
                          F.softmax(teacher_scores / T, dim=1)) * (alpha * T * T) + \
                          F.cross_entropy(y, labels) * (1. - alpha)
    return loss

# Distillation training loop
for epoch in range(num_epochs):
    student_model.train()
    for inputs, labels in dataloader:
        teacher_output = teacher_model(inputs).detach()
        student_output = student_model(inputs)

        loss = distillation_loss(student_output, labels, teacher_output, T=2.0, alpha
            =0.7)

        optimizer.zero_grad()
        loss.backward()
        optimizer.step()
```

Employing these techniques during the model optimization phase can significantly enhance the performance of your models during inference. This not only provides faster response times but also enables deployment in environments with constrained resources.

10.7 Quantization and Sparsity

Quantization and sparsity are essential techniques for optimizing machine learning models, especially when deploying on resource-constrained environments such as mobile devices or embedded systems. These methods help to reduce the memory footprint and computational complexity of models, enabling faster inference and lower power consumption.

Quantization involves approximating the floating-point numbers used in the model weights and activations with lower precision representations such as 8-bit integers. This simplification can significantly reduce the size of the model and speed up inference with minimal loss in accuracy. Sparsity, on the other hand, exploits the presence of zero values in the model parameters or activations, allowing further reductions in memory usage and computational load by skipping zero-multiplications.

1. Quantization Techniques

In PyTorch, quantization can be applied using different approaches such as static quantization, dynamic quantization, and quantization-aware training.

Static Quantization: Static quantization converts the model weights to lower precision once training is complete. The following code snippet demonstrates how to perform static quantization in PyTorch:

```
import torch
from torchvision import models

# Load the pre-trained model
model = models.resnet18(pretrained=True)
model.eval()

# Specify quantization configuration
model.qconfig = torch.quantization.get_default_qconfig('fbgemm')

# Prepare the model for quantization
model_prepared = torch.quantization.prepare(model)

# Calibrate the model to determine scale and zero-point
calibration_data = torch.randn(100, 3, 224, 224)
model_prepared(calibration_data)

# Convert the model to quantized version
model_int8 = torch.quantization.convert(model_prepared)

# Save the quantized model
torch.save(model_int8.state_dict(), 'quantized_model.pth')
```

Dynamic Quantization: Dynamic quantization is applied during runtime, which means weights are converted to lower precision when the model is being executed. This approach is particularly useful for models with RNNs or LSTMs. The following example shows dynamic quantization applied to an LSTM model:

```
import torch
from torch import nn

# Define an LSTM model
class LSTMModel(nn.Module):
    def __init__(self):
        super(LSTMModel, self).__init__()
        self.lstm = nn.LSTM(input_size=10, hidden_size=20, num_layers=2)
        self.fc = nn.Linear(20, 1)

    def forward(self, x):
        x, _ = self.lstm(x)
        x = self.fc(x[-1])
        return x

model = LSTMModel()

# Apply dynamic quantization
model_quantized = torch.quantization.quantize_dynamic(
    model, {nn.LSTM, nn.Linear}, dtype=torch.qint8
)

# Save the quantized model
torch.save(model_quantized.state_dict(), 'dynamic_quantized_model.pth')
```

Quantization-Aware Training: Quantization-aware training integrates quantization into the training process to minimize accuracy loss. Although it demands more effort and computational resources during training, the resulting models often perform better in terms of accuracy compared to post-training quantization methods. The following example shows how to implement quantization-aware training:

```
import torch
from torch.quantization import QuantStub, DeQuantStub

# Define a simple feedforward network
class QuantAwareModel(nn.Module):
    def __init__(self):
        super(QuantAwareModel, self).__init__()
        self.fc1 = nn.Linear(28 * 28, 128)
        self.relu = nn.ReLU()
        self.fc2 = nn.Linear(128, 10)
        self.quant = QuantStub()
        self.dequant = DeQuantStub()

    def forward(self, x):
        # Quantize input
        x = self.quant(x)
        x = self.fc1(x)
        x = self.relu(x)
        x = self.fc2(x)
        # Dequantize output
        x = self.dequant(x)
```

```
        return x

model = QuantAwareModel()

# Specify quantization configuration and prepare the model
model.qconfig = torch.quantization.get_default_qat_qconfig('fbgemm')
model_prepared = torch.quantization.prepare_qat(model)

# Simulate training process
optimizer = torch.optim.SGD(model_prepared.parameters(), lr=0.01)
loss_fn = nn.CrossEntropyLoss()

for epoch in range(5):
    # Training step (example with random inputs and targets)
    inputs = torch.rand(64, 28, 28)
    targets = torch.randint(0, 10, (64,))

    optimizer.zero_grad()
    outputs = model_prepared(inputs)
    loss = loss_fn(outputs, targets)
    loss.backward()
    optimizer.step()

# Convert the trained model to a quantized version
model_int8 = torch.quantization.convert(model_prepared)

# Save the quantized model
torch.save(model_int8.state_dict(), 'qat_quantized_model.pth')
```

2. Sparsity Techniques

Sparsity focuses on exploiting the zero values in the model parameters or activations to improve efficiency. PyTorch supports techniques like zero pruning, low-rank factorization, and structured pruning.

Zero Pruning: Zero pruning removes model weights that are below a certain threshold, effectively setting them to zero. This can be illustrated as follows:

```
import torch
from torch.nn.utils import prune

# Define a simple model
model = nn.Sequential(
    nn.Linear(784, 128),
    nn.ReLU(),
    nn.Linear(128, 10)
)

# Apply L1 unstructured pruning to the first fully connected layer
prune.l1_unstructured(model[0], name='weight', amount=0.2)

# Check sparsity
sparsity = float(torch.sum(model[0].weight == 0)) / float(model[0].weight.nelement())
print(f'Sparsity: {sparsity:.2f}')
```

```
Sparsity: 0.20
```

Low-Rank Factorization: Low-rank factorization decomposes weight matrices into the product of smaller matrices, reducing the dimensionality and computational cost. This technique can be approximated using Singular Value Decomposition (SVD):

```
import torch
from torch import nn

# Define a linear layer
linear_layer = nn.Linear(784, 128)

# SVD factorization
u, s, v = torch.svd(linear_layer.weight)

# Keep only the top 'rank' singular values
rank = 10
u_reduced = u[:, :rank]
s_reduced = s[:rank]
v_reduced = v[:, :rank]

# Reconstruct the approximated weight matrix
reconstructed_weight = torch.mm(torch.mm(u_reduced, torch.diag(s_reduced)),
    v_reduced.t())

# Assign the approximated weight to the layer
linear_layer.weight = nn.Parameter(reconstructed_weight)
```

Structured Pruning: Structured pruning removes entire neurons, filters, or channels, resulting in a more compact architecture. This type of pruning can be accomplished in PyTorch using custom pruning methods or tools like the PyTorch Pruning Library.

Quantization and sparsity, when appropriately applied, significantly enhance the efficiency of machine learning models without a substantial impact on accuracy. These methodologies are key to ensuring the successful deployment of PyTorch models in real-world applications where resources may be limited.

10.8 Using ONNX for Interoperability

ONNX, which stands for Open Neural Network Exchange, serves as an open format designed to make deep learning models portable across various frameworks. The primary objective of ONNX is to provide a unified, open source format for AI models, facilitating their interchange between AI tools. In deploying PyTorch models, the utilization of ONNX enhances model adaptability and cross-framework compatibility, allowing a seamless transition between different systems without significant overhead.

Converting a PyTorch model to the ONNX format is straightforward. PyTorch provides native support for exporting models to ONNX, which involves capturing the model's computational graph and converting it into the ONNX format. The following steps illustrate the systematic process to achieve this:

First, ensure that the PyTorch model is in an evaluation mode. This is essential because certain layers like dropout and batch normalization behave differently during training and evaluation.

```
import torch
import torch.onnx

# Assume model is an instance of a PyTorch neural network.
model.eval()
```

Next, define a dummy input that matches the shape of the data the model processes. This input acts as a placeholder to trace the model's computational graph.

```
# Dummy input for the model with the appropriate shape
dummy_input = torch.randn(1, 3, 224, 224) # Example for an image input
```

Now, the model can be exported using the torch.onnx.export function. This function requires the model, the dummy input, and the desired output file name.

```
# Export the model
torch.onnx.export(model, dummy_input, "model.onnx")
```

This results in the creation of a file named model.onnx in the specified directory. This ONNX file encapsulates the model's structure and parameters in a standard format.

To verify the export process, the ONNX file can be loaded and checked using the ONNX runtime. This validates that the conversion was successful and the model maintains its expected performance.

```
import onnx

# Load the ONNX model
onnx_model = onnx.load("model.onnx")

# Check that the model has a valid schema
onnx.checker.check_model(onnx_model)
print("The model was successfully converted to ONNX format.")
```

Utilizing the ONNX format opens up several deployment possibilities. One significant advantage is the ability to integrate with the ONNX Runtime (ORT), a high-performance inference engine for deploying ONNX models on different hardware backends.

To run inference with ONNX Runtime, initialize an inference session. This session handles the model loading and execution on the chosen hardware.

```
import onnxruntime as ort

# Initialize an inference session
session = ort.InferenceSession("model.onnx")

# Prepare the input and run inference
input_name = session.get_inputs()[0].name
output_name = session.get_outputs()[0].name
result = session.run([output_name], {input_name: dummy_input.numpy()})

print("Inference result:", result)
```

To leverage the full capabilities of ONNX Runtime, one can utilize its optimization features, which include hardware-specific optimizations and graph transformations aimed at reducing latency and increasing throughput. This ensures that the model runs efficiently on different platforms, including CPUs, GPUs, and even specialized accelerators.

When deploying a model to a cloud platform, the ONNX format ensures that the model can integrate with various services. Most modern cloud AI services, including Azure Machine Learning, Amazon SageMaker, and Google AI Platform, support ONNX models natively, enabling efficient and scalable deployment of machine learning workloads.

Moreover, ONNX fosters collaboration and model sharing in a diverse tooling ecosystem. Researchers and practitioners can create models using PyTorch, export them to ONNX, and allow their utilization in another framework, like TensorFlow, without the need for extensive reimplementation.

In addition to its utility in model deployment, ONNX also supports a rich ecosystem of related tools and libraries. ONNX Model Zoo provides a repository of pre-trained models in the ONNX format, allowing practitioners to leverage existing architectures and weights for their applications. Furthermore, ONNX converters facilitate the transformation of model formats between different deep learning frameworks, enhancing the versatility of AI workflows.

10.9 Deploying on Edge Devices

Deploying machine learning models on edge devices involves running inference directly on hardware such as smartphones, IoT devices, and embedded systems. This allows for real-time data processing, reduced latency, and decreased dependency on network connectivity. PyTorch models can be optimized and adapted for various edge hardware specifications. This section details the steps required to deploy a PyTorch model on edge devices, with particular attention to model optimization, conversion to target formats, and integration with edge device environments.

The first step in deploying on edge devices is optimizing the model. Edge devices often have limited computational resources, so it is crucial to minimize the model size and enhance its efficiency. Techniques such as quantization, pruning, and sparsity play vital roles here.

```
import torch
import torchvision

# Load a pretrained model
model = torchvision.models.mobilenet_v2(pretrained=True).eval()

# Fuse model layers for quantization
model.fuse_model()

# Apply dynamic quantization
quantized_model = torch.quantization.quantize_dynamic(
    model, {torch.nn.Linear}, dtype=torch.qint8
)

# Saving the quantized model
torch.save(quantized_model.state_dict(), 'mobilenet_v2_quantized.pth')
```

Conversion to an appropriate format is the next step. Many edge devices support the ONNX (Open Neural Network Exchange) format, which facilitates interoperability across different frameworks and optimized inference on varied hardware.

```
import torch
import torchvision

# Load the quantized model
model = torchvision.models.mobilenet_v2(pretrained=False)
model.load_state_dict(torch.load('mobilenet_v2_quantized.pth'))

# Set the model to evaluation mode
model.eval()

# Dummy input tensor
dummy_input = torch.randn(1, 3, 224, 224)

# Export to ONNX
```

```
torch.onnx.export(model, dummy_input, "mobilenet_v2.onnx",
                  input_names=["input"], output_names=["output"])
```

With the model in ONNX format, the next task is to integrate it into the edge device environment. Frameworks such as ONNX Runtime, TensorFlow Lite, and others support running ONNX models efficiently on edge hardware.

```
import onnxruntime as ort
import numpy as np

# Load ONNX model
session = ort.InferenceSession("mobilenet_v2.onnx")

# Prepare input
input_name = session.get_inputs()[0].name
input_shape = session.get_inputs()[0].shape
dummy_input = np.random.rand(*input_shape).astype(np.float32)

# Perform inference
outputs = session.run(None, {input_name: dummy_input})

print(outputs)
```

For certain edge platforms, converting to an even more specialized format is necessary. For instance, TensorFlow Lite for mobile and microcontrollers or NVIDIA TensorRT for Jetson devices deliver significant performance improvements. Below illustrates converting an ONNX model to TensorFlow Lite format:

```
import onnx
import tensorflow as tf

# Convert ONNX to TensorFlow
model = onnx.load("mobilenet_v2.onnx")
from onnx_tf.backend import prepare
tf_rep = prepare(model)

# Convert TensorFlow model to TensorFlow Lite
converter = tf.lite.TFLiteConverter.from_concrete_functions([tf_rep.tf_func])
tflite_model = converter.convert()

# Save TensorFlow Lite model
with open("mobilenet_v2.tflite", "wb") as f:
    f.write(tflite_model)
```

The above steps exemplify a typical workflow for deploying models on edge devices. It is essential to comprehend the specific requirements and constraints of the target device when performing these operations. Effective deployment on edge devices leads to enhanced user experiences, seamless real-time processing, and a reduction in dependency on cloud-based resources. Various edge device ecosystems, such as Android Neural Networks API (NNAPI), Apple's CoreML, and Google's

Edge TPU, provide tailored solutions for specific environments, ensuring that the deployment is optimal for the given hardware.

10.10 Monitoring and Maintaining Deployed Models

Once a model is deployed, it is imperative to continuously monitor and maintain it to ensure its optimal performance. This section covers various strategies and practices for monitoring deployed models, detecting and diagnosing issues, and maintaining models through updates and retraining.

Efficiently monitoring a deployed model involves several key aspects: tracking performance metrics, detecting data drift, logging errors, and ensuring system health. Performance metrics help in understanding how well the model is performing in a real-world environment. Common metrics include accuracy, precision, recall, F1-score, and latency.

- **Tracking Performance Metrics:** Regularly tracking performance metrics is essential for evaluating the model's accuracy and reliability. Performance should be tracked on both a per-request basis and periodically (e.g., daily or weekly aggregates). It is possible to log these metrics and visualize them using monitoring tools such as Prometheus and Grafana.

```
from prometheus_client import start_http_server, Summary, Counter
import time

REQUEST_TIME = Summary('request_processing_seconds', 'Time spent processing
    request')
REQUEST_COUNT = Counter('request_count', 'Total number of requests')

@REQUEST_TIME.time()
def predict(input_data):
    REQUEST_COUNT.inc()
    # Model inference logic
    result = model(input_data)
    return result

if __name__ == '__main__':
    start_http_server(8000)
    while True:
        # Simulate model prediction
        predict(random_input_data)
        time.sleep(1)
```

```
# Prometheus will run on http://localhost:8000/metrics to collect metrics.
```

Detecting data drift is another crucial aspect of model monitoring. Data drift occurs when the statistical properties of the input data change over time, which can affect the model's performance. By utilizing tools such as Alibi Detect or Azure Machine Learning, it is possible to continuously monitor input data for drift.

- **Detecting Data Drift:** Implementing continuous data drift detection ensures that any changes in the underlying data distribution are quickly identified, allowing for timely intervention.

```
from alibi_detect.cd import KSDrift
import numpy as np

# Assume features_train is the training data used for model training
cd = KSDrift(features_train, p_val=0.05, update_X_ref=True, X_ref_window
    =10000)

def monitor_data_drift(new_data):
    preds = cd.predict(new_data)
    if preds['data']['is_drift']:
        print("Data drift detected!")
    else:
        print("No data drift detected.")

# Simulated live data feed
for new_data in live_data_feed:
    monitor_data_drift(new_data)
```

```
# The output will indicate whether a data drift is detected in the live data feed.
```

Logging errors and analyzing logs is paramount to diagnose issues. Logs should encompass all aspects of the model serving pipeline including request data, model predictions, errors, and system health metrics.

- **Logging Errors and Diagnosing Issues:** Utilize logging libraries such as Python's built-in logging library to record detailed logs for every request made to the model, including any errors that occur during inference.

```
import logging

logging.basicConfig(filename='model_serving.log', level=logging.INFO)

def predict(input_data):
    try:
        # Model inference
        result = model(input_data)
        logging.info(f'Input: {input_data}, Prediction: {result}')
        return result
    except Exception as e:
```

```
        logging.error(f'Error during prediction: {e}')
        raise e

# Simulated prediction cycle
for data in test_data:
    predict(data)
```

The entries in 'model_serving.log' will contain detailed logging information.

Ensuring system health involves monitoring resource usage such as CPU, memory, and disk usage. This can be achieved using system monitoring tools such as Nagios or New Relic. Resource utilization metrics help identify bottlenecks and scale the infrastructure as needed.

Model maintenance involves updating and retraining the model to adapt to new data and requirements. This includes re-evaluating the model periodically, retraining using recent data, and deploying updated models seamlessly with minimal downtime.

- **Updating and Retraining Models:** Implement version control for models using tools like DVC (Data Version Control) and CI/CD pipelines for automating the retraining and deployment process.

```
stages:
  - test
  - build
  - deploy

test:
  stage: test
  script:
    - python -m unittest discover tests

build:
  stage: build
  script:
    - dvc repro
    - dvc push
    - docker build -t my_model:latest .

deploy:
  stage: deploy
  script:
    - docker run -d -p 5000:5000 my_model:latest
```

GitLab CI/CD will run the tests, build the model, and deploy the Docker container.

By integrating comprehensive monitoring, logging, and maintenance practices, it is possible to ensure that deployed models remain reliable, efficient, and adaptive to changing data and requirements. Continually evaluating and updating models helps in maintaining their efficacy and accuracy over time. It is critical for practitioners to incorporate these strategies into their deployment workflow.

Made in United States
Orlando, FL
04 November 2026

90201051R00164